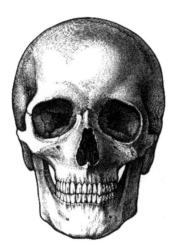

"Remember, never take no cut-offs and hurry along as fast as you can."

Virginia Reed

Survivor of the Donner Party

FORLORN HOPE

A Haunted History of the Donner Party

TROY TAYLOR

AN AMERICAN HAUNTINGS INK TITLE

On the Way to the Summit (The Donner Party). ca. 1891. William Gilbert Gaul, artist. Oil paint on canvas. Collection of the Oakland Museum of California, Kahn Collection.

This Book is Published By:
American Hauntings Ink
Jacksonville, Illinois | 217.791.7859
Visit us on the Internet at http://www.americanhauntingsink.com

978-1-7352706-6-1
First Edition - March 2021

Printed in the United States of America

TABLE OF CONTENTS

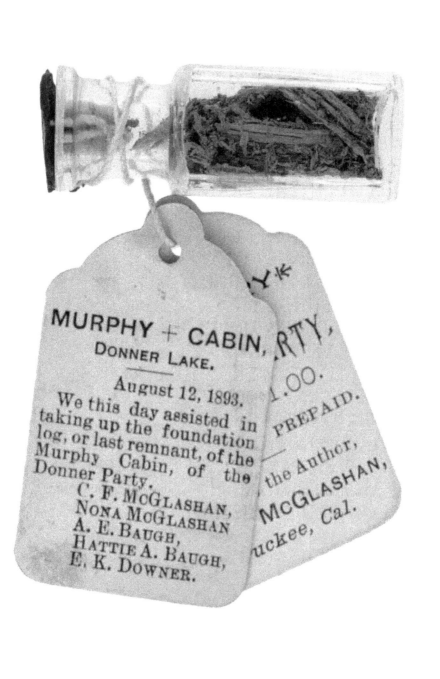

MURPHY + CABIN,
DONNER LAKE.

August 12, 1893.
We this day assisted in
taking up the foundation
log, or last remnant, of the
Murphy Cabin, of the
Donner Party.
C. F. McGLASHAN,
NONA McGLASHAN
A. E. BAUGH,
HATTIE A. BAUGH,
E. K. DOWNER.

RTY,
1.00.
PREPAID.
the Author,
McGLASHAN,
uckee, Cal.

The voice of a woman wails from the place where a ruined cabin once stood. It pierces the night, just as it has done for nearly two centuries. As travelers passed by the place where the shelter once stood, they sometimes saw the woman, staring at them as their wagons rumbled past. They knew not to speak to her - they had been warned. None dared approach the woman in the pale dress with the hollow eyes and the ravaged face. Her expression was one of madness, but it was not the insanity they feared.

It was the fact that she was dead.

Her spirit haunted the trail. She remained at the place where she met her fate. After her husband had perished, she lost her mind to grief and ran wildly through the woods, searching for someone - anyone - who was left alive. But she fell into a stream and her clothing froze. Shivering and weak, she stumbled to a cabin from which a ribbon of smoke curled from the chimney. She found shelter there - and she found death.

When rescue finally came for the survivors who were trapped in the snow and ice of the mountains, the woman was gone. Only her bones remained. They had been picked clean of their flesh by a man whose own sanity had been devoured by hunger.

And yet her spirit remains. She is trapped here by the lies that accompanied her death. A man later claimed that he had not killed her - that she had succumbed to a fever that followed her fall into the river, but this man had eaten others, all too weak to fend for themselves.

The woman cries for their souls - and for her own.

1. "A DESPERATE UNDERTAKING"

Restless people with a hunger for land began moving West in the early 1840s.

For most of them, it wasn't the first time they had moved west. They had traveled across the ocean to reach a new land. The original American frontier lay east of the Appalachian Mountains when the first colonists arrived from Europe, but they didn't remain in one place for long. Following the example of wilderness hunter Daniel Boone in 1767, a few adventurous families began to leave the settled colonies and cross the mountains to the west.

These emigrants - a nineteenth century word for the pioneers who crossed the continent - filled the Ohio River Valley, the lower Mississippi, and the old northwest of Illinois, Indiana, and Michigan. In the 1820s, the frontier along the muddy Mississippi was as far west as most dared to go.

The pioneers paused here for a time. Beyond the river, all the way to the Rocky Mountains, lay the desolate Great Plains, and beyond them, the ominous wall of the mountains. This was the land of the Louisiana Purchase, the land that Thomas Jefferson had paid Napoleon only $15 million for, sight unseen, in 1803. Many believed that the French had gotten the better end of the deal. There were almost no trees for houses or fences and scarcely any water for farm crops. The forbidding land broiled in the summer, froze in the winter, and the tall grass that choked the prairie bent before a wind that never seemed to stop blowing. No one from the East - a land filled with forests and rivers - had ever seen such an inhospitable place.

Children's geography books called this area the Great American Desert. In addition, the United States had designated the worthless region as "Indian land," because it wasn't good for anything else. This seemed to be proven by some of the men who braved the area, like Zebulon Pike, a U.S. Army explorer most famous for discovering Pike's Peak, who surveyed the region in 1806. He concluded that the Great Plains had been purposely put there by a merciful "Providence to keep American people from diffusion and ruin."

American expansion would go no further than one-third of the way across the continent - or so it seemed.

But those "restless people" could not be kept in one place. No tract of prairie, however bleak, could stop them from seeking better fortunes and room to grow. Somehow, the unknown lands of the West always seemed to promise something extra - blacker soil, bluer skies, and a brighter future. The urge to move west was described as an "itch in the brain, a restlessness in the feet, and a rising to the challenge of new land that no one else had settled."

Henry David Thoreau sensed this in the New England woods where, walking in circles, he could feel the pull. He wrote, "Eastward I go only by force, but westward, I go free."

A pioneer woman wrote something similar in her diary one winter's day in Dakota's Red River Valley: "When God made man, he seemed to think it best to make him in the East and let him travel West."

There was even a popular saying about it - "If Hell lay to the West, Americans would cross Heaven to get there."

The desire to see it was almost irresistible. Men and women began hearing amazing claims about the land along the Pacific Coast. As early as 1782, a British author named William Frederick Martyn had described California as a place where "a vast quantity of dew falls every morning which, settling on rose leaves, candies, becomes hard like manna, and possesses all that sweetness peculiar to refined sugar."

More recent reports were hardly less miraculous. Fur trappers, adventurers, and merchant seaman who traded with the Spanish colony brought back fabulous tales of California's perpetually sunny climate. No one, some claimed, ever got sick because the weather was so perfect.

The stories about Oregon were just as marvelous. By 1836, the land was inhabited by a handful of trappers, traders, and missionaries, but they all told of the lush, richly timbered peaks and valleys. Oregon was a "pioneer's paradise," an advocate of the region told a party of emigrants that was journeying there in 1843, "where the pigs are running about under the great acorn trees, round and fat, and already cooked, with knives and forks sticking in them so that you can just slice off a piece whenever you are hungry."

A less unnerving report - although just as enthusiastic - came from a former Boston man named Hall Jackson Kelley, who wanted to build a New England town beneath the towering evergreens of Oregon. "When improved and embellished by the white man," he wrote, "Oregon would become the loveliest and most envied country on earth. As far as producing qualities are concerned, Oregon cannot be outdone whether in wheat, oats, rye, barley, buckwheat, peas, beans, potatoes, turnips, cabbages, onions, parsnips, carrots, beets, currants, gooseberries, strawberries, apples, peaches, pears - or fat and healthy babies."

It's surely no surprise that caravans of wagons began heading West. It didn't matter to the emigrants that these lands remained wholly or in part the property of other nations. Both California and Oregon seemed to have been designed for American occupation and settlement. And Americans felt a kind of confidence - or less politely, an arrogance - that America would get them. Surely both Mexico and Britain would concede that all this land belonged by God-given right to the United States - by Manifest Destiny, as President James Polk might phrase it.

And, of course, that's how things turned out, due in large part to the persistence of the emigrants. The first push toward the Pacific began in 1841, when a party of 69 brave souls left Missouri for the Pacific Coast, led by a farmer named John Bartleson and a schoolteacher named John Bidwell.

There were 200 pioneers who headed west the following year. Another 1,000 crossed the plains in 1843, followed by 4,000 in 1844. By 1845, more than 5,000 were on their way toward the Pacific Ocean and by then, the magnetic pull of the West had convinced thousands more to join them. By the time the Donner and Reed Party left Illinois for the West, there were at least 25,000 emigrants each season who were leaving the eastern states behind to find their fortunes in the West.

But it wasn't just wild stories and Manifest Destiny that were prompting Americans to pull up stakes and leave the eastern states in the mid-nineteenth century. Many faced hard realities at home.

The wild stories from the Pacific coast convinced many emigrants - even those without a taste for adventure - to pack up and go West.

In 1837, the nation suffered its first major financial collapse. It was the result of reckless banking policies and feverish speculation on public lands during the Andrew Jackson administration. On May 10, just 67 days after Jackson left office, the major New York banks closed their doors and in the panic that followed, banks across the country did the same. Depression hit the country. Crop prices went down, farm surpluses clogged the produce markets, and farmers were unable to make the mortgage payments on their land. So, many of them left their debt behind, packed their wagons and headed west.

Slavery also caused many to flee the East. Some abolitionists found the institution to be so horrific that they pulled up stakes, loaded up their families, and moved everything they owned to new territories where slavery didn't exist. Many others objected to slavery because of economics. A typical farmer was always at a disadvantage against those who owned slaves. A man who didn't use slave labor could not raise crops as easily or as cheaply as a man who did. He was faced with the choice of either going broke or going West. Many chose the West.

Illness, disease, and health concerns drove many people to the open West, where both legend and logic suggested the air was cleaner. In the East, people died of typhoid, dysentery, tuberculosis, and other epidemics. Yellow Fever had so decimated the population of New Orleans and other Mississippi River towns that the regional death rate exceeded its birth rate for nearly a century. And in the 1830s, a cholera epidemic, which had started in Asia, spread through Europe, and came across the Atlantic on passenger ships, struck the East Coast and spread inland. It raged for almost two decades and killed at least 30,000 in 1850 alone.

Some emigrants fled to the West because of religious persecution. The Mormons were driven from homes in Ohio, Missouri, and Illinois before starting a migration to the Salt Lake Valley of Utah in the 1840s.

And then there were those - like the Donner Party - who simply went West with hopes for a bright future and the always present "hunger for land." It could be found there, perhaps west of the mountains in the golden lands of California and Oregon.

These emigrants - whatever the reason they had for going West -- rode saddle horses or trudged along on foot. Only the sick, some of the women, and the littlest children rode inside the wagons. There was simply no room for anyone else. The wagons were piled high with flour and beans; bacon and dried fruit; coffee and sugar; salt and vinegar; plows and axes; rocking chairs and chamber pots; cast-iron skillets and Dutch ovens; dresses and shirts; feather beds and quilts; water barrels and butter churns; violins and books. And the list went on.

As the emigrants traversed the plains to the mountains, many followed the Oregon Trail - a route already mapped out by fur trappers and other adventurers into the Rockies and followed by a handful of missionaries seeking to save the Indians of the Oregon country. By the 1840s, it was also leading thousands of pioneers to the unsettled Pacific Coast.

But this was no great highway across the West. It was simply a pair of parallel wheel ruts made by wagons across the sod of the prairies, the rock and rubble of mountain passes, and the sands of the desert. They were ruts that, when they arrived at a river they stopped and resumed on the other side, leaving the traveler to devise his own way across.

Even so, when Oregon officially became a part of the United States in 1846, the 2,000-mile trail was the longest highway in the country - and unquestionably the hardest. As one pioneer later wrote, "Once started on the journey, the problem was to finish. We didn't think much about the unborn generation who would profit by our venturesomeness. It was simply a desperate undertaking."

In those days, the westernmost edge of the country ended at the Missouri River. California appeared on the map as a northern province of Mexico. The Oregon country was a huge tract of wilderness that extended north from California, along the Pacific Coast to Alaska, and from the Pacific Ocean in the west to an eastern boundary running along the Continental Divide in

The wagon ruts of the Oregon - California Trail are still visible after more than a century and a half.

the Rocky Mountains, encompassing the present-day states of Oregon, Washington, and parts of Canada, Montana, Idaho, and Wyoming. No one knew for certain to whom this land really belonged. It was claimed by both the United States and Britain, who had signed an unusual treaty allowing for "joint occupation" in 1818.

That meant these overland pioneers really were emigrants. They left their own country for what was essentially a foreign land - a very uncivilized one - to build homes and farms and to start a new life.

"In prosecuting this journey," warned an 1849 guidebook to the West, "the emigrant should never forget that it is one in which time is everything."

No better advice would ever be given to the emigrants in the wagon trains that made their way to the mountains, meadows, and open ranges of the American West. Time spelled success for most of them and doom for many others during the middle decades of the 1800s.

Nothing had prepared these travelers for the ordeals of the trail. They imagined building new homes in the bright, shining lands of the West, but the strain of getting there proved to be far worse than any guidebook could have hinted at.

Life on the trail was a story of an increasingly difficult adventure, of failing food and water supplies, of bone-wrenching weariness, and accumulating miseries of every sort. The pioneers pushed overland, perhaps as slowly as 15 miles each day, and many of them lost sight of the vision that had set them on the road in the first place. It was replaced by reminders of the families that had preceded them -- the wolf-pawed graves of the dead, the rotting carcasses of mules and oxen, splintered wrecks of abandoned wagons, and once-precious household items that had been cast away like refuse once travel became too tough.

The weight of their own privations was enough, on occasion, to bring tears to the eyes of the women and to buckle the knees of the men, yet they kept going. After a few weeks on the trail, most of them had come too far to turn back. There was little choice but to keep going, putting one foot in front of the other.

One emigrant wrote, "The trail west is a treadmill."

Most pioneers summoned reserves of tremendous courage to continue on that treadmill, enduring everything from heat sickness to a mule kick to the shins. It was an unyielding determination that helped them to make the march of more than 2,000 zig-zagging miles, with constant detours for pasture or fresh water.

The distance in miles however, mattered less than the distance in time. It usually took about four and a half months to reach the far West, and the trip became a race against the seasons, in which timing made the difference between success and failure.

Late April or early May was the best time to depart, although the date had to be calculated with care. If a wagon train started too early in the spring, there would not be enough grass on the prairie to graze the cattle. On the other hand, a train that left after other trains had already departed would find campsites marked by trampled grass and fouled water holes.

And if there was one thing that all the guidebooks to western travel agreed upon -- it was not to get caught in the mountain passes when winter came to the high elevations. Such a dilemma would be sure to bring tragedy and disaster to even the most hardened group of travelers.

To reach a starting point in Missouri, a family from the East could either book passage on a steamboat for themselves, their wagons, and their livestock or - as was much more common - pile everything into a wagon, hitch up the team, and begin their overland trek from their own front yard.

Along the roads and turnpikes east of the Mississippi River, travel was relatively fast, campsites were easy to find, and supplies were plentiful. Then, in one river town or another, the emigrants would pause to gather provisions. Independence, Missouri, had been the first destination of many emigrants since 1827, but as more and more settlers pushed west, rival towns sprang up, like Westport and St. Joseph. The emigrants who journeyed to Missouri by riverboat often saved at least four days on the trail by staying on the paddle-wheelers until St. Joseph before starting off by land.

Wherever they began, the emigrants studied guidebooks and directions, asked questions of other travelers who were as clueless as themselves, and made final decisions about outfitting for the road ahead.

They had various - often conflicting - options. For example, either pack animals or two-wheeled carts or wagons could be used for the trip. These kinds of handcarts were used by the Mormons as they emigrated from Illinois to the Salt Lake basin.

A standard type of wagon chosen by families in the 1840s.

A family man usually chose a wagon. It was the costliest and slowest option, but it provided space and shelter for children and for a wife who was, more likely than not, pregnant. There were stories of top-heavy wagons blowing over in high winds or overturning on mountain rocks, sinking in the mud, or bogging down in the desert sand - but maybe if those things happened on a journey, they might happen to someone else. Most pioneers, especially those with farm backgrounds, believed it was a risk worth taking.

A new wagon could cost anywhere from $60 to $90 - which is $2,000 to $2,600 today - and a wise man would buy as many spare parts as he could afford. Wheels needed to be high for clearance, but this meant that it would be harder to maneuver. Wagons were unable to make sharp turns unless the front wheels were small enough to swivel under the wagon box. Wagon tongues often snapped in two when the draft animals - either horse or oxen - pulled too far left or right. The wheels themselves, unless they were exceptionally well-made, often broke. The dry air of the plains shrank the wooden spokes and rims of the wheels until the iron tires simply wobbled off. A blacksmith could fix a thrown tire by heating it red-hot and replacing it on the rim because, as it cooled, it would shrink to a snug fit. More unexpected breakdowns required quick thinking. In one instance, a caravan's cattle stampeded on the trail and wrecked the underside of a carriage and smashed three of the wheels. A dining room table was quickly cut up and turned into new wheels.

There was more thought that went into the wagons than merely as a conveyance. They had to provide a home for the families that owned them for months at a time, often under unusually harsh conditions. A wagon had to be light enough to not place too much strain on the animals that pulled it, and yet strong enough not to break down under loads that might weigh as much as 2,500 pounds. To meet these requirements, most wagons were constructed of hardwoods like maple, hickory, and oak. Because of its weight, iron was used only to reinforce parts that took the greatest pounding. These included the tires, axles, and hounds - bars that served to connect and provide rigidity to the undercarriage.

The cover of the wagon was its sole concession to passenger comfort. It was made up of heavy cotton or canvas and waterproofed with linseed oil. An inventive wife would often sew pockets and slings into the inner fabric for extra storage space. Supported by hickory bows, the inside of the wagon allowed for about five feet of headroom. The cover shielded travelers - sort of - from rain and dust and when the interior became stifling in the heat, the covers could be rolled back and bunched, allowing the air to circulate. In addition, pucker ropes at either end could be tightened to screen the inside of the wagon from prying eyes when the cover was in place.

The emigrants called their combination parlor-kitchen-bedrooms "prairie schooners." Not only did they resemble sailing ships but, on occasion, they were known to float. With its seams calked and its wheels removed, a wagon could be rowed across rivers that were too deep to be forded.

But regardless of whether they could float, the wagons were heavy and as the draft animals weakened and wearied, loads often had to be lightened. Many family heirlooms suffered the fate of the "massive bureaus of carved oak" that one emigrant sadly reported seeing along the trail in 1846.

But, as one guidebook reported, "a pioneer who exercised all due and proper diligence in traveling could cherish a reasonable hope that he will arrive at his journey's end safely and in season."

After choosing a wagon, the emigrant then had to select his draft animals. Horses were expensive, so travelers generally reserved them

Oxen - in addition to being the dumbest animals imaginable - were also slow, but they were the most reliable animals to pull the heavy wagons across the Great Plains.

for saddle riding. The real choice was between mules and oxen and any salesman with travel experience could make a strong case for or against either. A man risked his life and limb just getting acquainted with an unbroken mule, but once it was trained to the harness, a mule turned out to be smart, sure-footed, and durable. Oxen, though, could pull heavier loads, would eat anything, did not run away at night, cost less than a mule, and were less often stolen by unfriendly Native Americans encountered on the trail. Many emigrants swore by oxen, but the animals did have their drawbacks. Their cloven hooves sometimes splintered on rocky trails and took at least two weeks longer to make the trip west than mules. "They don't walk," wrote one exasperated pioneer, "they plod."

No matter what animal the emigrant chose, he needed plenty of them. Generally, at least two teams of mules or two yokes of oxen were needed to pull a loaded wagon. If more than this minimum could be had, so much the better. With extra animals to share the load, the chance that they would last the entire journey was increased. A few wealthier emigrants took several wagons and sets of oxen, and even hired teamsters to drive them. But most pioneers were not well-off - they were men of ordinary means with a wife and four or five children, all of whom pitched in to manage one wagon and perhaps four animals.

The wagons didn't hold much, but the trail ahead held even less. Because travelers knew that they had better take with them whatever they needed, they piled their wagons high with every bit of clothing, food, and furniture they believed essential.

Wagons were jammed with everything imaginable. Keep in mind as you look through this list that most wagons measured about 10-feet by 4-feet in size. In addition to all their goods, the smallest children usually rode in the bed, so room was needed for them, too. And no matter how carefully it was packed, it had to be unpacked every night so that the tent could be set up and food could be prepared.

Here's a basic list of goods and belongings that made their way West with most families:

- Blankets, pillows, and feather beds
- Tent, poles, stakes, and ropes
- Rifles, pistols, knives, and hatchets
- Gunpowder, lead, and bullet molds
- Flour, bacon, coffee, baking soda, corn meal, and tea
- hardtack, dried beans, fruit, and meat, rice, and eggs
- Molasses, vinegar, salt, pepper, and sugar
- Dutch over, kettle, skillet, coffee grinder, and coffee pot
- Tableware, water keg, matches, and butter churn
- clothing like socks, shirts, trousers, boots, and hats
- Dresses, brogans, sun bonnets, and goggles for the sun
- tools, ax, hammer, hoe, plow, shovel, and whetstone
- oxbows, axels, linchpin, spokes, wagon tongue, and rope

There were also generally handy items like:

- Surgical instruments, bandages, liniments, and medicines
- Chamber pot, wash basin, spyglass, needles, and thread
- lanterns, tallow, and candle molds

And, of course, the luxury items, which became the first items to be left along the trail when the wagons became too heavy to pull, broke down, or ran into trouble:

- Canned food
- Plant cuttings
- Books, family albums, and musical instruments
- Dolls, jewelry, china, silverware, and fine linens
- Iron stoves that wouldn't be found out West
- And furniture of all kinds - chairs, sofas, beds, dressers, armoires, pipe organs, pianos, you name it. Just about everything that

While the men drove the wagons and kept things moving, the women and children were in charge of meals, laundry, packing, cooking, building fires, collecting wood, and just about everything else that was needed to make sure the family traveled in as much comfort as possible.

might fit into a parlor or bedroom was found discarded along one trail or another in the mid-nineteenth century.

An emigrant named A.J. McCall found his fellow travelers' tendency to leave nothing behind to be ridiculous. He wrote, "They laid in an over-supply of bacon, flour, and beans, and in addition thereto every conceivable jim-jack and useless article that the wildest fancy could devise, or human ingenuity could invent - pins and needles, brooms and brushes, ox shoes and horseshoes, lasts and leather, glass beads and hawk-bells, jumping jacks and jews-harps, rings and bracelets, pocket mirrors and pocketbooks, calico vests and boiled shirts."

Usually, though, a packing list consisted of food that was chosen according to what would stay fresh and what would not. Some items didn't fare well. An emigrant named Alonzo Delano wrote of this issue: "We had been imposed upon in St. Louis to purchase bacon. But two days later, it began to exhibit more signs of life than we bargained for, having the tendency to walk in insect form."

He must have gotten a bad batch, though. Ordinarily, thick slabs of smoked bacon would keep as long as they were protected from the heat of the plains. Packing bacon in barrels of bran was one way of insulating meat. Similarly, eggs were often packed in barrels of corn meal to keep them from breaking. As the eggs were used, the corn meal was used to make bread. Coffee was consumed by both adults and children since it disguised the taste of most of the water along the trail.

One man wrote that he encountered water that was so bad that his horse "declined the water with decision" and drank coffee instead.

Some pioneers killed buffalo or antelope along the trail to provide meat for their party, but a more dependable supply came from herds of cattle that were led behind the wagon. They also used cows for milking purposes, too. Surplus milk was churned into butter simply by hanging it in pails beneath the jostling wagon. At day's end, the butter would be ready - no churning by hand necessary.

With wagons loaded and animals assembled, all that remained for the pioneers to do before departing was to organize themselves. Within the party, they would nominate candidates, hold elections, and set up temporary governments for the journey. Some of these trail governments were so complicated - and included courts of appeal, executive branches, and legislative bodies -- that they quickly collapsed, usually because the various officials exempted themselves from taking their turns at night guard duty, so the ordinary citizens threw them out of office.

Simpler set-ups were more common. They usually consisted of a wagon train captain and a few officials. The captain would then make most of the decisions, like when the party started out in the morning, when they stopped at noon-day, and where they camped for the night. Unfortunately, his reward was usually a lot of criticism for his poor judgment, especially if the party started later than it should have.

Finally, the day arrived when the wagons were given their last overhaul, the animals were ready, and the weather was promising. It was time to move out and the captain gave the signal. Slowly, the wagons rolled forward, each of them taking their assigned position in line. The "prairie schooners" lumbered on across the Missouri border and onto the open prairie. It was usually a moment of excitement, only tinged by memory of old homes and old friends that had been left behind.

In the 1840s, the United States was now behind them and the emigrants were on their way to the "promised land."

Since most wagon trains departed from western Missouri in the early days of May, they found the grasses of the plains to be thick and luxuriant - perfect for cattle grazing. The grasses covered the rolling mounds of Kansas, waving in the winds.

They also encountered the spring storms on the open plains, marked by lightning and often, a deluge of rain that caused the creeks and rivers to boil over their banks, obliterating all sign of the trail. One account told of a party that, arriving at a creek at day's end, decided to postpone their crossing until morning. It proved to be a terrible decision. A storm that came up during the night forced the group to remain stalled beside that creek for nearly two weeks before the waters went down enough to cross.

Even with bad weather, the emigrants usually had things easy during their first weeks on the trail, following it northwest toward Nebraska and the Platte River. It was a good place to learn to handle the "prairie schooner," to work out any kinks, and to adjust to the adventure on which they had embarked.

For many, it also became the first time they had encountered Native Americans. By the late 1820s, most of them had been driven out of the Eastern states and so the emigrant's arrival in the western lands meant coming face-to-face with a people most had been taught to fear. One traveler noted that, when passing through Indian country, "Every man displayed his arms in the most approved desperado style."

But dealing with the Native Americans of this region required more bargaining skills than expertise with guns. Some of the enterprising natives had established ferries across the larger rivers and did a good business, charging whatever the market would bear. Others pestered the emigrants for sugar, coffee, and whiskey. Under the heel of the U.S. government, most of the Indians of Kansas were a dejected, beaten people. Those travelers expecting the proud Indians found in the works of James Fenimore Cooper - on which many had been raised - were sorely disappointed.

During the initial leg of the journey, evenings in the campgrounds were given over to children's games, parties, music, and dancing. On Sundays, Oregon- or California-bound missionaries preached to those who would listen and gave bibles to those who would take them.

About two weeks out of Independence, the trail crossed the Big Blue, a tributary of the Kansas River. It was an often-changing river that could sometimes be forded, but at other times, required a ferry to cross it. Yet for those who were forced to wait to cross, it had the advantage of being one of the most welcoming campsites along the

Emigrants crossing at a river ferry in Kansas.

trail. Edwin Bryant, a former newspaper publisher from Louisville, described the spot in 1846: "We found a large spring of water, as cold and pure as it had just melted from ice. It gushes from a ledge of rocks, which composes the banks of the stream, falling some ten feet into the basin. Altogether it is one of the most romantic spots I ever saw. We named this the 'Alcove Spring' and future travelers will find the name graven on the rocks."

After the crossing, the trail continued into Nebraska to meet the Platte River, then turned west to follow its south bank. The Platte was a broad band of flowing silt, forming lazy curves from the Rocky Mountains to the Missouri River. The plains on either side of the Platte were covered with short grass, but empty of trees. Most of the timber had been burned off by the Native Americans of the region. What remained could be found on the small sandy islands in the river.

About three miles along the river, the banks on both sides of the Platte rose in sandstone cliffs, which grew taller as the trail continued west. It was a peculiar landscape to those who came from the forested areas in the East.

The emigrants also marveled at the prairie wildlife, like antelope, coyotes, bears, buffalo, and too many prairie dogs to count. The villages of the prairie dogs sometimes covered hundreds of acres and the busy lives of these little creatures intrigued the travelers.

During the 1840s, buffalo were still plentiful in this part of the country. Their numbers, though, diminished with the passing of each wagon train. They could be a nuisance when gathered in large herds.

A panoramic image of a herd of buffalo on the Plains.

The buffalo turned drinking water dark and muddy after ambling through it. Sometimes, the emigrant's oxen and cows wandered off with the buffalo herds, never to be seen again.

At first, the animals were shot and used wastefully. The emigrants usually brought the choice cuts of meat back to the wagons and left the bulk of the carcasses for the wolves. As the buffalo became fewer, they finally learned to make better use of the animals - cutting meat into strips and drying it for future use.

They also used them for warmth, in addition to food. The pelts could be used for blankets and with a lack of wood, the pioneers depended heavily on deposits of buffalo chips - dried dung - for heat and for cooking their meals. Their piles of waste could be found everywhere and when dried, it proved suitable for burning.

Trouble with the native population was also rare along this section of the trail. The Platte valley was in a sort-of "no man's land" between the warlike Pawnee to the north and the Cheyenne to the south. Meetings between the natives and the emigrants were generally peaceable affairs in which the meat was traded for tobacco, ironware, and the traveler's used clothing.

Nevertheless, precautions were always taken. The wagons were drawn up into a circular corral every night. This served the practical purpose of enclosing the livestock so they could graze - and keeping them safe from being stolen. The corral was formed by interlocking wagons, with the tongue of one extending under the rear wheels of the next. Before it was closed, the animals were brought inside and then the last wagon was rolled into place.

During the night, guards were posted around the edges of the corral. As the campfires burned low, the guards sometimes nodded off with exhaustion or fired off wild shots at unknown sounds in the darkness, disturbing the sleep of everyone in camp. But almost never in the history of Western migration did a native raiding party attack a circle of corralled wagons. Such a strategy would have assured heavy casualties among the attackers since the defenders would have been safe within their circular fortress and able to easily pick off any Indians that approached. Such battles - other than rare occasions - are the stuff of western films and bore little resemblance to real life.

But that's not to say that no emigrants were killed along the trail to the west. A single wagon traveling alone or straggling at the end of a long train would sometimes be attacked and robbed. Those who resisted were killed. Years after the "golden age of Western migration" in the 1840s and '50s, the Sioux and Cheyenne, in response to attacks by the U.S. Cavalry, forced a closing of the trails to Oregon and California. There was simply too much bloodshed.

Less dramatic but far more common than attacks by Native Americans were the everyday trail hazards of accidents and disease - especially disease. At least 20,000 emigrants - about 1 out of every 17 who started West - were buried alongside the Oregon Trail. Most of them died from diseases that the pioneers traveled west to try and escape.

Cholera was the most frequent killer. The horror had spread up the Mississippi Valley from New Orleans, bringing with it diarrhea, fever, vomiting, convulsions, and death. It followed the emigrants across Missouri to Independence and St. Joseph and then on to the Platte River Valley. Only the higher elevations of the Rockies seemed to stop its spread, but by then, it had already claimed hundreds of lives. Fallen emigrants were buried in small - and sometimes large - cemeteries along the trail.

Death was so certain for those who contracted cholera that their companions often went ahead and dug their graves before the sick were even dead. The burials were stark and pragmatic. Since there was no lumber for coffins, the dead were wrapped in cloth and buried under rocks and packed earth - anything to keep the wolves out. But this rarely worked. They seemed able to dig the bodies out no matter what precautions were taken.

Over 400 miles west of the Missouri River - and after at least a month on the trail - the emigrants arrived at the confluence of the

The North Fork of the Platte River

Platte's north and south forks. To reach the north fork, which the trail followed, they had to cross the south fork. Depending on when they needed to cross, the south fork might be anywhere from a half-mile to a mile wide, which created significant problems. At times of high water, wagon wheels were removed, and the wagon box became a flat-bottomed boat. It would often be waterproofed by nailing buffalo hides over it.

Even when the water was low, it was still a difficult crossing. Wagon beds were raised by putting blocks under them and then the river was navigated using a diagonal course. It usually took 45 minutes or more to cross it. In 1853, a woman named Phoebe Judson wrote, "We found the river so deep in places that, although our wagon box was propped nearly to the top of the stakes, the water rushed in like a mill race, soaking the bottom of my skirts and deluging our goods."

Beyond the river crossing, the trail changed dramatically and began to provide one adventure after another, which few of the emigrants were prepared for. First, it turned sharply uphill, then traveled 22 miles across a high, waterless plateau, which dropped off sharply toward the valley of the North Platte. Bringing the wagons down the steep incline was always treacherous. At the crest of the hill, the men locked the wheels by chaining them to the wagon boxes and then would slowly slide the wagons by ropes to the bottom of the grade. If a wagon broke loose - and many did - it would tumble down the hill and explode into splinters, flinging the family's belongings into the rocks and brush.

Getting to the bottom of the slope was worth it to most travelers, though, thanks to the wooded glen that waited there. Ash Hollow, as it was called, offered the first shade that most had seen after weeks of travel. It also provided an icy cold spring that allowed emigrants to fill their barrels with fresh clean water for the journey ahead.

Leaving the campsite behind, the trail followed the sandy banks of the North Platte for about 50 miles. The uphill climb through this part of the trail was slight but constant, and even in late June, the nights grew steadily cooler with the

Chimney Rock in Nebraska.

rising altitude. Far off on the horizon, the snow-patched Laramie Mountains - the stepping stones to the Rockies - began to appear.

Closer by, at various points along the trail, strange formations of earth and rock gained the attention of the travelers. The heaps of clay and volcanic ash were described as looking like "a cathedral in ruins." Perhaps the most eye-catching was the formation dubbed Chimney Rock, which thrust 500 feet into the air from a rock-strewn base.

Another 20 miles beyond it was Scott's Bluff, a weathered tangle of peaks, towers, and gulches. A fur trader named Hiram Scott had died there in 1828. No one knew how, so a number of legends grew up around the ominous-looking site - that he had gotten sick and was abandoned by his companions, that he had been murdered by Indians, or maybe killed by a grizzly bear, that his skeleton, when found, was twisted in a death agony or that it was propped against a rock where he died sitting up.

A wagon train that was running on schedule would reach the bluff in late June. Two days more brought the emigrants to Fort Laramie, a frontier outpost in what is now the southeast corner of Wyoming. In a passage that described the fort in one emigrant guidebook it was noted, "You are now 640 miles from Independence, and it is discouraging to tell you that you have not yet traveled one-third of the long road to Oregon."

In most cases, more than one-third of a man's supplies, and much of the strength of his mules and oxen - to say nothing of his patience - had been used up by this time. What was worse was that the road

Sutler's Store on the grounds of Fort Laramie - one of the last sources of supplies before the mountains for many westbound travelers.

beyond the fort truly began to ascend into the Rockies, further draining the stamina of the travelers and their animals. Some travelers never made it any further west than Fort Laramie.

Those that continued usually took a hard look at what they had brought with them and made some decisions about the road ahead - and how they wanted to lighten the load. This could mean dumping an iron stove, an anvil, heavy furniture, or even food. The road just beyond the fort was polluted with household goods and groceries. It was all stuff that had seemed beyond price in Missouri but now was valuable to no one.

The daunting stretch of the trail was mostly barren. At a distance, the mountainsides looked like green meadows, but up close, they turned out to be dry sand and rock, dotted by growths of sage and greasewood. A 50-mile trek would take travelers to the Sweetwater River - named, it was said, for the relief from the bitter and sometimes poisonous springs that had just been passed. The Sweetwater led the trail deeper into the Rockies and as it did, the scenery became always more breathtaking as the mountains began to loom overhead.

A favorite campsite along the Sweetwater was near a granite monolith known as Independence Rock, so called because wagon trains running on time seemed to always reach it around July 4. The rock became famous along the trail. Thousands of names, dates, and initials were chiseled or painted on it during the golden age of the western movement and few pioneers passed up the chance to add one more inscription.

The travelers shivered during the nights and mornings along this part of the trail. At a place called Ice Slough, which was 77 miles past

Wagon train at Independence Rock, the traditional point in the trail reached by most emigrants by July 4.

Independence Rock, a bed of ice lay about a foot beneath the surface even in the heat of noontime, and travelers often carved out large chunks of it for their water barrels. The presence of ice in midsummer indicated that the emigrants had reached an altitude above 7,000 feet. They had, in fact, reached the crest of the trail - the Continental Divide - at South Pass in the Wind River Mountains.

Many travelers found South Pass to be a disappointment. It was nothing like the dramatic gorge they had envisioned. Instead, the trail crossed a broad grassy meadow and then started to dip downward toward the Pacific Ocean. Travelers could not even be sure they had reached this milestone until they went another four miles and reached the landmark dubbed Pacific Springs. There they could celebrate their arrival at the eastern boundary of the Oregon Territory. There were still rugged mountains - the Sierra Nevada on their way to California or the Cascades going to Oregon - that lay between them and their destinations, but for the moment it was a thought they could put out of their minds.

After a night or two at Pacific Springs, the trains were again on the move. Soon, the emigrants would have to make a choice of trails. Some of them took the safe, roundabout route with plenty of water that dropped southwest to Fort Bridger.

Fort Bridger, described by emigrant Joel Palmer in 1844, "as shabby concern built of poles and daubed with mud," was home to legendary mountain man Jim Bridger who had been at home in the

Rockies since 1822. He had built the fort in 1843 to settle down and make a few dollars providing emigrants with supplies and fresh oxen.

Though it offered fresh water and good forage, the Fort Bridger route seemed a needless detour to many emigrants. They chose a shortcut - Sublette's Cutoff - which ran straight across a sunburned stretch of land with no grass. The only water available was on its far western side at the Green River. Those who braved the shortcut traveled through ravines and across dried-up alkali lakes. The route was not always clear in guidebooks of the day, but few lost their way because the trail was clearly marked by the bleached bones of abandoned animals. When they reached the other side of the cutoff, the melted snow water of the Green River had such a magnetic pull on the tired oxen that survived the trip that they would break into a frenzied gallop for the last few miles to the river. When travelers on the cutoff rejoined the main trail, they had an 85-mile, seven-day jump on those who had gone the long way past Fort Bridger.

From that point, the wagons moved northwest along the trail. In 70 miles, they passed Soda Springs, where the naturally carbonated water was able to raise bread. To some travelers, the water tasted like beer and, according to an emigrant named Alonzo Delano, it made good lemonade when mixed with citrus and sugar.

Just 55 miles later, at Fort Hall - built by Nathaniel Wyeth and later operated by the Hudson Bay Company - the wagon trains split up once again. This time, though, it was for good. A few miles west of Fort Hall, at the Raft River, the trail to California branched off from the Oregon Trail. The California Trail veered southwest through an arid, rocky landscape of sagebrush and greasewood into the fearsome Great Basin of Utah and Nevada. Eventually, after 525 more miles and a month of travel, they would reach the Sierra Nevada and if they stayed on time, they would cross the mountains before the first winter snows.

But they had to get through the Great Basin first.

Many called it "a killer of men." Isolated, almost barren, and covering an area of about 200,000 square miles, it formed a cauldron in which sand, clay, and circling mountains soaked up the sun's heat. In the middle of the kettle was the Great Salt Lake and the viscous Humboldt River, which oozed rather than flowed and eventually disappeared into a thick patch of alkali dust. In this bleak and terrifying place, the hopes of many of the pioneers dried up, too.

Strangely, the agents from the Hudson Bay Company at Fort Hall, encouraged emigrants to take the grueling route to California. Their motive was simple and self-serving, though - they wanted to delay the inevitable settlement of the fur-rich Oregon country for as long as possible. They told travelers that the trail to Oregon was a dangerous journey of roaring rivers, hostile Indians, famine, and winter storms - all of which was true.

And it got worse from there. About 300 miles of the trail ran along the Snake River's high, boulder-strewn south rim. Just getting drinking water meant climbing down into the river gorge and carefully getting back up again. By the time a man had made this dangerous journey, he generally needed another drink.

Beyond that was the formidable barrier of the Blue Mountains. After the mountains, the emigrants still faced either a dangerous 230-mile trip on rafts or boats down the Columbia River or an exhausting 250 miles by wagon over the Cascades to the Willamette Valley.

It was on the final leg of the journey that Oregon emigrants - just like their counterparts heading for California - faced the greatest dangers and had the limits of their endurance tested.

In the earliest days of travel to Oregon, there was no feasible wagon route over the mountains. That would come later. For now, it was a grueling and treacherous climb up steep trails and through mountain passes. It seemed much easier to travel along the mighty Columbia River, running close to Fort Walla Walla, which was near the trailhead. Many emigrants abandoned their wagons, built large boats, and braved the river - often with disastrous results.

By the time the pioneers began their river travels, they had been on the trail from Missouri for almost five months. There was still four weeks ahead of them, even on the river, and that final voyage proved to be the worst ordeal of all. The tired travelers left shore, only to plunge into several horrendous sets of rapids for which they had no experience. Tragedies frequently occurred, resulting in the destruction of boats, loss of belongings, and worse, settlers that were swept into the surging waters and were never seen again.

Thanks to the scores of emigrants that perished in the Columbia River, attempts were made to open alternate land routes across the

Stephen Meek, the former fur trapper and originator of what became known as the "Terrible Trail."

Cascades. Some of those attempts didn't go much better than navigating the river had turned out.

In 1845, Stephen Meek, a onetime fur trapper, persuaded 200 emigrant families to take an abandoned Indian trail through the mountains south of the Columbia. He claimed it was a shorter route. By the time the party emerged from the wilderness two months later, 75 of the emigrants were dead. Some died of starvation while others were poisoned by drinking alkali water. The disastrous shortcut earned its place in history as "Meek's Terrible Trail."

In 1846, though, workers hired by Samuel Barlow of Illinois did complete a wagon road over the mountains south of Mount Hood and it soon became the standard emigrant route to Oregon.

The search for a shortcut also became an obsession on the trail to California, too. In 1846, about 300 pioneers took the California Trail south from Fort Hall, along the Humboldt River, and over the Sierra Nevada to the Sacramento Valley. Though they were plagued by hunger, thirst, and exhaustion, most of them reached their destination without serious misfortune.

But there was one now-infamous group of emigrants that did not.

They made every mistake that travelers could make - from overloading their wagons to being overconfident they could make up lost time after leaving home too late. Then, at Fort Bridger, they made one last bad decision - they decided to take an untested shortcut to California.

It would be this final mistake that earned the Donner Party its tragic place in the history of the untamed West.

2. A HUNGER FOR LAND

The Donners had always been a family who craved and cared for their land. To them, land was money. They tilled the earth, cultivated their crops, and dreamed of wild land and abundant harvests. It was a dream and a hunger that would always drive them west.

George Donner, Sr. was born in 1752 in Lancaster County, Pennsylvania, to German immigrants who eventually moved to North Carolina. When war broke out against the British in 1775, George and two of his brothers fought for American independence.

When the conflict was over, George went home, back to his farm, and back to his wife, Mary Margaret, and his first child, Ann Mary. Seven more children followed - Lydia, Elizabeth, George, Jr., Tobias, Jacob, Susannah, and John. The children worked almost as hard as their parents did. Rural life was never easy. There was always planting and harvesting to be done, as well as regular chores. The winters were worse with wood to be cut, fires to tend, game to hunt, and work animals to tend, no matter how much snow fell, how much ice covered the walkways, or how cold the nights were that allowed pails of water to freeze even close to the fire. As the oldest son, George, Jr. cared for his younger siblings, leading the boys on squirrels hunts and the girls to forage for wild grapes and hickory nuts.

The Donners worked various farms throughout the 1790s, but by 1795, began to get the urge to travel. At least one of the Donners had already followed the trail of the adventurous Daniel Boone and went west. In 1799, George, Sr. decided to uproot his family and look for new land in the west. He sold off all his property, except for a quarter acre that he reserved as a burial plot for his parents and older relatives.

In the early 1800s, George and Mary, along with family members that included George, Jr., and Jacob, moved to Kentucky, which speculators had been promoting as "the most fertile land in North America and probably the world."

The Donners traveled the most direct route west - through the Cumberland Gap of the Appalachian Mountains, across the edge of Tennessee, and along the popular Wilderness Road into Kentucky. They settled on farmland just south of Lexington, a fertile area that made all of them rich. They farmed, raised fine horses, and sought out wives and husbands from other families in the region.

On December 12, 1809, George, Jr. married Susannah Holloway, daughter of a local farmer. Like most young women of the time, Susannah had little education, but she knew how to work hard, keep a good house, and raise children, of which the couple had six - Mary, William, Sarah, Lydia, Elizabeth, and Susannah.

As the various branches of the Donner family grew, George Sr. and his sons acquired more land. However, they were ready to be on the move again - this time to neighboring Indiana. After the War of 1812, thousands of Kentuckians, many collecting land bonuses for their military service, crossed the Ohio River into Indiana. In 1818, just two years after Indiana became a state, the federal government purchased all the Delaware and Miami tribal lands and opened them up for legal settlement in 1821.

By April of that year, the Donner families - including George, Sr. and three of his sons, George, Jr., Jacob, and Tobias - settled in the northeastern part of Decatur County. Just after the move, Susannah, George, Jr.'s wife and mother of his children, died. His mother and his sisters-in-law helped care for his children as he settled the land.

The Donners should have been at peace now. They had new, rich land, new homes, and were respected in the neighborhood. But, like so many other families of the era, the Donners were always ready to pull up stakes and move on. Their incentive was not for lack of success. They simply wished to leave what was perceived as depleted land for new, more fertile ground. Poor farmers couldn't afford to leave their land, but the Donners could, and they did.

The need to be on the movie was always there, and it continued to pull them west.

In 1825, they came to Illinois. In those days, the state was only a handful of years old and was considered the western frontier by those in the East.

At first, nineteenth century settlers shunned the "dreaded prairies" of which Illinois had plenty. There were no trees there, only a thick grass that often grew as tall as a man on horseback, so most believed the ground would not be good for farming. So, they built their homes in the woods and spent countless hours clearing the timber for their farms - only to discover that the richest, darkest soil could be found beneath the grass, not the trees.

A photo believed to be George Donner as a younger man. There are no known photographs of any of his wives, including Tamzene, a figure that is central to the story of the Donner Party.

One of the problems with photographs of the figures in the story is that photography was still uncommon in the 1840s, so many of the survivors were not photographed until much later in life, so they appear older than they were at the time of the events in this book.

Illinois gained statehood in 1818 and throughout the 1820s, the ease of purchasing land from the government, along with waves of American migration, brought thousands of new settlers to the state, including the Donners.

George, Jacob, and other family members, including their father, George, Sr., ventured west and began buying 80-acre parcels of land in Sangamon County, Illinois, in the central part of the state. George, Jr. and his six children were established there by 1828, along with Jacob and their sister, Susannah, her husband, Micajah, and their five children. Another brother, Tobias, and his family also came west but eventually settled on a farm elsewhere in Illinois.

The Donner farm was near the Sangamon River, which provided water for farms in the summer and ice in the winter, which could be cut and stored for use throughout the year. The area was filled with massive oak and walnut trees, which provided plenty of firewood and lumber for building homes and businesses in nearby Springfield, which became the state capital in 1837.

It didn't take George long to find a new wife in Illinois. On January 10, 1829, he married Mary Blue Tennant, a widow with no children. Their daughter, Elitha, was born in 1832 and another daughter, Leanna, followed in 1834. By that time, some of the children from George's first marriage were on their own, including his son, William, who had married Elizabeth Hunter in 1832. In 1835, George's younger brother, Jacob, married George's sister-in-law, Elizabeth Blue, a divorced woman with two young sons. Jacob and Elizabeth went on to have five children of their own - George, Mary, Isaac, Samuel, and Lewis.

The Donners, happy and hard-working, continued to prosper in Illinois until George's second wife, Mary, suddenly died in 1837. That same year, a national bank crisis touched off a major recession that damaged Springfield's economy. The combination of his wife's death, the bank panic, and the Donner urge to be on the move resulted in George leaving Illinois for a time.

In 1838, George, his two youngest daughters, and his grown son William and his family packed up and asked relatives to care for their farms while they went off to the new Republic of Texas. George had heard tales about attractive offers of land in Texas and wanted to see the place for himself.

The Donners acquired some land south of Houston, near the Gulf of Mexico but had doubts about settling there for good. Besides finding the marshy swamp land poor for farming, they also had to contend with snakes, alligators, mosquitoes, a harsh, humid climate, and the constant threat of dysentery, cholera, and Yellow Fever.

And there was also the Karankawa Indians who, while their numbers were reduced, still resided in the area. They were reputed to be cannibals who practiced a ceremonial ritual that included eating their dead and dying enemies. Pirate Jean Lafitte had once referred to them as "demons from hell."

George planted his first crop but soon realized moving to Texas was a mistake. About the only good thing that happened there was the birth of William and Elizabeth's third child, a baby named George T. Donner in honor of his grandfather. He didn't plant a second crop. By 1839, after being away for less than a year, the clan returned to Sangamon County and their farm on German Prairie in the Clear Lake Township.

Soon after returning home, George rode out to visit his sisters, Lydia and Susannah, at their homes on nearby Sugar Creek. Along the way, he happened upon a woman and several children standing waist deep in the grass and flowers of a meadow. He climbed down from his horse, took off his hat, and introduced himself. It was the first time that he saw the face of Tamzene Dosier.

She had dark hair, blue-gray eyes, and was dressed simply but elegantly in a wide-brimmed hat and gloves. Barely five-feet-tall, she shook George's hand and later said that she immediately felt at ease in the presence of the big, bearded, broad-shouldered farmer. Tamzene told him that she was a schoolteacher at Sugar Creek and she and her students were on a botany field trip.

The first meeting between the two of them only lasted a few minutes, but George knew that it would not be their last meeting - and so did Tamzene.

Tamzene was 37-years-old when she met the older George Donner. Born in 1901 in Newburyport, Massachusetts, she was the youngest child of a wealthy sea captain named William Eustis and his wife, Tamesin. She had originally been named after her mother, who died when the child was only seven, but when she was older, she changed the spelling to Tamzene.

Her widowed father later married Hannah Cogswell, a loving stepmother who encouraged the little girl to follow her dreams. Tamzene was well-educated and a voracious reader. She spoke French, wrote poetry, and was schooled in art, philosophy, and mathematics. Her favorite subject was botany and she put her artistic talents into creating detailed drawings of the flowers and plants she studied.

After receiving her teacher's certificate, Tamzene accepted a position at a school in Maine. But the meager wages and a growing desire to leave New England caused her to become restless. She took another post at an academy in Elizabeth City, North Carolina, and moved south, far away from home and her family. She never regretted the decision, as frightening as she later admitted that it had been.

She was a strong and resilient young woman and by 1829 was not only teaching but was also the head of the Female Department at the academy. She was also nearly 30 and still single at a time when most women were married a decade earlier. Soon, though, she met a "young man of education and good family" named Tully Dozier. They were married on Christmas Eve 1829.

As Tamzene wrote to her sister, Elizabeth, "I do not intend to boast of my husband, but I find him one of the best of men - affectionate, industrious, and possessed of an upright heart. These are requisite to make life pass on smoothly."

Although Tully was not a "man of means," the two of them lived comfortably on his farm and Tamzene's teaching salary. Within two years, they were the parents of a baby boy that Tamzene lovingly described as being "a true copy of his father."

But her joy would not last.

In a letter to her sister on June 28, 1831, Tamzene noted that her son "has been very sick, and for a few days we feared we should lose him but at this time is in fine health and sitting upon the table as I write. He at one time scolds me for the ink stand and for another knocks my knuckles with a spoon." Tamzene also fretted about her husband's health. "I have had excellent health since I saw you, but Mr. Dozier had twice been reduced very low since we married. His precarious health and our strong dislike to slavery has caused us to determine upon removing to some western state. But not until next year."

Their move together never took place. An influenza epidemic changed Tamzene's life forever. Her son died on September 28 and Tully himself passed on December 24. Both had perished from influenza. To make matters worse, Tamzene had been pregnant at the time of her son's death and suffered a miscarriage a short time later. In despair, she wrote to her sister, but received no immediate reply. When a letter did finally come, Tamzene found it disappointingly short and less than comforting.

She now felt completely alone in the world. She threw herself into writing and settling her husband's estate until eventually, she and her sister reconciled. After that, she left her position at the academy and returned to the home of her father and stepmother in Massachusetts. She remained there until 1836, when she received a letter from her older brother, William, who had recently lost his wife. He asked Tamzene to move to his home in Auburn, Illinois, near Springfield, to tutor his two children. Tamzene jumped at the chance, made the move, and she proved to be so successful that she was soon asked to teach at the local school.

Dealing with a herd of unruly farm children was much different than teaching young ladies at a fancy academy, but Tamzene relished the challenge. One of her male students later recalled the moment when he met his new teacher, thinking how easy it would be to pick her up, toss her over his shoulder, and pitch her out the door. He changed his tune, though, after Tamzene took charge. "Her pluck had won our admiration and her quiet dignity held our respect, and we boys ceased to wonder at the ease with which she overturned our plans and made us eager to adopt hers. No teacher ever taught at Sugar Creek who won the affections and ruled the pupils more easily than she. She expected us to come right up to the mark; but if we got into trouble, she was always ready to help us out, and she could do it in the quickest way imaginable."

Her students loved the frequent field trips that she took them on to collect plant specimens. It was during one of these trips, three years after she had taken over the school, that she met George Donner.

George wasted no time in planning another meeting between them. He began making every effort to win the heart of the pretty schoolteacher. Fortunately for the lovestruck farmer, Tamzene was no longer in mourning for her late husband and was willing to try marriage again. George was almost 30 years older than she was, but he was a prosperous landowner in good health and was well-liked and admired in the community. Tamzene quickly learned that he was also a good and kind man.

They were married on May 24, 1839, in a quiet ceremony that was attended by family and friends. Tamzene became a caring mother to George's youngest daughters and friends with his older children and their spouses. Tamzene also gave birth to three more daughters - Frances, Georgia, and Eliza. Now with five daughters and a beautiful wife, George built a large stone house for them. Tamzene entertained friends, wrote poetry for the local newspaper, and delighted in watching the family's bees gather nectar from the field of wildflowers behind their home.

In 1840, Tamzene wrote to her sister: "I find my husband a kind friend, who does all in his power to promote my happiness and I have a fair prospect for a pleasant old age as anyone."

She told her sister about George's lifetime of rambling, from North Carolina to Kentucky, Indiana, Illinois, and Texas, and then added, "But his roving, he says, is over. He finds no place so much to his mind as this."

And George was right. He would not leave Illinois - for six more years anyway.

3. CALIFORNIA DREAMING

The cheap and fertile land that attracted the Donner family to Illinois was not the only thing that brought new settlers there. Another major reason to come to the state was lead. The great demand for this important mineral after the War of 1812 brought hundreds of miners to the Native American lands of northwestern Illinois, which at the time was the largest area of lead mining in the world.

One of the miners who flocked to the region was an eager young immigrant named James Frazier Reed. By most accounts, his family name was originally Reednoski, or Rynowski, until the late 1700s. That was when his ancestors had chosen exile over submission after Poland was divided among its powerful neighbors of Russia, Prussia, and Austria. After they fled the upheaval, they became the Reeds and moved to Ireland. They established themselves in County Armagh in Northern Ireland and James Reed was born there on November 14, 1800. His mother, Martha Frazier Reed, gave him the middle name Frazier to honor her lineage from the famous Clan Frazier of Scottish history.

James was a young boy when his father died, and he and his mother moved to America. They lived in Philadelphia for a time before settling in Virginia, where other members of the Frazier family had lived for many years after escaping the tyranny of the British crown. James attended school until he was nine, which was old enough to work.

Galena, where James Reed first began working in Illinois.

He moved in with the family of James Anderson Frazier, a maternal uncle, who employed him at his general store.

By the time he was 20, James was ready to go out on his own. He had heard stories of the lead bonanza in Illinois and Wisconsin and he dreamed of making more money than he'd earned as a clerk. He said goodbye to his mother and the rest of the Fraziers and headed west.

James soon arrived in Galena, a remote settlement that was surrounded by wilderness but was quickly becoming a mining center because of the very stuff that the town was named for - *galena*, the Latin word for lead ore. Carved into the steep, rocky hillside along the Fever River - a tributary of the nearby Mississippi River - the village began to thrive as men flocked there by land and steamboat to work the mines. In 1825, the busy river port was one of the largest towns in the state with more than 10,000 residents.

Miners like James Reed, who were too far from home and had no place to go once winter arrived and the steamboats and teams of oxen went south, had to carve caves out of the hillside or shiver in a hut during cold weather. The chill resulted in outbreaks of "cabin fever" that could be soothed by visiting brothels, saloons, and gambling dens. Liquor flowed freely. Bets were placed on cockfights and wolf fights and scores were settled by "stone duels." This meant that men would stand next to a pile of river rocks and throw stones at each other until one of them was "unconscious or dead." There were very few women in the camp - aside from the "soiled doves" in the brothels - so the men did their own cooking and washing.

The death toll in the winter months, usually caused by murder or frostbite, was only matched by the number of mining accidents that occurred in the season. If you mix in death from diseases like milk sickness, dysentery, pneumonia, and malaria, Galena could be a fairly unhealthy place to live.

But James endured. If was nothing like his home in Virginia, but he managed to prosper in northwestern Illinois. It's unknown whether he made his money scraping lead from the ground or whether he worked his way into a management position, but after a few years, he accumulated a substantial sum that allowed him to seek a greater fortune elsewhere. He moved south to Sangamon County in 1831, where he eventually became involved in several businesses.

Not at first, though. He had barely made it to Springfield when he was asked to return north with a rifle in his hands.

In the Spring of 1832, the short-lived Black Hawk War erupted in Illinois and Wisconsin. Black Hawk, a Sauk war leader, rallied a confederacy of Native Americans who were enraged that white farmers had plowed up their sacred burial grounds and planted corn on ancestral lands. The Sauk had lost the land in a treaty they considered invalid. Inevitably, violence broke out between the natives and the settlers, causing white residents to abandon their farms and seek shelter in larger towns or at army posts.

A call went out for volunteers to curb the behavior of the Indians. All white males between the ages of 18 and 45 were obligated to enlist in the state militia. James joined a scouting unit of mounted volunteers known as "Spy Company," led by a Springfield physician named Jacob M. Early. Besides James, others on the company's rolls included James Clyman, a veteran of the War of 1812 who had spent time as a mountain man in the far West; a rising star in Illinois politics named Stephen A. Douglas; Robert Anderson, a West Point graduate who would command Fort Sumter 30 years later at the start of the Civil War; and a gangly storekeeper from New Salem named Abraham Lincoln. Like the Donner family, Lincoln had come to Illinois by way of Kentucky and

One of Reed's close friends was a Springfield attorney named Abraham Lincoln. The two men had fought together in the Black Hawk War, but Reed would not be around to see Lincoln begin his rise in Illinois politics.

Indiana and like his new friend James Reed, he had only recently settled in Sangamon County.

The company saw no real military action during its few weeks of service. They were mustered out of service on July 10, 1832 in Wisconsin. Lincoln and Reed's soldiering days were over, but the two men became good friends.

Back in Sangamon County, James became involved in a variety of businesses, including a general store that provided enough of an income for him that he purchased a farm in late 1832. The following year, he opened a starch factory just northeast of Springfield at German Prairie, where the Donners lived and farmed.

Commercial starch was just making its way into households on the Illinois prairie. Until starch came along, cooked gluten paste was used to make men's shirt collars stiff and give body to the petticoats that were fashionable with ladies. Starch was a logical product since so many local farmers - like the Donners - grew corn and wheat. To solicit grain from farmers and at the same time offer an alternative method of payment to those who owed him money from other business ventures, James placed notices in the Springfield newspaper. He also offered to sell livestock, farm implements, oxen, and other goods in exchange for cash or wheat.

James became well-respected by his business associates, but he wasn't always well-liked. Many people were put off by him, saying that he was overbearing and arrogant.

But he did make friends over time. Among the closest to him were members of the Keyes family who, like Reed, had come to Illinois from Virginia. Humphrey Keyes had been an established landowner near the Shenandoah River in Virginia with a working plantation and slaves when his first wife died, leaving him with five children. He married Sarah Handley in 1803, and the couple had six more children.

In Springfield, Keyes's son, James, opened a tailor shop near the town square, which is probably where Humphrey met James Reed. They became close friends and by the time Humphrey passed away in 1833, Reed had become engaged to one of the older man's daughters, Elizabeth.

But that wedding never took place.

Tragically, Elizabeth died during a cholera pandemic that swept the entire country in 1833. There was no known prevention or cure for what was dubbed "the ghost on the stairs." At that time, doctors had no idea what caused the disease and were unable to treat it. Thousands died on the Illinois frontier, forcing towns of every size to enlarge or begin public burial grounds for the dead.

The disease not only claimed the life of Elizabeth Keyes, but it also struck her brother-in-law, Lloyd Backenstoe, a 23-year-old tailor who worked in James Keyes's shop. Lloyd left behind a widow, Margaret, and a one-year-old daughter, Virginia.

Born in 1814, Margaret - two years older than sister Elizabeth - had little time for grief. Apparently, neither did James Reed. Margaret was suffering from the illness herself when she gave her dead sister's fiancée permission to court her. She was, of course, well acquainted with James, a handsome young man who wore fine suits that had been sewn by her brother. He was practically part of the family already.

James and Margaret married on a cool October evening in 1835, following a short engagement. Margaret was still in poor health and the ceremony took place with the bride lying in bed and the groom standing next to her, holding her hand.

James became the legal guardian of his stepdaughter in 1836. Although he never formally adopted her, Virginia used his surname, and they had a very strong bond between them. Many people who knew the family commented that she was always treated as if she was his own child. When Virginia was grown, she recalled that James was "the most loving and indulgent stepfather that ever lived."

In the eight years that followed their marriage - and Margaret's recovery from cholera - their family grew larger. Martha Jane, who everyone called Patty, was born in 1838. She was followed by James, Jr. in 1841 and Thomas in 1843. Their widowed grandmother, Sarah

James and Margaret Reed. This photograph was taken in California, after the events that are chronicled in this book. Both were younger when the trip West occurred.

Keyes, also joined the Reed household and helped Margaret, who suffered from occasional migraines, with the children.

To most who knew him, James Reed - with his prosperous business, happy marriage, and brood of children - appeared to be in an enviable position. His various enterprises, including his store, his starch factory, and real estate investments, were doing well, and allowed him to expand into new commercial pursuits. So, James did not hesitate when he was offered another opportunity. It came from John Taylor, an early merchant and land speculator in the area, who platted a new settlement on the Sangamon River, just a few miles from Springfield.

By 1837, the idea of bringing a railroad to Illinois was no longer just talk and speculation. That year, the legislature, which included Reed's friend Lincoln, passed an internal improvement act that funded a network of train lines, starting with the Northern Cross Railroad, which was planned to run across Illinois from the Indiana state line to Quincy.

A contract to construct the rail line between Springfield and the Sangamon was awarded to James Reed. Plans called for the rail line to pass through Taylor's proposed town site, where he was selling lots for homes and businesses. It was also where James Reed had constructed a large mill on the river that would produce railroad ties.

All that was needed was to choose a name for the settlement. Only one name was suggested, and it was in honor of the man who employed so many in the area and gave the settlement its purpose - they called it Jamestown.

For a few more years, life was good for James and Margaret Reed. They had a new comfortable home in Jamestown, with plenty of room for Margaret's mother and the four children who were born over the next few years.

At Reed's mill on the Sangamon River, he stopped producing starch and hired more workers to help cut wooden ties for the railroad that was being touted as the first to operate in "the entire area west of the Allegheny Mountains and north of the Ohio River." Surveying began in 1837 on the first section of track that would link Meredosia, a tiny town on the Illinois River, to the new capital of Springfield, which was 59 miles away. Although the bank panic of 1837 had ended the funding for the state's internal improvement plan, political and business leaders remained optimistic that at least part of the railroad would be completed.

Grading along the right-of-way took all winter. By spring 1838, the construction crews were ready to start laying track, but a shortage of materials slowed things down through the summer. Iron for the rails had to be shipped from New Orleans to St. Louis, then had to go up the Mississippi and Illinois Rivers to Meredosia. By November, only eight miles of track had been completed.

It would take four years to complete that section of the line. Because of the prolonged national economic collapse that ravaged the credit of the Illinois government and reduced the value of its bonds, it was almost impossible for work to continue. The first train didn't roll into Springfield until February 15, 1842.

The public lined up eagerly as the Northern Cross began making three weekly trips between Springfield and Meredosia. One excursion of 30 Springfield residents, which including Abraham Lincoln's future wife, Mary Todd, a brass band, and a cargo of 205 barrels of flour, took the train 30 miles to Jacksonville for a celebration.

It's probably a good thing they didn't go any farther than that. It cost just 20-cents to ship a barrel of flour to the Illinois River, but passengers paid $2.50 --that's $75 today -- for the trip. It took more than two hours to travel the distance if there were no delays, which became more frequent. It wasn't long before farmers began complaining that the state-owned railroad was inadequate and inefficient for transporting their goods to market and that was nothing compared to what people were saying about using the train to travel.

Not only was it slow and costly, but it could also be dangerous and occasionally lethal. Accidents and derailments were common. Farmers were known to steal rails to use as sled runners or to pull up the wooden ties for building material. Rails at that time were strips of iron nailed to oak timbers. They were inexpensive but prone to failure. The pounding of the wheels shook the spikes loose and consequently, the iron strips would separate from the wooden base, curl upward, and shoot through the wooden underside of the carriages, sometimes injuring or even killing a passenger or a crew member. The railroad men called the curls of steel "snake heads." Trusted workers - the "snake spikers" - were assigned to patrol sections of track with sledgehammers and a leather bag of new spikes. If they spotted a snake head, they hammered it back down flat to the wood again and banged it into place. Despite their efforts, though, it was difficult for them to keep up.

As a result of these problems, James Reed saw his holdings start to shrink. Early in the struggle to build the railroad, he wisely decided to diversify. He partnered with John Weber, a skilled cabinetmaker, and they expanded the mill to produce more than just railroad ties. Soon, they were manufacturing furniture, chairs, and ornamental fencing, too. The two men advertised quality craftmanship and low prices and while cash customers were preferred, they also accepted "cattle, hogs, wheat, corn, potatoes, bacon, lard, butter, and eggs" in payment.

The mill thrived for several years until 1841, when John Weber lost his left hand in a buzz-saw accident. Fortunately for Weber, he was right-handed and was able to find work as a copyist for state land records because he certainly wasn't interested in working in the mill any longer.

This left James without a partner - a partner who had all the woodworking expertise. But he didn't give up. He started advertising for a man to take Weber's place as well as for timber cutters, oxen drivers, and men to operate the wood turner and lathe. People still needed lumber and the railroad still needed ties, but the sad news was that the Northern Cross Railroad was doomed.

Land speculator John Taylor wasn't giving up on the railroad quite yet, though. His sale of lots in Jamestown were far below what he'd hoped so he began trying to boost the railroad in 1843 by leasing the Northern Cross operation from the state. The tracks and train were in such poor condition, however, that the train could only travel six miles per hour, down from the 15 miles per hour from the previous year. The engines frequently failed so the trains often had to be pulled by mules and oxen, an embarrassment to the workers and to Taylor. He tried several different schemes to fix the problem but none of them worked.

By 1845, even the optimistic Reed had to admit the rail system was a disaster. The state continued to run the decrepit line until 1847, when it was auctioned off for $21,000 - a small fraction of its original cost. It eventually became part of the Wabash Railroad line.

After the railroad shut down, Jamestown fell on harder times. Taylor was unable to pay property taxes on the town, forcing the land to be sold. Reed tried to keep the mill going by grinding corn and wheat, but this didn't raise enough money to take care of his growing debt.

With his prospects growing dim, he turned to an old and trusted friend for advice - Abraham Lincoln. His friend from the Black Hawk War had made a name for himself in Springfield as a respected attorney and likely arranged a job for Reed as a U.S pension agent, dispensing government funds to military veterans in Central Illinois. He kept the job for less than a year. The income helped him to pay off some of his debts, but it wasn't enough. Desperate, Reed mortgaged the mill, along with some other real estate he owned, to the Sangamon County school commission for $1,000. He was now facing complete financial ruin, but even so, he refused to give up.

Historian Bernard DeVoto calls 1846 a pivotal "year of decision" in American history, when an increasing number of people made up their minds about the future.

This painting by John Gast - called "American Progress" became a symbol for Manifest Destiny. The figure floating above the scene is Lady Columbia, the symbol of the United States. Traveling west, she wears the Star of Empire on her brow. In one hand, she carries a book, bringing education to the West. In the other is a string of telegraph wire.

Railroad and emigrants follow behind her, while ahead, wild animals and Indians flee before her enlightening atmosphere. The Indians have left their teepees and the bones of the buffalo behind. To the East the skies are clear, representing the influence of civilization and technology, but to the west, over the Rocky Mountains, where the white man has barely reached, it is dark and unsettled.

It was a time when countless Americans began to generally accept the idea that God had bestowed on the United States the right to grow and prosper by advancing the country from coast to coast. The phrase "Manifest Destiny" came from magazine editor John L. O'Sullivan. He urged the annexation of Texas and complete control of the Oregon Territory, which had been shared with England.

Manifest Destiny became a phrase that was on everyone's lips. The federal government began encouraging easterners to move across the Mississippi River in greater numbers, promising natural resources, vast farmland, mineral riches, and timber forests.

Many were pushed West from the church pulpit. These were the latter days of the Second Great Awakening, the revival movement of the nineteenth century that gave birth to numerous churches, metaphysical cults, and movements like Spiritualism. Powerful figures told their followers that America had been chosen by the Almighty and was "destined to lead the way in the moral and political emancipation of the world."

The entwining of religion with Manifest Destiny served as a creation myth for the United States. It became engrained in the national consciousness that many Americans still accept to this day. The belief that God intended for the continent to be under the control of Christian Americans became official U.S. government policy. It created an incentive to take lands from those considered inferior to white Americans - the indigenous tribal people who were characterized as "savages" and Mexicans, who most believed were lazy and backwards. In short, Manifest Destiny became a convenient way to colonize the rest of the continent and wipe out anyone who got in the way.

In Illinois, the restlessness sparked by Manifest Destiny began to resonate but not everyone was ready to look elsewhere for greener pastures.

Despite their many years of movement, George and Jacob Donner had settled down as practical businessmen who were concerned about the success or failure of their business. They were not inclined to leave the Springfield area.

The same could also be said for James Reed, but his situation was different. He now had five children - Margaret had given birth to Gershom just before New Year's 1845 - and more responsibility. The new baby was sickly, which added to the pressure. Even with help from Sarah and the Reeds' oldest daughter, Virginia, the added stress caused an increase in Margaret's terrible migraines.

The new stress may have been the reason that Reed began thinking that a fresh start was in order. He began looking westward. Whether or not his friend Lincoln fully agreed with Reed, he could understand the attraction. Both men had received firsthand accounts from family members who had made the journey to the Pacific in the same wagon train in 1845.

William Levi Todd, Lincoln's nephew by marriage, and Robert Keyes, one of Margaret Reed's brothers, had joined a wagon train that left Springfield bound for the Oregon Territory. Reed and others in Springfield waited anxiously for news from the emigrants that took two months to arrive in the form of a letter from the caravan's leader, William Ide, which was printed in the local newspaper. By then, the group had made it to Fort Laramie.

The expedition then camped at Fort Hall, in present-day Idaho, to replenish supplies and trade for horses from some Snake Indians.

While at the fort, they had been approached by a fur trapper and trail guide named Caleb Greenwood, He hoped to persuade them to go to Alta California, then a province of Mexico, instead of Oregon. Greenwood - described by those who didn't like him, mostly because he was married to an Indian woman and had sons with her, as an "old mountaineer, well stocked with falsehoods - had a vested interest in diverting wagons to California. He had been hired as a recruiting agent to try and convince any settlers he encountered to veer southwest.

After the party listened to Greenwood's convincing spiel, a heated debate began that almost became violent. Finally, the matter was put to a vote and many of the emigrants - including Ide, Todd, and Keyes - decided on California.

With Greenwood and his sons in the lead, a company of about 100 struck out for the Sacramento Valley. When the caravan reached the slopes of the Sierra Nevada, they split into smaller groups, each one determined to find their own way over the mountains. Little by little, the various groups eventually straggled to safety with far fewer cattle than the number they started the journey with. It had been difficult, but all were thankful they had made the mountain crossing before the first snowfall.

William Todd and Robert Keyes wrote back home to alleviate the worry of the family left behind. Todd stayed on in the immediate area, but Robert Keyes made his way to Monterey, a major seaport and the capital of Alta California. He soon discovered that Monterey was too exotic for his tastes and in a letter to James Reed in October 1845, he complained about both California and the people who lived there. He stated that he was heading north to Oregon, where he had planned to go in the first place.

Keyes' letter didn't deter Reed, who was dreaming of starting over again in California, a place with a climate that would be better suited to his ailing wife. Once the urge to move west became planted in his mind, he quickly found others who were happy to join him, like George and Jacob Donner, who decided that pulling up stakes for new territory suited them after all.

The Donners and Reeds were not close friends, but they were acquainted through business dealings at Reed's mill and a common interest in community and social affairs. They simply couldn't resist the urge to travel once again. The Donners had caught California fever.

This came as a surprise to Tamzene Donner, who had been convinced that her restless husband would never contemplate moving again. She understood it, though. She knew her husband well and she worried about leaving Illinois, her beautiful home, her gardens, and her friends. But she knew there were new discoveries that awaited her in the West and once established, she decided, she would establish a school for girls and embrace her love for teaching.

On September 24, 1845, George Donner placed an advertisement in the newspaper of "A Good Farm for Sale." He would be parting with 240 acres, including 80 acres of timber, an orchard, a farmhouse with two brick chimneys, and a deep, clear well. Jacob Donner posted his farm for sale, too.

James Reed had little left to sell. California was his last chance. He had nowhere else to go. Worse, on December 10, 1845, his youngest child, Gershom, died at the age of only 11 months. His passing brought on more of Margaret's "sick headaches" and she was inconsolable for weeks. Eventually, she was able to cope with the idea of leaving her child behind because he was buried next to his grandfather. Years later, an inscription was carved into his tombstone that read "Touch not my little grave, mama is far away."

Death was not the only thing knocking on the Reeds' front door - there were also bill collectors. By early 1846, there were dozens of them. The final blow came in March when the circuit court ruled in favor of William Butler, who had sued Reed for $1,000 that James had borrowed but could not repay. Reed's land and his mill faced immediate foreclosure. There was simply nothing left.

As an inventory for all his property and goods was drawn up for public sale, Reed began preparing for what would become the biggest gamble he'd ever taken - the journey West.

There would be no turning back.

4. WESTWARD HO!

During the winter and early spring of 1846, the Donners and the Reeds made plans for their long trek from Illinois to California. They began seeking advice about the new land and the dangerous trail from anywhere they could find it. They found letters and bits of trail wisdom at community meetings and church services. George Donner wasn't much for attending church but Tamzene used every ploy that she could - including getting information about the trail - to get him there.

Jacob and his wife, Elizabeth - who went by Betsy - regularly attended services and were even given letters of introduction from their minister to use in California.

Reed took advantage of his Methodist Church contacts and he was also a Freemason who had been initiated into the Springfield Lodge. One of his chief sources of knowledge was a Masonic brother named James M. Maxey, who had left Springfield to run a general store in Independence, Missouri, a main departure point for wagon caravans. The town was the eastern terminal for both the Oregon-California and Santa Fe Trails, so he dealt with a lot of customers who spoke of their experiences.

His advice was practical and also a bit self-serving, since he advised Reed to get supplies at his store in Independence rather than Springfield. He did advise a "good family ox wagon" and an ample supply of muslin, calico cloth, ribbons, and beads to trade with Indians along the way. He stressed the importance of large oxen, as well as a good gun and a fast horse for hunting buffalo along the way.

From one of Maxey's letters, James learned that a large company of emigrants planned to depart from Independence in mid-May 1846. Maxey urged his friend to make sure that the wagons from Springfield arrived in Independence as early as possible to let the livestock rest and to be sure they bought plenty of supplies - from his store, of course.

Reed and the Donners compared notes and studied the books, guides, and maps that were available to them, including one written by explorer John C. Fremont, who conducted surveys of the Oregon Trail, the Oregon Territory, the Great Basin, and the Sierra Nevada Mountains of California. His book included detailed notes about finding drinking water, grazing grass, and information about various forts and Native American tribes.

Fremont's book also included an account of his harrowing winter of 1843-1844, when his expedition traversed the Sierra Nevada mountains in the snow. Although none of his men perished, more than half of their horses and mules died. The men ate the dead animals and, on advice from local Indians, survived on acorns, pine nuts, grasses, and wild onions. One of Fremont's entries noted, "We had tonight an extraordinary dinner - pea soup, mule, and dog."

Reed and the Donner also relied heavily on another bestseller that was published in 1845 - the *Emigrant's Guide to Oregon and California* by a young real estate promoter named Lansford W. Hastings. The Ohio native had financial and political connections in Alta California - which seem to have been his only qualifications for writing the book. According to Bernard DeVoto, the 23-year-old "wrote a book without knowing what he was talking about."

Hastings idealized the American settlers in California as hard-working and honest and with few faults. Indians and Mexicans, on the other hand, were depicted as stupid, lazy, and dishonest. His book had no value as a guide or travel planner. It mostly just promoted the land and climate of the West Coast. There was no practical value to it, but it did inspire Reed and the Donners and they kept it close at hand.

That was, as it turned out, a fatal mistake.

Finally, in March 1846, George Donner sold his property after several months on the market. He deeded shares of his land to his grown children and reserved 110 acres in case his five younger children ever decided to return to Illinois.

On March 26, an advertisement appeared in Springfield's *Sangamo Journal:*

WESTWARD HO!
FOR OREGON AND CALIFORNIA

Who wants to go to California without costing them anything? As many as eight young men, of good character, who can drive an ox team, will be accommodated by gentlemen who will leave this vicinity about the first of April. Come boys! You can have as much land as you want without costing you any thing. The government of California gives large tracts of land to persons who have to move there. The first suitable persons who apply will be engaged. The emigrants who intend moving to Oregon or California this spring from the adjoining counties, would do well to be in this place about the first of next month. Are there not a number from Decatur, Macon County, going?

G. DONNER and others
Springfield, March 18, 1846

The headline was bold, but the response was not. The Donners received few applicants. Work as a teamster could be brutal and it was never-ending. The main task was to make sure the wagon train stayed on course. Like most people in the party - aside from the very old and the very young - there was no riding in the wagon. A teamster walked alongside, cracking the whip to keep the oxen moving forward. They made camp every night to feed and water the livestock and the others in the party. Those who signed on where usually young single men who were looking for adventure - or running away from something.

The Donner brothers and James Reed had three wagons each, all pulled by teams of heavy oxen. The wagons were jammed with provisions, household furniture, books, clothing, and all the essentials the families believed they needed. In other words, those things I mentioned in the first chapter that often ended up left on the side of the trail.

And it got worse. The largest and most extravagant wagon was the one the Reed family provided for Grandma Keyes, who was mostly an invalid by then and confined to bed. She refused to stay behind in Springfield because she couldn't bear to be separated from her daughter and grandchildren, and wanted to see her son, Robert, who had journeyed west the year before. The entrance to her two-story wagon was on the side, like the door on a stagecoach. Although Hastings' guide - along with every other reliable source - cautioned against bringing heavy items that would slow down a wagon, Reed installed an iron cookstove in the wagon with a vent that ran out through the top. It also had spring-cushioned seats and comfortable bunks on the lower level. This wagon was dubbed the "Pioneer Prairie Palace" by the family and worse things by others in the party, who laughed and made wisecracks about it. They had never seen anything like it - and for good reason because it had no place on the trail.

Of course, it was just one of many bad decisions that would be made on the journey to California.

For weeks leading up to their departure, the Donners and Reeds were treated to farewell dinners by friends and loved ones. By April, all the teamsters had been hired, the wagons were nearly loaded, and the last will and testaments had been signed and sealed.

It was finally time to leave.

James Reed was especially eager to get the wagon wheels turning. He was completely broke - on paper, at least. Four lots that he still owned in Springfield were sold to pay his back taxes. In a last-ditch effort to satisfy his creditors, Reed, with help from Lincoln, drafted a list of those to whom he owed money and how much, as well as an inventory of his belongings, real estate holdings, and credits.

Bankruptcy papers were filed in probate court and a justice of the peace named William Lavely was assigned to oversee the public sale. Luckily, Reed was able to convince Lavely - a fellow Freemason - to leave 300 pounds of bacon and two barrels of pickled pork - off the list. The meat was quietly loaded onto a waiting wagon and Reed signed the bankruptcy papers on April 13, 1846, just one day before the party left Springfield.

As you might imagine, the bacon and pork were not the only things of worth that vanished from Reed's bankruptcy settlement. The overland expedition to California was an expensive effort. Substantial funds had been needed to outfit the wagons, purchase oxen, and buy supplies. Although bankrupt in the eyes of the court, Reed managed to hide quite a lot of cash. He was confident that once he was in California - and out of reach of bankruptcy courts in Illinois - he would put his hidden cash to work for him again.

He also hedged his bets in other ways. He wanted to ensure a warm reception and smooth transition in California. He had attained the rank of Royal Arch Mason, so he packed all his Masonic regalia, including his badges of honor, fraternal apron, collar, sash, and gloves. He petitioned Illinois congressional delegates to help him win an appointment as "Sub Indian Agent West of the Rocky Mountains." At the last minute, he also used connections to get a letter of introduction from Illinois Governor Thomas Ford, which was delivered just before his departure.

The only letter of introduction any of the Donners carried was from Jacob's country preacher. But the Donners did have a substantial amount of surplus cash squirreled away for expenses. Eliza Donner later wrote, "A liberal sum of money for meeting incidental expenses and replenishing supplies on the journey, if need be, was stored in the compartments of two buckskin girdles, to be worn in concealment on a person. An additional sum of $10,000, cash, was stitched between the folds of a quilt for safe transportation. This was a large amount for those days, and few knew that might parents were carrying it with them."

It was a "large amount" and would translate to about $338,000 today. I expect this was much more than James Reed had managed to hide from the bankruptcy court but the difference between the two families was that the Donners never felt the need to flaunt their worth, as Reed usually did - which had gotten him in financial trouble in the first place. This was only one of the many contrasts between the families - more of which would become apparent on the trail.

The inventory of staples and supplies were checked and re-checked in the days before departure. The list included 200 pounds of flour for each person 10 and older and 100 pounds of each younger child. They packed coffee, sugar, bacon. Salt, rice, pepper, corn meal, 50 pounds of dried apples and peaches, a strong tent, and a "good rifle with five pounds of powder and 12 pounds of lead for each man."

Much of what they packed would not be used until they reached California, including farm implements, seeds, furniture, and other supplies. Tamzene Donner brought a substantial number of books, knowing they would be scarce in the new country. Virginia Reed later noted, "Certainly no family ever started across the plains with more provisions or a better outfit for the journey."

For bartering with the Native Americans they might encounter, they brought bolts of inexpensive cotton prints, blue calico, and yellow and red flannel.

Virginia Reed in a photograph obviously taken much later in life than the events of this book. However, since we will be hearing from Virginia quiet often in these pages, the reader can see what she looked like at the time of her writings.

They also had ribbons, handkerchiefs with brightly-colored borders, glass bead necklaces, brass rings, and pocket mirrors. To use when negotiating for land with the Mexicans, they packed finer fabrics, like bolts of muslin, silk, satin, and velvet.

There were attempts made to lighten the large Reed wagon's load, but not many. Virginia Reed wrote, "Our clothing was packed - not in Saratoga trunks - but in strong canvas bags, plainly marked. Some of mama's young friends added a looking glass, hung directly opposite the door, in order, as they said, that my mother might not forget to keep her good looks."

On April 14, 1846, the nine wagons were loaded and finally ready to leave Springfield. The first steps of the journey began just before dawn - and then it took them two days just to get out of town. It became quickly clear to the emigrants that the overland journey to California was not going to be made in a hurry.

The center of what came to be called the Donner Party was made up of the Donners and Reeds and their employees. The George Donner family was made up of George, 60; his wife, Tamzene, 44; their three children - Frances, 6, Georgia, 4, and Eliza, 3; and George's two daughters from his second marriage - Elitha, 14, and Leanna, 12.

Traveling with Jacob (Jake) Donner, 56, were his wife, Betsy, 45; their five children, George, 9, Mary, 7, Isaac, 5, Samuel, 4, and Lewis, 3; and Betsy's two sons from her previous marriage, Solomon, 14, and William, 13.

Author's note: *It's tough for many of us today to imagine driving across country with children this young in an automobile. Now imagine yourself doing it - with your children -- for months in a covered wagon.*

Hired as teamsters to work the Donners' wagons were Noah James, 16, a cousin of William Herndon, Abraham Lincoln's law partner; Samuel Shoemaker, 25, who may have been from Ohio; John Denton, 28, a gunsmith from England who had become friends with the Donners in Springfield; and Hiram Miller, 29, a blacksmith from Kentucky.

The Reed contingency was made up of James Reed, 46; his wife, Margaret, 32; and their three children, Martha, 8, James, Jr., 5, and Thomas, 3; Margaret's daughter from her previous marriage, Virginia, 12; and Margaret's mother, Sarah Keyes, 70.

The Reeds had five employees with them, including two siblings: Eliza Williams, 31, a deaf woman who had worked for the Reeds for several years as a cook; and Baylis Williams, 25, Eliza's half-brother and an albino who, because of his condition, slept in the wagon during the day and tended to livestock and campfires at night. Reed also hired teamsters - Milt Elliott, 28, a Kentuckian who had worked at Reed's mill for so long and was so close with the family that he often called Margaret "Ma," even though she was only four years older than he was; Walter Herron, 27, from Virginia; and James Smith, 25.

Virginia Reed vividly remembered her last time in Springfield. She wrote, "Never can I forget when we bade farewell to kindred and friends. The Donners were there, having driven in the evening before with their families, so we might get an early start. Grandma Keyes was carried out of the house and placed in her wagon on a large feather bed, propped up with pillows. Her sons implored her to remain and end her days with them, but she could not be separated from her only daughter. We were surrounded by loved ones, and there stood my little schoolmates who had come to kiss me goodbye. My father with tears in his eyes tried to smile as one friend after another grasped his hand in a last farewell. Mama was overcome with grief. At last, we were all in the wagons, the drivers cracked their whips, the oxen moved slowly forward, and the long journey had begun."

"We were full of hope," Virginia recalled, "and did not dream of sorrow."

At the George Donner home, the children were scrubbed and dressed in new traveling clothes made from sturdy homespun cloth. Three big wagons with canvas tops were waiting in the yard. Feed boxes had been attached to the back of one wagon for their favorite saddle horses, Fanny and Margaret.

The Donners joined the group as it rolled into Springfield, pausing briefly in the public square so that a few friends could wish them well. Abraham Lincoln was not among them. James Reed had hoped he would be, but Lincoln was traveling the law circuit on the day the family left town. Mary Lincoln was there, however, offering good wishes to the Reeds and apologies for her husband's absence.

James Reed had tried hard to convince Lincoln to pack up his family and join the wagon train. But Mary had no interest in moving west and Lincoln, only a few months away from being elected to the U.S. Congress, knew that a move to California would effectively derail his political career.

It was late afternoon by the time the handshaking, hugging, and farewells were over. The party only made it as far as the western edge of town before stopping to set up camp for the night.

They camped in a grove on a wooded hill near the home of Thomas Mather, a prominent city leader who, in 1849, would take over Reed's ill-fated Northern Cross railroad company. The hill where the

The writings of Eliza Donner will also be frequently referenced throughout this book. This photograph was taken much later in her life. She was only three-years-old when the wagons left Springfield, Illinois.

Donner Party camped that night would one day be the location of a new state capitol building.

Eliza Donner wrote, "Mr. Reed and family, and my uncle Jacob and family, with their traveling companions and cattle, were already settled there. Under father's direction, our own encampment was soon accomplished. By nightfall, the duties of the day were ended, and members of our party gathered around one fire to spend a social hour."

As supper was prepared, the hired teamsters got to know each other and the children from all three families began to get better acquainted. A short time later, a party of eight riders approached the camp. They were members of the Springfield Reading Society, coming for one last visit with Tamzene Donner. Among them were brothers Simeon and Allen Francis, close friends of Lincoln and publishers of the *Sangamo Journal*. They wanted to convince Tamzene to serve as their correspondent and send letters back home to be published in the newspaper. She promised to do so.

Bottles of brandy and other spirits were passed around, but others were tucked away for safekeeping until July 4. On that date, the Reeds and Donners promised, no matter where they were on the trail, to face east toward Springfield at noon. At the same time, their friends back home would come to this hill and face west. Miles apart, they would lift their glasses in a toast.

Early the next morning, before anyone had stirred except for Baylis Williams, who was tending the fire, Margaret Reed slipped out of the campsite in the pre-dawn darkness. A short distance away was the Old City Graveyard, Springfield's earliest burial ground, just west of the newly opened Hutchinson Cemetery. Margaret sought out the gravesites of her beloved father and that of Gershom, the little boy who had died before his first birthday. She had no idea if she would ever stand in that same spot again.

By the time she returned to camp, the wagons were packed, and preparations were made for the journey to finally leave Springfield. Besides the families and the teamsters, three other people accompanied them on the first leg of the trip. Gershom and James Keyes, concerned about their ailing mother, Sarah, rode with the party for several days. William, George Donner's grown son, helped drive the cattle and stayed with the group all the way to Independence.

They headed west on the Jacksonville Road and Virginia Reed later wrote of riding next to her father on his handsome gray racing mare, Glaucus. According to Greek mythology, Glaucus was a nobleman who fed human flesh to his team of chariot horses because he believed it made them swifter and bolder. In the end, the horses turned on him when his chariot overturned, and they ate him alive.

The irony of the name of Reed's horse would eventually become apparent.

The Donner brothers and James Reed estimated that it would take their caravan at least three weeks to reach Independence. There, they planned to replenish their supplies and join a larger wagon train that was heading to California. That leg of the trip, they believed, would take four to six months.

The travelers wrote little about the first leg of the journey, perhaps finding the Illinois and Missouri countryside to be so familiar that they didn't feel like their adventure began until after they left Independence. Even Virginia Reed noted, "Nothing much of interest happened until we reached what is now Kansas."

Unfortunately, except for a few letters, the writings of Tamzene Donner did not survive. She was the one person in the group who likely recorded her daily observations of the trail. There have been rumors for years about a "lost journal" kept by Tamzene, but if it's out there, it's never been found. As she had promised - and thanks to obliging eastbound travelers who dropped off her letters at whatever post office they could find - Tamzene faithfully sent dispatches from the trail back to Springfield to be published in the newspaper. But, when publisher Allen Francis became a U.S. consul and moved to Canada, rodents invaded his storage boxes and destroyed all Tamzene's letters and writings.

Shortly after the Donners and Reeds departed, though, a letter written home from California by William Todd did survive. The young man had left Springfield with one of Margaret Reed's brothers the previous year. In his letter, he described some of the hardships of the trip and offered some advice for anyone else thinking of making the journey - "If there are any persons in Sangamon who speak of crossing the Rocky Mountains to this country, tell them my advice is to stay home."

The letter wasn't published in the newspaper until August 13, 1846, long after the Donner-Reed Party was past the point of no return.

The caravan spent several days traveling west to Jacksonville, an early contender for the state capital and named in honor of Andrew Jackson. They camped one night in the city's public square and then traveled out of town, past Illinois College and the newly opened State School for the Deaf and Dumb.

West of Jacksonville, they took a southwesterly path that took them past Winchester and along the rolling hills that followed the valley of the Illinois River. Until then, the wagons had encountered only creeks that could be crossed on bridges or forded at shallow points. The Illinois was their first major river crossing and they ferried across it to the village of Florence, a task that took several hours to get all the wagons and animals from one side to the other. The trip then resumed along a gravel road that took them past the village of Barry to the broad valley of Hadley Creek. Just before Kinderhook, the last village they would encounter before leaving Illinois, they began crossing the bottomlands of the Mississippi River.

They crossed the mighty river at Hannibal aboard two steam ferries. It took the better part of a day to load and unload and to make several round trips across the river. Once safely across, they continued toward Independence.

By early May, the emigrants had become used to their daily routine. They were anxious to get beyond the familiar prairie and the rolling hills. They pushed hard across Missouri, stopping to rest at small settlements, and crossing the Missouri River at Lexington, which was then a major shipping port for farmers and the largest city west of St. Louis.

The route from Lexington followed the old Santa Fe Trail, which had been started by trader William Becknell in 1821. The Donners and Reeds knew that it would carry them into Independence, the westernmost city of the United States, where their journey would really begin.

5. ON TOWARDS INDIAN COUNTRY

On May 10, 1846, the Donner-Reed wagons rolled into Independence. They had been on the trail for 25 days before arriving at the "Mother of the West" and the "Queen City of the Trails" as the settlement was alternately called.

The town had been founded in 1827 and, thanks to its geography, became the epicenter of western migration. Typically, wagon trains did not leave until early May, when there was enough green grass to provide grazing for draft animals, and when they did, Independence offered access to the Santa Fe, Oregon, and California Trails.

Reed immediately sought out his old Masonic brother, James Maxey, who ran a general store in town. Maxey and his business partner, William S. Stone, were happy to sell goods to some familiar faces.

When the wagons reached the public square, the emigrants were overwhelmed with what they saw around them - men and beasts at work, air filled with the smells of manure, tobacco, and wood smoke, and the sounds of voices that spoke English, German, Italian, and various Indian languages like Osage, Kaw, Chickasaw, and Choctaw.

Emigrant Jessy Quinn Thornton described Independence as a "great Babel on the border of the wilderness." He and his wife also arrived in May 1846. They were eager to leave the United States. He

By the early 1840s, Independence had been established as one of the most important links between the East and the West. It could be a little overwhelming for emigrants that had been on the road for a few weeks.

had been practicing law and editing a newspaper in Palmyra, Missouri, but as staunch abolitionists, they had first moved to the free state of Illinois but then decided to strike west for Oregon.

Thornton, his invalid wife, two hired men for the wagons, and his dog arrived in Independence and he noted in his trail diary, "Most of the emigrants had already departed. Some had assembled at Indian Creek; a few were still in this place not yet prepared to depart. Among these, I became acquainted with Messrs. James F. Reed, George Donner, and Jacob Donner, together with their wives and families, all from the neighborhood of Springfield, Illinois, and all of whom proposed to go to California."

Thornton told Reed and the Donners that he was waiting on some other emigrants to arrive and expected to leave within the hour. He urged them to leave as soon as possible and join his party on the trail, where an even larger caravan waited for them on the Kansas River. Thornton's advice made good sense to them and they agreed they would all likely meet again soon.

But the Reeds and Donners were all too excited by what they found in Independence to leave too quickly. The children especially, after three weeks on the trail, were delighted by the sights and sounds. The clamor was enough to give Margaret Reed one of her crippling migraines but fortunately, their campsite was not far away at a public spring on the edge of town.

The following day, Margaret rested in a tent with the family dog, Cash, while her mother napped in the big wagon's feather bed. Supplies were loaded, children were entertained, final meals were eaten in civilized conditions, and preparations were made for the next leg of the adventure.

That adventure began at sunrise on the morning of May 12. Gershom Keyes bid his mother and sister goodbye. He had ridden all the way from Springfield with William Donner, but now it was time for the two men to return home. They stayed with the wagons for a short distance and then headed east toward Illinois.

Eliza Donner wrote, "Near the outskirts of town we parted from William Donner, took a last look at Independence, turned our backs to the morning sun, and became pioneers indeed to the far West."

The nine wagons and herds of livestock followed the Santa Fe Trail out of town. It was an easy road to follow. It had been worn down by thousands of oxen, mules, horses, and steel-rimmed wagon wheels over the span of more than two decades. This would be their route for a few days until they reached the junction where the emigrant trail split off to the northwest.

Emigrants headed for Oregon and California began their journey on the old Santa Fe Trail, which ended in what would be the American Southwest.

It was slow going. Torrential rains turned the trail into a swamp of thick, sticky mud that clung to the wagon wheels and bogged down the oxen. All the animals - and their owners - struggled to move in the mess.

It was suggested that wagons try and travel at least 18-20 miles each day, although 8-12 miles was still acceptable. Yet according to the diary of Hiram Miller, a Donner teamster, by the end of the party's first day on the road, they managed to only go four miles before stopping for the night.

Early the next day, despite more rain, they pushed harder and covered more miles. By evening, as they huddled around campfires to dry their clothes, they had traveled about 16 miles.

Unknown to the tired and wet travelers, that same day, the United States - in the spirit of Manifest Destiny - declared war on Mexico. Before the company had left home, Mexico had ended diplomatic relations with the United States. On April 23, Mexico declared war, vowing to defend its territories but without taking the offensive. Tensions heightened as General Zachary Taylor moved south of the Rio Grande while the Mexican Army moved northward. By early May, battles had been fought and men had died on both sides. Although the Donners and Reeds didn't learn of the war immediately, they knew it was inevitable.

On May 15, they arrived at a well-used campground on Hart Grove Creek, not far from where it emptied into the Big Blue River. They rested there for two nights and then crossed the Big Blue. They were inexperienced but knew the dangers of fording streams. A wagon could get stuck or overturn, animals could be swept away, and axles could break. Less than a week earlier, a wagon from another group had capsized in high water at the same spot. The Donners and Reeds made it through without much trouble.

After four days on the road, they stopped for the last time in Missouri at a small settlement known as Little Santa Fe. Once the site of a Native American village, it had become a popular stop on the Santa Fe Trail because of the abundance of grass and water and a last-stop tavern, where travelers could get a wheel fixed by a blacksmith, replenish a supply of axle grease, and buy whiskey.

On May 16, only a few miles past Little Santa Fe, the Donners crossed the line that took them out of the United States and into present-day Kansas. They had entered a vast expanse of land that the United States had designated permanently as Indian Territory. It was a giant reservation for native people and considered the best solution for what was known for many years as the "Indian problem."

The land had been chosen as a Native American sanctuary in the 1820s because the "Great American Desert" didn't seem to be good for anything else. It was a flat, treeless, arid land that was unfit for white settlement and any kind of farming. Of course, this was all pure myth, largely spread by politicians and business leaders in the East who feared that westward expansion would diminish their wealth. In time, it would become the farmland of the Great Plains, but in 1846, it was nothing more but another obstacle on the way to California.

That night, they camped for the first time in Indian Country at Lone Elm, where there was a spring and grass as high as a man's waist. Although the site was originally known as Round Grove, it had been used by travelers for years and, so, by the time the Donners and Reeds arrived, most of the firewood was gone and only a single elm tree was left standing.

On May 17, the emigrants reached the fork in the road where the trails divided. The road to Santa Fe went left and the Oregon and California Trails veered to the right. At the junction, there was a crude signpost that read "Road to Oregon." It seemed hardly worthy as a designation for one of the most important intersections in western history.

Since the time the Donner Party had left Independence, the group's intention was to catch up with the larger wagon train they had been told about by Jessy Thornton. Reed and the Donner brothers believed in strength in numbers, especially in the unknown regions along the trail. This led to them breaking camp early on the morning of May 18, pushing on and barely stopping at noon to have lunch. By the time they stopped that night, the camp was buzzing with excitement - they were getting close to the Kansas River, where the larger caravan was waiting.

While the Donners and Reeds were crossing the plains, newspapers across the country were filled with news of the Mexican War. Meanwhile, the U.S Congress had approved an act to establish military posts as protection from Native Americans along the road between Independence and the Oregon Country.

One of the most apprehensive members of the Donner Party, as far as the Native Americans went, was Virginia Reed. Back in Springfield, as the Reeds prepared for the journey, she spent many winter nights listening to her grandmother, Sarah, tell stories about white settlers who were taken prisoner by "savages," including Sarah's own aunt, who had remained a captive for five years before making her escape.

"So, when I was told that we were going to California and would have to pass through a region peopled by Indians, you can imagine how I felt," she later wrote.

On May 19, Virginia and the rest of the caravan met their first Native Americans on the trail. The meeting was early in the day as the wagons and herds were nearing the banks of the Kansas River, which was still known then as the Kaw River. Virginia, riding her pony, was seized with fear when she saw them, even though none of them were even brandishing a weapon.

"The first Indians we met were Kaws who kept the ferry, and had to take us across the Kaw River," she wrote. "I watched them closely, hardly daring to draw my breath, and feeling sure they would sink the boat in the

Members of the Kaw Nation. The Kaw were the first Native Americans feared by the Donner Party but would not be the last.

middle of the stream, and was very thankful when I found they were not like grandma's Indians."

Although Virginia identified the Indians at the river crossing as Kaw, others said they were "French-Indians," or Shawnee. But Virginia and the others were not really concerned with their tribal affiliation. As was the case with most white travelers, despite the diversity of the hundreds of different tribes, all Indians were alike to them and were considered "savages" that should be treated with caution.

The crossing of the river, which was swollen with the spring rains, took some time. The livestock and horses had to swim the river while the wagons were moved by two flatboats that were pushed by hand using long poles. Each boat could only take two wagons at a time, at the cost of $1 per wagon. Once they were safely on the other side, the emigrants continued for five miles until they reached Soldier Creek.

It was there that they found the larger caravan they had been chasing. From that point on, the Donners and Reeds and most of their entourage remained intact, but the party would never be the same. The numbers ebbed and flowed, with some people dropping out and others joining them along the trail.

The Donners and Reeds became part of the Russell Party, named for William Henry Russell, a loud but likable attorney and politician who had acquired the courtesy title of "Colonel" in Kentucky, where he'd been born in 1802.

Russell had been a lawyer for years, serving a brief stint in the Kentucky legislature, and was married to a Baltimore woman named Zanette Freeland. He was also

This photograph is believed to contain the only known image of William Henry Russell in existence. It was inscribed to John Fremont from four of the "Old California Battalion" in 1848. The men were not identified but based on the age and resemblance to late family members, Colonel Russell is thought to be the third man from the left.

Courtesy of the Natural History Museum of Los Angeles County, California.

a close friend of Henry Clay, the orator and statemen who represented Kentucky in the U.S. Senate and House of Representatives.

His friendship with Clay had inspired Russell's curious nickname of "Owl." According to the story behind it, Russell had been stalking game in the woods when he heard a group of owls hooting and took their cry as a question that was being posed to him. He jokingly called out, "Why, it is I, Colonel William Henry Russell of Kentucky, bosom friend of Henry Clay!" From that point on, friends called him Owl Russell. The moniker stuck after he moved his family to Fulton, Missouri, and after he was appointed by President William Henry Harrison as U.S. Marshal of the District of Missouri in 1841.

But Russell yearned to see the much talked-about land of California, and in May 1846, he assembled a caravan in Independence. At Soldier Creek, he again faced the task of making sure the party that showed up could work well together. Before being accepted into the larger caravan, the new arrivals had to pass muster. This was standard for any wagon train and it was a way to weed out potential troublemakers.

Already that day, several other travelers had tried to join the group and had been turned away. The day before, a party headed by Reverend James G.T. Dunleavy, a Methodist preacher, was expelled from the Russell Party. The excuse given was that Dunleavy's especially large herd of cattle would slow down the rest of the group.

James Reed believed his family and the Donners were definitely worthy of joining Russell's caravan, but he wasn't taking any chances. As soon as the wagons came to a halt, he brushed off the trail dust, washed up, trimmed his beard, and went looking for Owl Russell to get approval. He took with him his letter of endorsement from the governor of Illinois. Russell, who considered himself an excellent judge of character, was impressed.

The question of the Reeds and Donners being allowed to join the party was put to a vote and was approved unanimously.

The teamsters that worked for the Reeds and Donners put the cattle out to pasture before going out to hunt and fish. The women and girls washed piles of clothing in the creek and spread them out on rocks and brush along the stream.

Eliza Donner wrote, "We children, who had been confined to the wagon so many hours each day, stretched our limbs, and scampered off on Mayday frolics. We waded the creek, made mud pies, and gathered posies in the narrow glades between the cottonwood, beech, and alder trees. Colonel Russell was courteous to all; visited the new members and secured their cheerful endorsement of his carefully prepared plans of travel."

The outlook for the months ahead certainly looked bright. They were filled with optimism about the trip West.

They wondered what could go wrong. At that moment, it seemed that nothing could.

6. DEATH ON THE TRAIL

After a night of celebrating the addition of the Donners and Reeds to the Russell Party, the caravan set out before dawn on the morning of May 20, 1846.

Before the emigrants returned to the trail, James Reed wrote a quick letter to his brother-in-law, James Keyes, back in Springfield. He included an update on his mother-in-law, Sarah, who remained bedridden in the Reed family wagon. He wrote, "I am afraid your mother will not stand it many weeks, or indeed days, if there is not a quick change. Margaret this morning is good in heart. She was visited by several of the caravan and Russell came with me last night to have an introduction to my family. I have been talking this moment with your mother. She says she feels very much like she is going to die. One of her eyes pains her so much and she is so blind that she cannot take her coffee or plate if it is not set near her this morning. She cannot eat anything. I am of the opinion a few days will end her mortal career."

But there was no time to rest - the journey had to continue. The wagons began to roll again. Eliza Donner later recalled the diversity of the people in the caravan and the many occupations represented. "The government of these emigrant trains was essentially democratic and characteristically American," she wrote. She described Colonel Russell as "the head of a representative body of pioneers, including lawyers, journalists, teachers, students, farmers, and day laborers, also a minister of the gospel, a carriage maker, a cabinet-maker, a stone-mason, a jeweler, a blacksmith, and women versed in all branches of women's work."

Several members of that "representative body of pioneers" went west for a new identity, while others were seeking land or wealth or trying to regain their health. Others merely wanted an adventure. A few, like James Reed, were starting over. Farmers, like the Donners, sought what they felt was their natural inheritance of land. They saw land ownership as synonymous with success. Going to California was their natural right, they believed, their Manifest Destiny.

It would become obvious in the months to come that they did not share a common sense of what they were seeking, other than the mutual goal of getting to California. Still, they all knew there was safety in numbers - everyone on the trail was vulnerable.

As it happened, Owl Russell was not the only person of consequence in the emigrant party. Edwin Bryant, the former Louisville newspaper publisher - mentioned earlier - was a key leader in the wagon train.

Bryant had briefly studied medicine but when he discovered how easily writing came to him, he became a journalist. Perhaps it came to him naturally - he was the cousin of celebrated journalist and poet William Cullen Bryant. By the 1840s, though, he had grown weary of the newspaper business and decided to make a journey west and write a book about his experiences. In April 1846, Bryant and two

Former newspaper publisher Edwin Bryant

friends boarded a steamboat for St. Louis and then traveled up the Missouri River to Independence. They arrived on May 1 and started west right away, picking up other emigrants along the trail. After a few days, they reached the camp of Colonel Russell, where Bryant was greeted warmly. He was also a friend of Henry Clay.

Another key member of the party was a 27-year-old Louisiana native named Andrew Jackson Grayson. He was accompanied by his wife, Frances, and their infant son, Edward. When the Graysons joined the larger group, Edwin Bryant was impressed with Grayson and his wife. Many years later, Frances had warm memories of the time. "I was as full of romantic adventures as my husband," she recalled. "The trip across the plains was one of the most enjoyable episodes of my life."

Lilburn W. Boggs, the controversial former governor of Missouri became another key member of the Russell Party.

Another high-profile emigrant as Lilburn W. Boggs. The Kentucky man was a veteran of the War of 1812 and a former Missouri governor whose second wife, Panthea, was a granddaughter of frontiersman Daniel Boone. His first wife Julia Ann Bent, had died in 1820. She had been the daughter of Silas Bent, a Missouri Supreme Court justice, and the sister of William and Charles Bent, well-known traders on the western frontier. They established the famous Bent's Fort, a massive adobe post that became the hub of mercantile trade along the Santa Fe Trail.

Lilburn Boggs had been a trader on the Santa Fe Trail for years, making him perhaps the most experienced of the emigrants in the party. Even after entering Missouri politics and serving as a state senator, lieutenant governor, and governor, he was unable to stay away from the West.

But Boggs also had controversy in his past.

In 1838, while serving as Missouri governor, Boggs had ordered all Mormons purged from the state. This led to his attempted assassination on May 6, 1842, in Independence, where he operated a store. Rewards were offered for the apprehension of the assailant, who most assumed had been sent by Mormon leader Joseph Smith. They were undoubtedly right - the Mormons had called for "blood atonement" against Boggs. Publicly, though, Smith denied any involvement, but almost immediately, his most loyal and dangerous bodyguard - Orrin Porter Rockwell - became the chief suspect. Smith and Rockwell became fugitives and were charged in the shooting. Smith stayed on the run and was never brought to trial, but Rockwell was arrested in St. Louis in 1843 and spent nine months in jail before his trial. The charge of attempted murder was dismissed for lack of evidence.

It took Boggs nearly a year to recover from his wounds, during which time he was successful in his bid to return to the Missouri senate, but he soon tired of politics. In May 1846, Boggs, his wife, Panthea, their son, William, and his wife, Sonora, left Independence for California.

Traveling along with Boggs when he joined the Russell group was Jessy Thornton and his wife, Nancy, who had met the Donners and Reeds earlier in the month. Although there would turn up to be many discrepancies in his account of the journey, a book written by Thornton in 1848 was the only full account of the Donner Party for at least 30 years.

On the morning of May 20, the Donners and Reeds' first day with the Russell Party began. As the wagons creaked off on the trail, there was not a cloud in the sky. At noon, the teams rested, and the families ate their dinner on the prairie grass.

Moments later, though, the day changed.

Eliza Donner recalled when it happened. "Suddenly a gust of wind swept by; black clouds drifted over the face of the sun; ominous sounds came rumbling from distant hills; and before our effects could be collected and returned to cover, a terrific thunderstorm was upon us. We were three hours distance from our evening campground and our drivers had to walk and face the buffeting storm in order to keep control of our nervous cattle."

The rain pounded the emigrants until they could reach the knoll where they would camp for the night. They were exhausted and soaked. Many of them, especially the men, were short-tempered. There could be no fires until wood could be gathered from an area about a mile from camp. When burned, it smoked so badly from its dampness that the evening meals were "late and rather cheerless," Eliza wrote.

But she added, "Still there was spirit enough left in those stalwart hearts to start some mirth-provoking ditty or indulge in good-natured raillery over the joys and comforts of pioneering. Indians had followed our train all day, and as we had been warned against leaving temptation within reach, the cattle were corralled early, and their guards doubled. Happily, the night passed without alarm or losses."

The rain continued all night. It finally let up near dawn, when the caravan planned to pack up and continue on the trail. At first, no one stirred, aside from Baylis Williams, who kept stirring the fires and provoking them to flame. The last shift of night guards was still sipping the coffee he'd made. The emigrants were wrapped in blankets and sheltered in their tents and wagons. Even the dogs still slept. Almost every family had at least one dog, and most had several. The Reeds had five dogs - Barney, Tyler, Tracker, and Trailer - and a lapdog that belonged to Virginia named Cash. The relentless rain had made the dogs anxious, but once they'd been fed, they dutifully curled up under the wagons.

Edwin Bryant had been on watch until the early morning hours. "The howls and sharp snarling barks of wolves; the mournful hootings of the owl; and the rush of the winds through the tree-tops of the neighboring grove, are the only sounds disturbing the deep solitude of the night," he wrote, expertly evoking the scene.

The wagon train had only traveled eight miserable miles the day before. Bryant was excited to see what a new day would bring. He added, "The views from the high elevations of the prairie have, as usual, been strikingly picturesque. The country we have passed through for the last one hundred miles, presents even greater attractions to the eye than any that I have ever previously seen. What the climate may be in winter, or how it may affect the health of the settlers in summer and autumn, I have no means of judging."

Edwin likely should have been wondering less about the country they were passing through and more about what the cold months would be like in the terrain ahead. That week, reports from Fort Laramie in the Wyoming Territory were just reaching St. Louis. Heavy snow had fallen in the western mountain ranges during the winter. But, like the others, Edwin wasn't worried. He was confident they would be basking in the California sun long before any snow fell.

It was slow-going once the wagons started to roll that day, thanks to the mud caused by the previous day's rain. Around noon, the party arrived at a narrow creek that had no crossing point, only steep banks on both sides. The caravan came to a halt while a plan was devised. The emigrants lowered the wagons with ropes down one side and then pulled them up with double teams on the other. It was nearly

4:00 p.m. before they were finished. A mile later, they made camp for the night.

They had only traveled about six miles that day, but spirits were high - at least it wasn't raining.

The end of the day became a bit brighter for Lilburn Boggs when his brother-in-law, Alphonso D. Boone, with his seven children and 11 wagons, caught up with the caravan. They had been following a few days behind and the celebration when the two branches of the family reunited pleased everyone.

After the evening meal, the men brought out their tobacco and pipes and, to mark the arrival of the Boones, started passing around a jug of whiskey. Soon, a shooting contest was proposed with targets set up in a meadow at 80 and 100 yards away. It would be good practice for the buffalo that would be found on the plains

Alphonso D. Boone, later in life than when the events of the book take place. He was an acclaimed descendant of famous frontiersman Daniel Boone.

ahead and, besides, it wasn't every day that a man could brag about being in a shooting match with a descendant of Daniel Boone. Several sharpshooters took their turn but, in the end, W.B. Brown, a Kentuckian, proved to be the best shot of the evening.

As Edwin Bryant wrote, "The day has been delightful, and a more cheerful spirit seems to prevail in our party than usual."

But it didn't last. By morning, there was a lot of grumbling in the camp about the slowness of such a large caravan. As a result, 13 wagons, half of them from Jackson County, Missouri, decided to move on alone. This was the second division in the party since it started. Many believed there would be more. Bryant noted, "A restlessness of disposition, and dissatisfaction from trivial causes, lead to these frequent changes among the emigrating parties."

Bryant was also unhappy about how slow things were moving, but not unhappy enough to strike out on his own. There were plenty of others who were complaining, notably the single men who were frustrated by the travelers who were encumbered by families, overloaded wagons, and livestock.

One of the loudest was George W. McKinstry, a 36-year-old man from New York. His decision to head west to California was reached after reading some newspaper articles about it. He kept a diary of the caravan's progress in May and June 1846.

Another young man who chronicled part of the journey was George Curry, a seasoned traveler who had spent most of his childhood in Venezuela. Curry was well read and began a long career in journalism, starting out as an apprentice printer. In 1843, he moved to St. Louis and became the co-editor of the *St. Louis Weekly Reveille,* which was published six days a week. When he left for California, he became a correspondent for the paper, although only a handful of his dispatches survive.

In one of them, he wrote, "Life on the plains far surpasses my expectations; there is a freedom and nobleness about it that tends to bring forth the full manhood. A man upon the horizon-bound prairie feels his own strength and estimates his own weakness. His is alive to everything around him."

Others in the group soon figured out the main reason that Curry had such a positive attitude - he had fallen in love with 24-year-old Chloe Boone, the oldest daughter of Alphonso Boone. Their casual flirtation soon turned into a full-blown romance.

For the first time since leaving Independence, the emigrants encountered a large number of Indians on May 22. They were Kaw, or Kanza, -- the "People of the South Wind" - who gave Kansas its name. The nation was always in motion, moving because of tribal disputes, the edicts of their chiefs, or most importantly, in pursuit of the great buffalo herds that kept them alive. The Kaw had been resistant to the settlers who tried to force their children into the white man's school and speak his language. When the Russell Party encountered the Kaw, they were moving away from a group of meddling missionaries and whites who had tried to force their leaders into signing treaties to cede their lands.

Several Kaw riders were spotted that day and by late afternoon, the caravan stopped to camp along Black Paint Creek, which was close to two sizable Kaw encampments.

There was little kindness or sympathy for the Kaw among the emigrants. They had been taught not to trust any Native Americans, no matter how friendly they might appear. Edwin Bryant called them "unblushing and practiced beggars" and wrote of young Kaw men trying to trade ponies for whiskey. Among the "troublesome" visitors he met was Hard Chief, a leader of about 55 years of age and "of commanding figure, and of rather an intellectual and pleasing expression of countenance."

Hard Chief promised Bryant and the other emigrant leaders that in exchange for gifts, he would ensure that none of his people would steal from the wagon train's herds of camp. It was a bribe they couldn't afford not to pay. Even so, they posted extra guards throughout the night. The only incident was caused when guards confronted two Kaw men in the camp, but they were released when it was discovered they were trading a pony for four gallons of whiskey.

The next morning, Hard Chief and his wife waited patiently for their reward - there had been no thievery during the night. In a rare instance of white men keeping their word to Native Americans, a large supply of bacon, flour, and other items were given to Hard Chief for distribution to his people.

Before leaving camp, the emigrants again faced a creek with steep banks and muddy water. This time, they cut down small trees and brush and used it to fill the stream bed. When all the wagons and livestock were across, the party began making good time across the open plains.

Some of the younger Kaw men, their faces painted with vermilion, rode along as an escort. During a short rest stop, one of the Kaw spotted some bright blue flowers among the tall grasses. He used a stick to dig up a root about the size of a chicken's egg. As he peeled off the rough brown husk on it with his knife, he revealed a white tuber that he presented to Bryant. It was what came to be called a "prairie potato." Plains Indians boiled it, roasted it in embers, or crushed it into a powder to flavor soup. They also ate it raw, which was how Edwin Bryant first sampled it. He said that "its flavor is more agreeable than that of the finest Irish potato."

Tamzene Donner was thrilled with not only this discovery but with all the fauna and flora of the prairie. She reveled in the plants that she had never seen before, and she found others in the party who were equally impressed and eager to explore the world around them. They searched for specimens, overturned rocks, and went into the woods to gather mosses, roots, and flowing plants. Tamzene spent as much free time as she had making pencil and watercolor studies of the flowers and plants she gathered.

On May 23, the party met up with four weather-beaten trappers from the Rocky Mountains, accompanied by several Delaware Indians. They were headed back east, and their saddles and pack animals were loaded with freshly killed game and large sacks of furs. The emigrants were envious, but the trappers told them not to despair. Just ahead, "one of two hundred miles," they said, they would find herds of bison on the Platte River that would give them plenty of fresh meat.

The caravan - and the Kaw who rode with them - established a camp later that day close to a spring of pure, cold water.

They pressed on the following morning. It was the Sabbath but as Jessy Thornton wrote, there was "no rest for man or beast." Later in the morning, they came upon the carcasses of two dead oxen that had been left beside the trail by an earlier wagon train. There was an unsettling feeling that traveled through the caravan, even though it had been strung out over a few miles for most of the day. Many of the wagons were slow to arrive at the campsite that evening with several people complaining of feeling ill and feverish.

Edwin Bryant wrote, "I am beginning to feel alarmed at the tardiness of our movements, and fearful that winter will find us in the snowy mountains of California, or that we shall suffer from the exhaustion of our supply of provisions. I do not fear for myself, but for the women and children of the emigrants. Singular as it may seem, there are many of our present party who have no just conceptions of the extent and labor of the journey before them. They appear to be desirous of shortening each day's march as much as possible, and when encamped are reluctant to move, except for the benefit of fresh grass for their cattle, and a more convenient and plentiful supply of wood for the purposes of cooking."

When the caravan returned to the trail on May 25, James Reed and his daughter, Virginia, rode ahead of the wagons, as they did on most mornings. Virginia later wrote, "In our party were many who rode on horseback, but mama seldom did. She preferred the wagon, and did not want to leave grandma, and could hardly be persuaded to leave grandma's side. Our little home was so comfortable, that mama could sit reading and chatting with the little ones, and almost forget that she was really crossing the plains."

Most women tried their best to avoid the dust, heat, and rain of the trail, as well as the cursing used by the teamsters to keep their oxen teams making good time. Staying inside the wagons also kept the women out of sight, thanks to

Women -- the largely unsung heroes of the emigrant trail - were the ones who really kept things moving, even under the most hazardous conditions.

the fact that the emigrants were always worried that curious Indians might want to carry them away. That was what the men believed - the women mostly dismissed the idea.

Eliza Donner later recalled, "The staid and elderly matrons spent most of their time in the wagons, knitting, and patching designs for quilts. The younger ones and the girls passed theirs in the saddle. They would scatter in groups over the plains to investigate distant objects, then race back, and with song and banter join husband and brother, driving the loose cattle in the rear. The wild, free spirit of the plain often prompted them to invite is little ones to seats beside them, and away we would canter with the breeze playing through our hair and giving a ruddy glow to our cheeks."

They moved through open country, with hardly a tree in sight. Around noon, they reached Vermilion Creek, which had steep banks on the east but a much gentler slope on the west. It was the largest stream they had forded since the Kansas and the crossing took several hours.

They stopped to camp later that afternoon on high ground, which turned out to be lucky. No sooner had they pitched the tents and circled the wagons than a terrible thunderstorm broke out. Sheets of rain and howling winds drove everyone to cover. The wind was so brutal that some of the wagons were nearly overturned. It only lasted for a half hour but made a frightening impression on the entire camp. When it was over, though, the trail dust had been washed away, leaving everyone feeling fresh and clean for the first time in days.

The next day, they continued over the rolling prairie. Three miles from their previous camp, they came to a small stream that was easy to cross, despite the rains of the evening before. The caravan climbed a long, low ridge and then made it to the tops of the bluffs that overlooked the Big Blue River. Its name was a misnomer - it wasn't blue; it was the color of prairie mud. The water was filled with branches, broken limbs, and fallen trees of all sizes.

And somehow, the party had to cross it.

Owl Russell called a meeting with James Reed, George Donner, and Lilburn Boggs to discuss the situation. The river was much too swollen, and the current too swift, to attempt to cross it. They were going to have to wait until the water had a chance to recede.

Even though the delay would slow them down, most of the party was ready for some rest. They found an ideal site with a fresh spring, stands of cottonwood, willow, and elm for firewood, and plenty of tall bluestem grass on which the animals could graze.

By the afternoon of May 26, most of the women and girls were scrubbing mounds of laundry in kettles over fires on the banks of a small creek that was close to camp. The bachelors, of course, had to do their own laundry. As one man groaned, "I find I have done my own work badly and am much fatigued." I'm sure the women would have rolled their eyes at this.

While the single men worked - and likely reconsidered their marital status - others looked for game to shoot but had no luck. Others tried fishing the Big Blue River, but the current was too strong. Only one large catfish made it into a skillet.

Later that evening, Boggs, Reed, Donner, and several others discussed the bylaws and regulations that governed the party, which, as Edwin Bryant pointed out, were rarely enforced. So far, no major disagreements had occurred, and the leaders were optimistic about the journey ahead.

That optimism likely waned a bit that night when another thunderstorm drenched the camp. Many feared their tents would be blown away. Edwin Bryant was grateful for the surrounding bluffs and timber that helped to break the wind. He wrote, "The whole arch of the heavens for a time was wrapped in a sheet of flame and the almost deafening crashes of thunder, following each other with scarcely an intermission between, seemed as if they would rend the solid earth, or topple it from its axis. A more sublime and awful meteoric display, I never witnessed or could conceive."

More rain meant it was going to take even longer to get across the river. Many were restless and irritable. A band of disgruntled single men - already unhappy with the slow movement of the caravan - decided the time had come for some leadership changes.

On May 27, an early morning meeting was held. Although initially called to discuss the regulations that had been talked about the previous night, the proceedings turned ugly. Robert Ewing, one of Bryant's traveling companions, was disappointed about not being appointed to a leadership role, let out a stream of curses that were mostly directed at Owl Russell. Ewing then moved to appoint a standing committed to try the caravan leaders, "when charged with tyranny or neglect of duty by any individual of the party." A vote was called and, to the surprise of many, the motion carried. Stunned and outraged, all the officers, including Russell, immediately resigned. Ewing nominated Boggs to take over as the leader, but the former Missouri governor quickly declined.

The wagon train was suddenly without any leaders.

Edwin Bryant quickly stepped forward. He knew that most of the party still supported Russell and knew that most of the people who voted didn't understand Ewing's measure. So, Bryant made a motion of his own - a reconsideration of the vote. His motion was accepted, and the new vote completely reversed the situation. Russell and the others were now back in charge.

With the defeat of Ewing and the "young men," as the dissenters were sympathetically called, a semblance of order returned to the camp.

This seemed like the perfect time for Tamzene Donner, the Thorntons, Bryant, and other nature lovers to duck out of the encampment and explore the surrounding woods and prairie. Andrew Grayson brought back a huge supply of prairie peas and then he and a few others went in search of a honey tree. They proved to be good bee trackers and returned to camp that afternoon with several pails brimming with golden wildflower honey.

Alcove Spring, where Edwin Bryant - and many other emigrants - left their names behind over the years.

It was during this delay that Bryant found the fabled "Alcove Spring," an icy-cold spring that fed the water of the small stream the party was camped on. He left behind his name and the date carved into the rock - as scores of other emigrants would do in the years to come.

A quiet night passed, with no further storms. The camp woke up on May 26 to find that the river had dropped 15 inches while they slept. After breakfast, a call for volunteers went out. The plan was to build a large raft for ferrying the wagons across. The men quickly went to work with hammers, axes, and other tools.

Russell devised a plan to construct a rope ferry consisting of two large dugout canoes united by cross timbers so wagons would be loaded onto the raft. Then, with ropes attached at both ends, the craft could be pulled back and forth across the river by the strength of the men. Two trees were felled, trimmed, and moved into place. The next step involved hollowing out a pair of canoes that were 25-feet long. They worked on the raft all day and returned to camp in the evening, exhausted, hungry, and in desperate need of rest.

But that night was anything but restful for the Reed family. They were on deathwatch around the feather bed in the wagon. The first member of the Donner Party to die had reached the end of her journey. Near dawn on May 29, Sarah Keyes, took her last breath.

Edwin Bryant wrote, "The event, although it had been anticipated for several days, cast a gloom over our whole encampment. The construction of the ferry-boat and all recreations were suspended, out of respect for the dead, and to make preparations for the funeral."

James Reed dug a grave beneath an imposing oak tree, while others cut down a cottonwood and built a coffin for Sarah. John Denton, the teamster who traveled with the Donners, found a smooth, flat stone and carved Sarah's name and date of death onto its face.

Margaret and her daughters washed Sarah's body, combed her hair, and dressed her in her best gown. Before the coffin lid was nailed shut, James Reed snipped a lock of Sarah's hair. He gave it to Patty, the little girl who had been closest to her grandmother, and she treasured it for the rest of her life.

A funeral procession was formed, and Sarah was conveyed to her final resting place in what Bryant called, "this desolate but beautiful wilderness." After a song and a short sermon, the coffin was lowered into the ground, the grave was closed, and covered with prairie sod and wildflowers.

Believed to be a photograph of Sarah Keyes, the elderly mother of Margaret Reed, who passed away while the emigrants were waiting to cross the Big Blue River.

Virginia Reed wrote about this mournful day. "It seemed hard to bury her in the wilderness, travel on... but her death here, before our troubles began, was providential, and nowhere on the whole road could we have found so beautiful a resting place."

Although gloom hung over the camp in the wake of Sarah's death, there was some good news, too. The river was continuing to fall. Work continued on the raft and was launched to a chorus of cheers. The floating of the wagons began. "She floated down the stream like a cork and was soon moored at the place of embarkation," Edwin Bryant wrote.

Each crossing that day was difficult and dangerous. The current was so strong that even near the bank, where the water was only a few feet deep, it took tremendous effort to pull in the raft and secure it. To make matters worse, the banks were so steep on the east side that the wagons had to be let down with ropes and then carefully secured on the raft. There was only one accident - one of the canoe floats was swamped during a crossing - but there was no serious damage or loss, except for precious time. Repairs were made and operations resumed, but by nightfall, only nine wagons had made the river crossing.

The ferrying process began again early the next morning, May 31. The river had fallen at least another seven inches but moving the wagons and swimming the livestock across the river was just as dangerous as the day before. Everyone pitched in and worked quickly - even as rain clouds began to darken the sky.

The rain moved in, along with dark skies and a chilling wind that dropped the temperature into the forties, and it didn't stop until nearly 10:00 p.m., just as the final wagon made the crossing. The men had been working for 15 hours straight, often in freezing water up to their armpits. They were cold, badly cramped, and shivering violently as they trudged along to their new camp, about a mile from the crossing. The men were so tired that after gathering wood and circling the wagons into the makeshift corral, they fell asleep by the fire without eating their supper.

The next morning was the first of June, but it felt like a morning in November. A chilly wind blew from the northwest causing coughing and complaining as everyone dug through their wagons for heavier shirts and coats.

Margaret Reed was stricken with one of her painful migraines as she wept at having left her mother behind in a prairie grave. As happy as everyone was to leave the Big Blue River behind them, they were saddened by the sounds of Margaret's piteous weeping coming from inside the Reed family wagon.

Edwin Bryant made a note of another kind that morning. "We are now in the territory of the Pawnee," he wrote, "reported to be vicious savages, and skillful and daring thieves. Thus far we have lost nothing of consequence and met with no disaster from Indian depredation or hostility."

But Indians were not the biggest concern. Tensions within the Russell party were every bit as dangerous as Pawnee warriors. On the last night of the river crossing, two teamsters got into an argument that turned into a knife fight. They were both disarmed before any serious blood was drawn. There were still many of the men who refused to follow Russell's authority and continually defied the caravan leaders and openly fought amongst themselves. Gossip and rumor --- as dangerous as a rattlesnake - spread around the evening campfires and turned friends into enemies.

A quarrel that had been simmering for a few days boiled over between Jessy Thornton and John B. Goode. Both men - Jessy and his wife and Goode alone - were headed to Oregon. Back in Independence, the men had become partners. Thornton financed the wagon, Goode had purchased the oxen, together they hired two teamsters. Problems flared between them almost as soon as the caravan started across the prairie. Goode decided that Thornton was spending too much time collecting botanical samples and not putting in his share of labor maintaining the wagon.

On June 1, Goode had reached his limit. He threatened to remove the oxen from the wagon and leave Jessy and his sickly wife, Nancy, along the trail. Late that night, the caravan's appointed council met to try and arbitrate the dispute. Tempers flared, punches were thrown, and Thornton and Goode had to be separated.

After a few hours of sleep, all the men were summoned to a meeting to consider a plan that would prevent further problems. In the end, it was decided that the two men who were fighting over their wagon and oxen - and the other 18 or 20 wagons also bound for Oregon - should "in a respectful manner and friendly spirit" leave the Russell caravan en route to California. This was put to a vote and it was unanimously passed. The Oregon emigrants immediately withdrew their wagons from the corral and proceeded on their way.

The departure caused a lot of sadness for both groups. Many of the women broke into tears. After several weeks, bonds had been formed between mothers from both sides. Likewise, many children were saddened to lose their friends and young women were distraught at being separated from the young men who had been wooing them. Most of the anxiousness and tears were unnecessary, though. Although from this point in the journey the Californian and Oregon parties were divided, they stayed fairly close together much of the way. They were usually only a day's ride apart, which allowed them to visit back and forth along the trail.

Charles Stanton wrote about the departure of the Oregon emigrants from the Russell Party. "Friendships and attachments had been formed which were hard to break; for, ever since, our company is

This unfortunate drawing of Charles Stanton is the only likeness of a man who would prove to be one of the most heroic members of the Donner Party.

nearly deserted by the young men everyday riding out on horseback, pretending to hunt, but instead of pursuing the boundless deer or fleet antelope, they are generally found among the fair Oregon girls."

At age 35, Stanton was a bachelor but quite a bit older than the young men hired as teamsters. He had read Lansford Hastings' guide to Oregon and California and was convinced he could change his life through travel. As far as we know, even though he drove a Donner wagon, he was not employed by the family. It's more likely that he'd paid George Donner to transport his belongings and helped out however he could. He became a friend of the family, especially to Tamzene, with whom he shared a passion for botany and geology.

But no one was off looking for plants in the early days of June. The unseasonable weather wasn't conducive to collecting specimens. It was still cold and many of the emigrants, especially the children, were sick with colds and fevers. In addition, as Bryant had written, they were now in Pawnee country and when gossips in the caravan spread rumors of Indian sightings, it put everyone on alert.

On June 2, they encountered Indians - a small party of Shawnee who were returning home from a hunting trip along the Platte River. Two of them spoke English and that night, they were invited to camp with the caravan. The Indians sold the party some dried buffalo tongues and jerked meat and slept wrapped in furs and blankets next to the fire.

Dawn on June 3 arrived with even colder temperatures. Before the Shawnee left camp, the emigrants gave them a large bundle of letters that were addressed to family and friends back east. They also supplied them with enough bacon, flour, coffee, and sugar to make it the rest of the way home. The two groups parted on good terms and the Shawnee vanished over the horizon to the east.

Despite this friendly encounter, though, the party stayed vigilant. They scanned the ridges and occasional groves for any sign of the Pawnee and for something that might actually be worse - Mormons.

The Mormons had not forgotten that they had been driven out of Missouri by Lilburn Boggs, who was still traveling with the Russell group. After Mormon leader Joseph Smith had been shot and killed by a mob in Illinois in 1844, Brigham Young was appointed as the new prophet and president of the church. He was committed to a plan conceived by Smith, who had envisioned the Mormons establishing a kingdom in the West. Thanks to continued persecution, the Mormon exodus from Illinois began ahead of schedule. They crossed the frozen Mississippi River in February 1846 and traveled across Iowa.

They were headed to the far West - just like the Russell party was.

7. THE NEW COMMAND

The endless days of open prairie and the discomfort of the trail took a toll on everyone in the party. Disease, injuries, and broken-down wagons forced many to fall behind. Many joined other caravans, but others gave up and went home. The stress and indecision about final destinations resulted in the constant change in size of the wagon train. Bickering was inevitable. Worries about the weather, marauding Indians, vengeful Mormons, and fear of the unknown kept nerves frayed and tempers short. Not every argument was settled amicably. When that occurred, it usually led to families or individuals breaking off from the main party.

Occasionally, it led to violence.

On the evening of June 3, exchanged words over next to nothing with some men who had recently joined the caravan turned into a brawl. When fists had no effect, they drew knives and guns. Edwin Bryant wrote, "But not for the interference of William Kirkendall, who was standing near at the moment and rushed between the parties, one or both would probably have been killed."

The fight came at the end of a chaotic day. While fording a river that afternoon, a wagon had overturned. A pregnant woman and her daughter were thrown from the wagon without serious injury, but the long wooden wagon tongue had snapped and everything in it - clothing, supplies, food, and bedding - were soaked and covered with mud. Bryant wrote that the wagon belonged to a "German immigrant named Keseberg." It would be the first mention of a family that would become an important part of the story of the Donner Party.

Johann Ludwig Christian Keseberg - who was known as Lewis - had been born in Germany in 1814. He married Elizabeth Zimmerman in 1842 in a Protestant church, despite opposition because the bride was Catholic. Less than a year later, Elizabeth gave birth to twin daughters, Ada and Mathilde, and the family traveled to America in 1844. Two months after arriving in New York, though, little Mathilde died. The Kesebergs then moved to Cincinnati, where Lewis worked in a brewery until the family decided to go west. Writings from the trail about Keseberg described him as a tall,

Lewis Keseberg in a photograph taken much later in his life, long after the events of the book. Unfortunately, it doesn't offer an accurate representation of what he looked like during these events but it's the only image that we have.

handsome man with blond hair. He was also said to have an aptitude for language.

The Kesebergs had left Ohio with two wagons. One of them was driven by a Belgian emigrant named Hardcoop, whose first name is unknown. He was about 60-years-old and had been a knife-maker in his native city of Antwerp.

Keseberg made very few friends on the trail, with the exception of Heinrich Lienhard, a Swiss man who was party of a caravan just ahead of the Russell group. Keseberg was a standoffish man with a terrible temper. He was usually quiet, but when angry, he shouted at his wife, his daughter, his teamster, his animals, and just about anyone who crossed his path. Lienhard recognized Keseberg's shortcomings but still maintained a friendliness with him. He had confessed to Lienhard that his temper was "a source of considerable embarrassment to him. After his anger subsided," Lienhard wrote, "he always realized his mistake and was extremely penitent. He gave every indication of being an honorable man."

The other German-speaking emigrants in the party traveled together and kept to themselves. Among them was a couple named Wolfinger - possibly Jacob and Dorthea - about whom little is known. According to camp gossip, they were wealthy and the pretty wife's appearance seemed to validate this. She was recalled as a "tall, queenly lady" who wore fine clothing and jewelry, even on the rough trail.

Two men traveled with them - Joseph Reinhardt and Augustus Spitzer. They were partners and rode with the Wolfingers at least part of the way to California. Like the other Germans, they had little to do with the others in the caravan.

By June 4, the caravan hadn't had fresh meat in days. Things were so grim that some of the men on horseback, probably led by James Reed, pursued a wolf for miles. They came close to shooting it, but because of the many ravines, the animal eluded them.

Around noon, though, scouts spotted a large herd of antelope in the distance. A party started out immediately on the best horses, but the herd easily outdistanced the hunters.

That evening, the hunters made camp on the Little Blue, not far from a patch of oak, cottonwood, and hickory trees. Andrew Grayson slipped quietly into the woods and brought down a deer. It was field-dressed and taken back to camp, where every bit of the roasted venison was consumed. Edwin Bryant wrote, "This is the first game of consequence that has been killed since we commenced our journey, and it was a luxury highly appreciated after subsisting so long upon salted meat."

Spirits buoyed by fresh meat, the emigrants made good time on the trail for the next few days, and while attempts to hunt continued, they were unable to kill anything larger than a jackrabbit. There were plenty of antelopes around, but they stayed well out of distance for even the best man with a rifle. They were getting close to buffalo country and all eyes kept watch on the horizon for any sign of the big, shaggy beasts.

They may not have found game to eat, but the mosquitoes and gnats found plenty to feast on. They continually harassed both humans and beasts. At night, the emigrants allowed their tents to fill with campfire smoke. They might spend the night coughing but at least the pests would leave them alone. Horses and cattle got no relief at all. They were continually covered by clouds of mosquitoes. Grazing cattle were so aggravated that they pulled their picket pins out of the ground and tried to run away. The horses cried in pain all night and, the next morning, blood was found running down their flanks. The dogs howled and scratched themselves raw.

Mothers were worried about the bites from mosquitoes and ticks that covered the skin of their families. For days at a time, the caravan was plagued by sickness, mostly fever, chills, and severe diarrhea.

The trail could be a brutal place but in the midst of the problems, compassion was also present. On June 7, one of the axles broke on a heavily-loaded wagon that belonged to Edwin Bryant and some of the other single men. Some of the travelers simply rolled past the stranded wagon without a second glance but finally, someone stopped to help.

That man was William H. Eddy, a carriagemaker from Belleville, Illinois. He was about 28-years-old when he left Illinois in the spring of 1846 with his wife, Eleanor, and their young children, James and Margaret. They eventually joined up with the Russell Party. Eddy earned a reputation for being good with his hands, a skilled hunter, and a likable, friendly man. He proved himself to everyone who didn't know him already when he stopped and repaired the broken wagon.

Bryant wrote, "This would have been a most serious disaster, detaining us probably a whole day, but for the fact that we had brought with us from Independence duplicate axles. The tools with which we had provided ourselves in the event of accidents were now found to be indispensable. The damage was fully repaired, and our wagon as strong if not stronger than before at sunset, when we started for camp."

The Russell Party pushed hard during the first week of June. They were mindful of the time that had been lost at Alcove Spring and hoped to make it up. They traveled from 18-20 miles each day, following the trail northward into what would someday be Nebraska. They were anxious to make it to the Platte River, one of the great milestones of the journey. The emigrants knew when they arrived there, the trail would turn in the direction of their dreams - due west.

For several days, the caravan moved steadily northwest to Thirty-Two Mile Creek, which had gently sloping banks and shallow fords. There had been good water and forage for the most recent leg of the journey but soon the thick grass gave way to shorter ground cover, fewer water holes, and little wood for fires.

Late in the afternoon on June 9, the wagon train reached the Platte River valley. After descending the bluffs, the party made camp at the river's edge, opposite long wooded Grand Island, which was formed by the Wood River and a channel of the Platte.

Along the trail in the Platte River Valley

It was a wide, open area, with little to see but the curving ribbon of the river as it stretched out into the distance. After spending several days there, Edwin Bryant wrote, "The general aspect of the scenery is that of aridity and desolation. The face of the country presents here those features and characteristics which proclaim it to be uninhabitable by civilized man."

That first night at the Platte River, the Russell Party feasted on their first antelope meat, brought down by Andrew Grayson.

On the morning of June 9, the wagons moved westward, following the broad yellow stream that was flanked by a dusty trail they would follow for a month to the higher country of what would someday be Wyoming. The river often spread out to nearly two miles wide, even though it was often so shallow that a man could wade across it "without wetting his pants, if well rolled up above the knees."

That evening, one of the hunters came back to camp with a skull that he had found in a meadow that was littered with human bones. It was decided that the skull had belonged to an Indian man who had likely been killed during a battle between warring tribes, although honestly, they had no idea.

The skull became an object of macabre fascination and many emigrants came to the man's tent to see and hold it. But others urged the man to get rid of it - the skull could only bring bad luck.

It was a dark omen for what lay ahead.

The journey continued on June 10. Each new day brought new discoveries for the party. When they found the primarily treeless landscape offered little wood for fires, they turned to the alternative fuel of buffalo chips, just as other emigrants had done in the past and would continue to do long after the Russell Party was gone. The

When there was no wood for fires, the women and children would gather large quantities of buffalo chips to burn.

vast herds left endless "deposits" behind them and when dried out, burned as well as wood.

As soon as the wagons stopped for the night, women and children carrying pails and sacks hurried to gather buffalo chips for the fires. It was not unusual to see the women carrying them in their aprons. The sun-dried piles burned so quickly that it often took two or three bushels to cook a meal but, fortunately, there seemed to be an endless supply.

For the first few days on the Platte, the chips were the only sign of buffalo that the party found. No herds had yet been seen. Hunters turned to other sources for fresh meat and anything that crawled, walked, or flew was considered fair game.

The river was an important migratory bird corridor and many species ended up on a spit or in a stew pot. There were ducks and plovers that were hunted as they fished near sandbars, as well as curlews and snipe that were eaten with cheese and dry biscuits.

The emigrants were also known to make meals of the numerous prairie dogs that scampered about and poked their heads out of the entrances to their underground dens. These little rodents got their name from early travelers who thought the little animal's warning call sounded like a dog bark. They lived in large colonies called towns, which were networks of tunnels that ran for hundreds of yards. After exploring a prairie dog town along the Platte, emigrants shot a few of them and the camp's supper included their meat, which was said to be "tender and flavorful."

The stew pots filled with small game enlivened the daily diet, but buffalo was still on everyone's mind. On June 11, the travelers encountered a group of hunters from Missouri and Kentucky who were trying to navigate down the Platte, which was no easy task since it was so shallow. The tired men tied up their two boats - loaded with buffalo skins - to a cottonwood and spent the night in the emigrant camp. They talked of large herds in the area and assured the emigrants they would find them soon. In the morning, the hunters traded some of their skins for some basic staples like bacon, flour, and coffee and were on their way.

On June 12, as the caravan continued westward, Lilburn Boggs' son, William, rode off across the Platte with Andrew Grayson to look for buffalo. Edwin Bryant and William Kirkendall headed into the hills, where they found antelope, but were unable to get close enough to shoot at them. They got turned around and spent most of the rest of the day trying to find their way back to the wagon train.

That evening, James Reed rode in with the carcass of a large elk that he had shot that afternoon. He gladly shared it with everyone, who devoured the tender meat and hunks of fat.

The next day, Boggs and Grayson returned with choice cuts from a buffalo cow they had killed about 15 miles from camp. The emigrants had already planned to stay an extra day in camp making wagon repairs, so they were happy to feast on buffalo. The morning fires were stoked with new chips and some branches from a nearby cottonwood and soon, plates were filled with generous portions of buffalo steak and ribs. Right then, they decided there would be no more suppers of plover and prairie dogs.

The emigrants of the 1840s were the first white settlers to see the vast herds of buffalo on the Plains. By the end of the century, they would be mostly gone.

Over the next few days, the party came upon herds of bison that stretched as far as they could see. Edwin Bryant wrote in a letter to a friend, "We are now in the midst of buffaloes, and buffalo meat is as plenty as blackberries. I have seen not less than 1,000 of these animals today, without going off from the wagon trail. I assisted in shooting one about two hours ago. He fell about 200 yards from our encampment tonight."

The buffalo hunts continued, mostly led by James Reed, gathering more meat than the emigrants could possibly eat. They began drying and smoking it, putting it aside for the journey to come.

Although hunting was successful, some of the emigrants faced serious problems that had no easy solutions. On the morning of June 14, the party had traveled only about five miles before three men from another emigrant caravan about 30 miles ahead rode back looking for Edwin Bryant, who they'd heard had medical training. They wanted Edwin to come to their camp to tend to a seriously injured Missouri boy whose family was bound for Oregon. The boy had fallen off a wagon and his leg had been crushed beneath a wheel. The men also told Bryant that several people in the camp were laid up with fevers and other illnesses and wanted him to help them, too.

Edwin knew he was out of his element. He had studied medicine briefly in his youth but was in no way qualified to act as a doctor, especially when it came to life-threatening injuries. Somehow, his brief time in medical school had been inflated by rumor to seem as if he had practiced medicine. He had no surgical instruments and assured the men that he wouldn't be of any service to someone who was suffering.

But the men were desperate and refused to take no for an answer. Finally, Bryant rode several hours with them to their camp. When they arrived, he was rushed to the Garrison family wagon, where seven-year-old Enoch Garrison was laid out on some planks. Edwin was stunned when he learned from the boy's mother, Margaret, that the injury had occurred a week before and that the wound had only been dressed one day earlier when the boy complained that he could "feel worms crawling in his leg." His mother discovered that the leg was swarming with maggots - gangrene had set in.

Edwin discovered that two former members of the Russell Party were already there - Jessy Thornton and Reverend Josephus Cornwall, the minister who had officiated at Sarah Keyes' funeral. They had ridden over that morning so Cornwall could preach at a neighboring encampment. When they arrived, the injured boy's mother begged Jessy to amputate the gangrenous leg. He declined but had told them about Bryant's time in medical school.

Edwin quickly examined the boy and determined that from knee to foot, Enoch's leg was in a state of decay. Edwin and Jessy talked and both men decided that the boy would soon die. He would not survive an operation. When they explained this to the mother, she became hysterical. She begged Edwin to amputate the boy's leg. Edwin wrote, "I told her again that all efforts to save him would be useless, and only add to the anguish of which he was now dying."

But Margaret Garrison refused to listen.

Finally, a French-Canadian cattle driver named Frederic Derusha volunteered to perform the surgery. He claimed that he had worked in a hospital and had witnessed many operations, including amputations. The only tools that he had to work with were a common butcher's knife, a carpenter's handsaw, and a shoemaker's awl that would hold the arteries. "I could not resist a shudder when I saw the preparations made for the butchery of the little boy," Edwin later recalled.

Laudanum, a popular opium-based painkiller was given to Enoch several times, but with little effect. According to his brother, the little boy took his mother's hand and said, "Goodbye mother, I am going to heaven."

Derusha made an incision just below the knee and began to saw. Just before he cut through the bone, he changed his mind and decided that the amputation should be above the knee instead. A tourniquet had been applied to the boy's upper leg and it did stop most of the bleeding. Jessy Thornton wrote in his journal, "The boy bore his sufferings with the most wonderful fortitude and heroism. He seemed scarcely to move a muscle. A deathlike paleness would sometimes cover his face, and there cannot be a doubt that the pain was most intense but, instead of groaning, he used words of encouragement to the almost shrinking operator, or some expression of comfort to his afflicted friends."

At last, an hour and 45 minutes after the initial incision, it was over. The limb was severed, the arteries secured, and a flap of skin was folded over and bandaged. And then, within minutes, Enoch's eyes rolled back, and he died.

While Thornton and Cornwall tried to console the Garrison family, Edwin was asked to deal with the dead boy's father, Abraham, who was lying in his tent. The man had been in great pain for days, unable to move because of what Edwin diagnosed as inflammatory rheumatism, likely brought on by wading through streams and exposure to the cold rains of the previous week. His intense pain, now combined with the news of his son's death, had overwhelmed him and he begged Edwin to find him some relief.

Edwin dug into his bag and left the man some medicine, giving him stern instructions not to deviate from the dosage directions unless the man wanted to die. Bryant wrote, "The propensity of those afflicted by disease on this journey is frequently to devour medicines as they would food, under the delusion that large quantities will more speedily and effectually produce a cure. The reverse is the fact, and it is sometimes dangerous to trust a patient with more than a single dose."

Edwin was then asked to examine at least six other people who were complaining of various ailments. He did what he could, offering sensible advice or some of the medicine he carried with him. He encountered one young man that he was sure had heart disease. He wrote, "I told him there was nothing I could do for him; that the journey might affect his cure, but that no medicine I possessed would have any other than an injurious effect." He later learned that five days after his visit, the man's heart gave out and he was buried along the trail.

When the task that he didn't want was completed, he accepted an invitation from Jessy Thornton to accompany him a mile or so to their camp for supper. There he was greeted by several more of his former traveling companions and Jessy's wife, Nancy, who served a stew of bison and antelope. Later that evening, Edwin and the Thorntons were invited to a wedding ceremony. Jessy reluctantly agreed to go, even though he thought wagon train marriages were a bad idea. He noted in his journal, "I cannot say I much approve of a woman marrying on the road. It looks so much like making a sort of hop, skip, and jump into matrimony, without knowing what her feet will come down upon, or, whether they may be wounded or bruised."

The pretty bride, 15-year-old Mary Lard, married Riley Moutrey, 22, a teamster hired to drive one of the Lard family's wagons. The service was held at the Lard tent, presided over by Reverend Cornwall. There were only a few candles, the wedding cake was plain, and there was no music or dancing. Edwin wrote, "The company separated soon after the ceremony was performed, leaving the happy pair to the enjoyment of their connubial felicities."

When Edwin and the Thorntons left the wedding, they looked across the plain and saw the distant torches and lanterns of Enoch Garrison's funeral procession. The emigrants had gotten into the habit of secretly burying the dead at night and leaving their graves unmarked because a rumor had made the rounds that Indians made a habit of opening the graves of white settlers. They didn't - but it was a hard rumor to dispel.

While Edwin and the others were watching the distant scene, a man rode up with news that there was a big celebration going on at his neighboring camp when a woman had just given birth to a baby boy.

Edwin Bryant never forgot that moment.

"I could not but reflect upon the singular occurrence of the events of the day. A death and funeral, a wedding, and a birth, had occurred in the wilderness, within a diameter of two miles, and within two hours' time. And tomorrow, the places where these events had taken place would be deserted and unmarked, except for the grave of the unfortunate boy deceased. Such are the dispensations of providence - such the checkered map of human suffering and human enjoyment."

As Edwin Bryant had written, the caravan rolled on down the trail the following day, getting ever closer to Fort Laramie, the next major marker along the road.

The emigrants wrote letters home and few concerns about them reaching their intended recipients. What Edwin Bryant called a "sort of post office communication" proved effective for reaching the outside world and other wagon trains. They exchanged news with other travelers and passed letters to those who were going east. Letters and messages were often left along the trail for those going either east or west to pick up. They might be greetings and words of cheer to those who were following, or advertisements for lost cattle.

Tamzene Donner wrote a letter to a friend at home on June 16 and so did Edwin Bryant. He described his experiences with the sick and dying at the Oregon Party camp, his success hunting bison, and how life outdoors had changed his looks. "If you were to see me now you would scarcely know me. Indeed, when I look in the glass, I do not exactly recognize myself. I am as dark, apparently, as the darkest Indian I have ever seen, and bear in many respects a great resemblance to them. My health has generally been good, although there is much sickness among the emigrants." He also hinted that he and some of the other single men would soon leave the Russell Party to get away from the slow-moving family wagons.

Owl Russell, who had been fighting off chills and a fever, also finished a letter on June 16 that he had started more than three days before. It was addressed to William F. Switzler, the publisher of the *Missouri Statesman*. In it, he noted, "We find thousands of buffalo, and kill more than we can eat, it is really a fine sport."

He also vented his frustrations as the busy captain of the caravan. "Well, it is a queer life we are living, all our teams are oxen, and our travel of consequences is vexatiously slow not averaging more than 16 or 17 miles a day. My duties as commandant are troublesome beyond anything I could conceive of. I am annoyed with all manner of complaints."

As luck would have it, a company returning from the Oregon Country arrived in camp that same day. They already had 840 letters from Oregon and from their stop at Fort Laramie, but there was more than enough room for a packet of letters from the Russell Party. The company was made up of 15 men led by Joel Palmer. They had no horses but rode mules and horses. This greatly reduced their time of travel - a fact that did not go unnoticed by Edwin Bryant and the other single men.

Some of the men who traveled with Palmer regaled the caravan with stories of attacks and degradations by the Pawnee. The stories further stirred the imaginations of the Russell Party emigrants and caused Owl Russell no end to his own sleepless nights. His guards had no trouble sleeping, though. He had written in his letter handed off that day, "I keep up a regular guard, and if I could only keep the militia from falling asleep on their post, I should be secure against surprise."

Palmer and his men rode out the next morning, anxious to see their loved ones at home. They took a few last-minute letters and rode east. They planned to return to Missouri, do their courting in the winter months, and return to Oregon with new wives in the spring. "Oregon is no place for bachelors," a reporter once wrote.

On June 17, the Russell Party left their camp at the convergence of the South Platte and North Platte. By that afternoon, they had journeyed 17 miles and had reached the upper ford of the South Platte, which was often referred to as the California Crossing. The river was rising, so it was important for all the wagons to get across it that day. They did it - the last wagon crossed at sunset. Virginia Reed wrote, "We had no trouble crossing the Platte, the only danger being quicksand. The stream being wide, we had to stop the wagon now and then to give the oxen a few moments' rest."

That evening, two or three buffalo were killed and early the next morning, a large bull was easily shot near the camp while it was grazing among the cattle. As Russell had written in his letter home, the emigrants often wastefully killed more than they needed, just for sport. It was the beginning of a wave of destruction that would haunt the Plains Indians, who used the herds not only as a major food source but everything else the tribes needed, from shelter to clothing, weapons, utensils, and ceremonial objects. Every part of the buffalo was used - hide, hair, flesh, blood, bones, and internal organs.

On the evening of June 18, following a supper of buffalo steaks and tongues, word spread throughout the camp for everyone to gather for a meeting. Although some were surprised, most knew what was coming - Owl Russell was stepping down from his role as the leader because of his poor health.

The assembled company voted to accept his resignation. Lilburn Boggs, the former Missouri governor, was called forward and Edwin Bryant moved to elect Boggs as the new captain. The motion was adopted unanimously and led by Bryant; Russell was thanked for his service. All the subordinate officers who had served under Russell, which included George Donner, then resigned out of courtesy to the new leader. Each man was given a vote of thanks.

The caravan departed early in the morning of June 19 while rumors were circulating through the party that perhaps a dozen of the single men were contemplating striking out on their own. Before the gossip could be verified, the new captain got the caravan moving and what was now called the Boggs Party was headed west.

8. PARTING WAYS

The Boggs Party, with its newly chosen captain, traveled more than 20 miles on June 19. After climbing some steep hills and navigating harsh terrain between the North and South Platte Rivers, the wagons slowly climbed a twisting path into the valley of the North Platte. They stopped at the mouth of Ash Hollow - named for the scattering of ash trees there - which was a common place for caravans to rest on their journey west. There was lush grass, plenty of wood, and a natural spring with sweet-tasting water. Emigrant diaries often described the hollow as one of the most idyllic places they found on the trip west.

After the camp had been set up, the children gathered wild currants and gooseberries while the women began preparing meals. Tamzene Donner and her fellow botanists collected some of the spring-fed vegetation, while others explored the deserted log cabin in the hollow that had provided shelter for some trappers that had been snowed-in there during the past winter. It had been dubbed the "Ash Hollow Hotel" and the walls were covered with messages from travelers. A recess in the wall contained a bundle of letters that were requested to be taken back east for delivery. A few of the Boggs Party added their own letters to the stack, hoping they'd be picked up soon by a traveler or trader heading back to the States.

Later that evening, a meeting was held to finalize plans for breaking away from the main caravan. Among those who proposed leaving were Edwin Bryant, George McKinstry, William Kirkendall, Benjamin Lippincott, Robert Ewing, and several others. Most were single men who could move faster on their own and all of them were frustrated by the caravan's slow pace. Bryant wrote of the meeting: "A party of eight or ten persons, including myself, had determined on our arrival at Fort Laramie, to change our mode of travel, provided we could make suitable arrangements. If mules could be obtained for packing, our design was to abandon our oxen and wagons, and all baggage not absolutely necessary to the journey. This would enable us to proceed with much greater expedition towards the point of our destination."

The next morning, Bryant and the others left for Fort Laramie, which was about 150 miles away. Later in the day, they overtook a wagon train captained by Gallant Dickerson, the same company that had gone out on its own on May 22, the day the Donners and Reeds joined the Russell Party. They accepted an invitation to spend the night in the camp and then rode on the next morning.

Meanwhile, the Boggs Party was also proceeding through the arid river valley, angling over to the North Fork of the Platte and staying close to the south bank. After spending weeks on the grassy plains, the changes in the landscape were rather dramatic to the members of the caravan. They began to see the optical phenomenon of mirages for the first time in the journey. At times, the mirages appeared to be bodies of water, animal herds, trees, and even buildings as they danced and shimmered far ahead of the wagons on the horizon. Mirages on the open prairie fooled everyone, not just emigrants. There were reports of them from Native Americans, mountain men, soldiers, and scouts.

The travelers also came upon rock formations like nothing they had seen before. In the glaring sun and the afternoon shadows, they often took on the form of castles, chimneys, and churches. The first formation they saw - two massive formations of sandstone, clay, and volcanic ash - was known as McFarlan's Castle until the 1830s, when emigrants began calling it Courthouse Rock because it was said to look like the new courthouse then being built in St. Louis. The Boggs Party camped near the two monoliths on June 22 and several of the emigrants

Scott's Bluff in Nebraska

visited the site and scratched their names and the date into their towering walls.

Ahead of them was the most noted landmark on this leg of the journey - Chimney Rock. Bryant and his group camped there on their trip. Because there were so few of them, every man had to stand guard duty. Bryant stood watch early in the evening and it was a memorable experience. He later wrote, "The dark masses of clouds that had been rising from the west for many hours continued to become more and more threatening. I have never before witnessed such brilliant displays of electricity or heard more deafening crashes of thunder."

It took the rest of the caravan two more days to arrive at Chimney Rock. They also etched their names on the base or as high as they dared to climb up the column of stone.

On June 24, the party reached Scotts Bluff, the gigantic rock formation that had been named for old fur trapper Hiram Scott. They made camp at Fremont Springs and several of the party found the names of explorer John C. Fremont and his guide, Kit Carson, engraved on the rock in 1842.

The travelers broke camp once again on June 25 and began rolling toward Fort Laramie - considered the point of no return for emigrants on the way to California and Oregon. They continued to follow the North Platte River, unknowingly entering what would someday be the state of Wyoming on June 26.

Despite its name, Fort Laramie - situated on the lower Laramie River - was not a military garrison at that time. It was an outpost of the American Fur Company and a gathering place for trappers, traders, settlers, and Native Americans. Fort Laramie supplied a vast region of the central Rocky Mountains to the west and the sprawling buffalo

Although Fort Laramie was the natural stopping point for many emigrants, the Boggs Party followed advice to stop at Fort Bernard instead. They had likely heard that the traders at Fort Laramie were "a set of mean swindlers."

region to the east, where a trade in buffalo robes was replacing the demand for beaver pelts.

For the past two days on the trail, the emigrants started to see the first glimpse of the Rocky Mountains rising from the morning mist. They were becoming increasingly excited about the mountains and about their eminent arrival at a place that would offer their first taste of "civilization" in weeks.

On the afternoon of the 26th, though, Boggs ordered the wagon party to stop just eight miles from Fort Laramie at Fort Bernard, a smaller trading post on the North Platte. Established only one year before, it had become competitive because westbound travelers came to it first. The owners of Fort Bernard had started undercutting the prices at the larger post and an intense rivalry had developed between them. When the Boggs Party arrived, the trading post was doing a brisk business with wagon trains, selling them goods at 30 to 40 percent less than could be found at Fort Laramie.

Writer and adventurer Francis Parkman, who was close with members of the Sioux nation, called the traders at Fort Laramie "a set of mean swindlers" and the "natural enemies" of the emigrants. He said they were "plundered and cheated without mercy."

In August 1846, long after the Boggs Party had departed, a mysterious fire burned Fort Bernard to the ground. Although never proved, it was widely believed that some men from rival Fort Laramie had started the fire.

When word spread along the trail that gatherings of Sioux, with large herds of horses, depleted the meadows around Fort Laramie, the grassy bottomland along the river at Fort Bernard became an attractive alternative.

Boggs had another reason for stopping at Fort Bernard - it was the site chosen for a rendezvous with the men who had left the main party earlier. Edwin Bryant and the others had arrived days before and had become familiar with both posts, especially with the mule stock each had available. They were now waiting there for their former traveling companions, who brought the men's oxen and wagons to exchange for trail mules and supplies.

When the Boggs Party arrived, Bryant and the others gave them a rousing welcome and reclaimed their wagons. That evening, all the emigrants, trappers, and traders were entertained at a supper. The traders from the post passed around jugs of a potent liquor concoction that they had dubbed "Taos Lightning."

Despite the supper and a night of hard drinking, many of the emigrants camped at Fort Bernard rose early the next morning. Bryant completed his trade of a wagon and three yokes of oxen for seven sturdy mules with packsaddles. He - along with his companions - spent the rest of the morning nursing hangovers and going through their baggage, taking out only the essentials.

That morning, while Tamzene Donner and Margaret Reed "botanized among the cottonwoods," George Donner wrote a letter to a friend back home, describing the scene at Fort Bernard. "We arrived here yesterday without meeting any serious incident. Our company are in good health. Our road has been through sandy country, but we have

Sioux warriors in a photograph taken long after the passing of the Donner Party through Wyoming.

as yet had plenty of grass for our cattle and water... There are 206 lodges of Sioux expected at the fort today on the way to join warriors on the march against the Crows. The Indians all speak friendly to us. Their ornaments are tastefully arranged, consisting of beads, feathers, and a fine shell they got from California, bark variously colored and arranged, and the hair from scalps they have taken in battles."

Eliza Donner also wrote about the Sioux warriors in the camp "smeared with war-paint, and armed with hunting knives, tomahawks, bows and arrows," and their huge herd of horses. She added, "Many of the squaws and papooses were gorgeous in white doe skin suits, gaudily trimmed with beads, and bows of bright ribbons. They formed a striking contrast to us, travel-stained wayfarers in linsey dresses and sun-bonnets. Many of the white men connected with the fort have taken Indian wives and many little children played around their doors."

At noon on June 27, the Oregon wagon train that included Jessy and Nancy Thornton and others from the former Russell Party arrived at Fort Bernard and set up camp. Jessy and Nancy were warmly greeted by their old traveling companions, who were washing clothes and hanging them to dry in trees along the river.

Later that same day, a small party of men, women, and children arrived at Fort Bernard from the west. The leader was a seasoned mountain man and trail guide named James Clyman - who had spent time in the same militia company with James Reed and Abraham Lincoln during the Black Hawk War.

At the time, no one realized that Clyman would give the emigrants the best advice offered to them during the entire journey. Clyman was delighted to see Reed among the men at the fort and the two had a happy reunion.

Born in Virginia, Clyman had led a life filled with danger and adventure. He had fought in the War of 1812 and had already traveled to the Rocky Mountains before he got involved with Reed in the Black Hawk mess. He returned out west after the brief conflict, where he cut new trails, trapped and traded, fought hostile natives, faced grizzly bears, and came through more or less intact. He was an oddity among the rough men of the West. He read anything he could find and particularly loved the works of Shakespeare and the poetry of Lord Byron.

Reed's old friend, James Clyman, in a photo that was taken long after the events in the book. It's obvious that Clyman's years as a mountain man took a toll on him in his old age.

His current expedition had started in April, about the time the Reeds and Donners left from Springfield. Clyman had just finished a bear hunt when he decided to join some travelers going to Illinois and Wisconsin. One of the men in the group was none other than Lansford Hastings, the author of *The Emigrant's Guide to Oregon and California*, the poorly researched book that the Reeds and Donners built their trip around. They had all read it, cover to cover, before leaving Illinois.

After getting to know him, Clyman considered Hastings nothing more than a schemer with big dreams. He had never crossed the Sierra Nevada, but was telling other folks how to do it. Hastings, mindful of this as well as his opportunity to sell land in California to eager newcomers, thought it was wise to travel the route that he was advertising to others. While on the trip, he planned to encourage all the wagon trains he met along the way to forget about Oregon and go to California instead.

Clyman seriously questioned the feasibility of the proposed cutoff through the Wasatch Mountains that Hastings had promoted in his book. This route would pass south of the Salt Lake and then go across the salt flats to rejoin the California Trail at the Humboldt River. Hastings - never having been there - was sure this shortcut would save travelers a lot of time. Clyman didn't agree.

Finally, Hastings and Clyman parted ways. Hastings decided not to go any farther but to greet approaching caravans and keep them on the right path. Clyman and the others from the party continued east and as they met other caravans, he told all of them the hard truth about what was ahead - a hard, tedious, often brutal journey awaited them. There were no shortcuts. Stick to the trail, no matter how difficult it seemed.

Clyman told Reed, the Donners, Bogs, Bryant, and others the same thing. They talked late into the night and they listened intently to Clyman's recommendations about the westward journey. A few of them - namely Edwin Bryant - took Clyman for just another frontier character and paid little attention to his advice. Others listened and some decided to change their destination from California to Oregon.

James Reed, though, was not one of them. He didn't doubt his old friend's wisdom, but he was convinced that the best way to reach California was by using the shortcut Hastings had written about in his guidebook: "The most direct route, for the California emigrants, would be to leave the Oregon route, about 200 miles from Fort Hall; thence bearing west southwest to the Salt Lake; and thence

The Emigrant's Guide to Oregon and California by Lansford Hastings was the book that James Reed and the Donners constantly referred to in their journey - despite the warnings of men like James Clyman, who knew that Hastings was a fraud.

continuing down to the bay of San Francisco, by the route just described."

Those few lines had immediately seized Reed's attention during his first read of the book. He was convinced the cutoff was the way to go. He didn't listen to Clyman when he tried to tell him otherwise. As Clyman later wrote: "I told him to take the regular wagon track and never leave it - it is barely possible to get through if you follow it before early snowfall and it may be impossible if you don't."

But Reed had responded, "There is a nigher route, and it is of no use to take so much of a roundabout course."

Clyman tried again to make Reed see the danger and recklessness of diverting from a proven trail in the middle of the wilderness, but it was no use.

The two men parted on good terms but there was nothing left to say on the matter of the shortcut through the Wasatch.

Reed would, of course, later wish that he had listened.

The Boggs Party began moving again on the morning of June 28. The party was behind schedule when it returned to the trail. There was now a sense of urgency to their movement. It wasn't panic, but everyone seemed to know that they had to keep moving.

That was only part of the tension that had seeped into the group, however. After that night around the fire with James Clyman, nothing was the same for the emigrants ever again. The seeds of doubt had been sown between them and those seeds would eventually turn into anger and dissension.

Some of the emigrants, including Lilburn Boggs, had been swayed by Clyman's advice, especially his warning about avoiding Hastings' shortcut. They knew that when the time came, they would choose the proven route. For the time being, though, all they wanted to do was to make up for lost time. Boggs remained, at least in name, the captain of the caravan in late June and early July, but many of the emigrants had started to call themselves the "California Train."

While the wagons were rolling along the dusty road, Edwin Bryant and the other eight men were setting off on their mules. Bryant wrote in his journal, "Not one of us had ever seen a mule packed before this morning. Some New Mexicans who came in with the trading party gave us our first lesson, and it was a very valuable one, although experience and necessity, the best of tutors, instructed us afterwards, so that many became adept in the art and handling of packing mules."

This seemed to give the expedition a rather inauspicious start, but Bryant was quick to point out that there was much to learn. "The mules, stupid as we regarded them, knew more about this business than we did; and several times I thought I could detect them in giving a wise and silly leer, as much as to say, that we were perfect novices, and if they could speak, they would give us the benefit of their advice and instruction. A Mexican pack mule is one of the sagacious and intelligent quadrupeds that I have ever met with."

Later in the morning, the caravan passed Fort Laramie. A contingent of Sioux who were camped there watched the emigrants pass by. The caravan only traveled a few miles up the Laramie fork before camping for the night. This was against advice that had been given to them by some of the Sioux they had met at Fort Bernard. They had suggested that the emigrants keep moving because tensions had increased with the Crow and fighting could happen at any time.

Eliza Donner had written about something that had unnerved her earlier in the day. "Before we got out of the country of the Sioux, we were overtaken by about 300 mounted warriors. They came in stately procession, two abreast; rode on in advance of our train; halted; opened ranks; and as our wagons passed between their lines, the warriors took from between their teeth green twigs, and tossed them toward us in pledge of friendship, then turned, and as quietly and solemnly as they had come to us, rode toward the hills. A great sigh of relief expressed the company's satisfaction at being left alone; still no one could feel sure that we should escape a night attack."

Virginia Reed also had memories of the Sioux they encountered on June 28, which was her birthday. She had turned 13 and marked the occasion by riding along with the train on her horse, Billy, accepting birthday greetings from the well-wishers among the wagons.

As she rode, Virginia and her pony caught the eye of some of the Sioux warriors who had been camped near Fort Laramie. She wrote, "The Sioux are fine looking Indians, and I was not in the least afraid of them. They fell in love with my pony and set about bargaining to buy him." Virginia might not have realized it at the time, but they were bargaining to buy her, too. Soon, it became apparent.

She wrote, "They brought buffalo robes and beautifully tanned buckskin, pretty beaded moccasins, and ropes made of grass, and placing these articles in a heap alongside several of the ponies, they made my father understand they would trade them all for Billy and his rider. Papa smiled and shook his head; then the number of ponies was increased and, as a last tempting inducement, they brought an old coat, that had been worn by some poor soldier, thinking that my father could not withstand the brass buttons."

James Reed managed to carefully convince the Sioux that he couldn't possibly trade his daughter and her cherished pony for anything. The Sioux were good-natured about his refusal.

And I would guess that the migraine that was starting to build inside Margaret Reed's skull quickly went away.

Virginia's encounter with the Indians had been a friendly one, as most of them were during the early part of the journey. Most had become accustomed to them and felt as Tamzene Donner did when she wrote in a letter to a friend, "We feel no fear of the Indians."

But not everyone felt that way. Eliza Donner often spoke of them with fear, but then she was only a small child at the time. Others remained wary. They believed that it was only a matter of time before open conflict erupted between the Native Americans and the white intruders. And they were right about that. The Kaw and the Sioux had been friendly to the emigrants because they were passing through, not staying. These white people were the problem of tribes in California and Oregon, not the problem of those on the Plains.

It wouldn't' be long before that changed. As more and more hunters and settlers came streaming west, the great herds of buffalo began to vanish. With each passing year, the natives, especially the Cheyenne and the Sioux, became more and more hostile to the whites. Eventually, that would lead to bloodshed. Before the Civil War, though, disinterest and a fear of the United States military - of which they had a confused idea about its power and strength - kept them from making open war on emigrants who were passing through their lands.

On July 1, the wagon train that was headed to Oregon - which included the Thorntons and Bryant's pack mule party - camped close to the Boggs group. The next day, Bryant came over to visit. One of his group, persuaded by stories he'd heard at Fort Bernard, had decided to change his destination, and had left Bryant with an extra mule. He convinced a teamster named Hiram Miller, one of the original men who had joined in Springfield, to join his band of mule riders.

The Boggs Party moved on. On July 3, they traveled 18 miles and camped along Beaver Creek, where they found plenty of grass, water, and firewood.

The next day was July 4 and trail tradition claimed that wagon trains had to reach Independence Rock by that day if they wanted to safely arrive in California before the winter snows. The party was more than a week away from that landmark.

Even so, they decided to celebrate the holiday at Beaver Creek. Bryant's mule expedition, the Oregon party, and the Boggs group joined together on the morning of July 4. Bryant wrote, "Our united parties convened in a grove near the emigrant encampment. A salute of small arms fire was discharged. A procession was then formed, which marched around the corral, and returning to the grove, the Declaration of Independence was read, and an address was delivered by Colonel Russell. A collation was then served up by the ladies of the encampment, at the conclusion of which, toasts suitable to the patriotic occasion were given and drunk with much enthusiasm, a discharge of muskets accompanying each sentiment."

James Reed provided most of the liquor for the many toasts. Keeping his promise to his friends back in Springfield, he broke out a special bottle of brandy. He faced to the east at the preordained time and raised his glass, while the folks in Illinois faced westward and drank a toast to his success from their own bottle.

Patriotic songs were sung, all to the accompaniment of fiddles, flutes, and drums. After a feast of roasted buffalo, bread, and beans, Bryant summed up the day in his journal by saying, "the glorious fourth was celebrated here in this remote desert with more spirit and zest than it usually is in the crowded cities of the States."

Bryant and the other mule riders, including newest recruit Hiram Miller, rode off in the afternoon. Thornton and the other Oregon emigrants did the same, picking a new campsite farther along the trail.

Although time was of the essence, the California group decided to stay put for another night. The teamsters and the men made repairs to the wagons and harnesses, the women washed clothing and bedding, and the children played in the meadow along the creek.

When they finally departed on July 6, Reed wrote, "We left camp much rested and our oxen moved off in fine style." Soon after leaving, they encountered a large party of Sioux. The wagons were strung out for some distance, leaving them mostly undefended if the Indians decided to attack. Virginia Reed wrote, "They could have massacred our whole party without much loss to themselves."

Some of the men were alarmed, brandishing rifles to show that they were prepared to defend themselves but, once again, the Sioux proved to be no threat. They were simply curious about the strange people crossing their land.

Virginia later recalled, "Their curiosity was annoying, however, and our wagon with its conspicuous stove-pipe and looking-glass attracted their attention. They were continually swarming about trying to get a look at themselves in the mirror, and their desire to possess my pony was so strong that at last I had to let one of the drivers take charge of Billy. This I did not like, and in order to see how far back the line of warriors extended, I picked up a large field glass which hung on a rack, and as I pulled it out with a click, the warriors jumped back, wheeled their ponies and scattered. This pleased me greatly and I told my mother I could fight the whole Sioux nation with a spy-glass, and, as revenge for forcing me to ride in the wagon, whenever they came near trying to get a peep at their war-paint and feathers, I would raise my glass and laugh to see them dart away in terror."

The emigrants tried to speed up their pace. They crossed the North Platte River. During this time, hunters killed eight buffalo, which was more than enough to feed everyone.

As the caravan made its way to the Sweetwater River, Alphonso Boone, brother-in-law of Lilburn Boggs, rode up to say that he and his company, headed for Oregon, had just killed eight buffalo, and invited those who wanted more meat to take all they liked. The caravan was halted for two hours while riders went to collect the best cuts of the meat.

The next day, the emigrants heard gunfire in the distance and were joined by Boggs' young son, William, who had just killed two buffalo. A short time later, James Reed charged into camp in pursuit of a buffalo bull that he had wounded. He shot it down in front of a cheering crowd.

With all this extra meat on hand, none of the emigrants could imagine that they would ever be hungry during the remainder of their journey.

At sunset on July 11, the caravan finally made it to the location they'd hoped to reach the week before - Independence Rock. They remained camped there for two nights.

During their stay, several of the men got together to look over the maps and guidebooks and to discuss plans for the rest of the trip. It didn't take long to see that not many minds had been changed in the past week. The differences in opinion about the route - whether to take

When the Donner Party finally reached Independence Rock, they were a week behind what was considered to be the best time to reach it. Things would not get any better from there.

the Hastings cutoff or not - had only deepened. But no one wasted any more time with arguing. Each man had to decide for himself and the decisions made that night ensured that some of these emigrants would become a dark and indelible part of American history.

The emigrants were roused from their sleep by a bugle blaring on the morning of July 13. The caravan was ready to leave Independence Rock and continue on towards the South Pass on the Continental Divide.

James Reed was anxious to return to the trail. He had been pleased to reach this point in the journey, and while he wished they were farther along, he was convinced they would make up some time by using the shortcut recommended in Lansford Hastings' book.

Reed must have also been a little concerned, too. Just the day before, the number of emigrants in their company had been greatly reduced when differences of opinion caused another division within the ranks. Thanks to reports from other travelers they'd met on the trail - as well as the warnings from James Clyman - several families had decided to go on their own to Oregon. The party included some of the most influential members of the caravan, including Lilburn Boggs, captain of the group.

One of those who remained, the Chicago man named Charles Stanton, wrote about the incident in a letter to his brother, "Today, a division of our company took place. Governor Boggs, Colonel Boone, and several other families went sliding out, leaving us but a small company of 18 wagons."

The letter continued, "Just as the new Oregon company was leaving, there was an important arrival - a single traveler, with his horse and pack mule, who had come all the way from Oregon. He gave the preference in favor of California. Of course, this pleased all of us who had not changed our minds and made some of the others feel a little chagrined that they had so suddenly changed the course. But Governor Boggs is actuated by different motives - he is afraid of the Mormons. He has heard they are on the route and thinks they will go to California. Should they do so, that will be no place for him. You may be aware that he was shot by Rockwell and came very near to losing his life. Consequently, he has something to fear."

While it's possible that Boggs was concerned about the Mormons, it's more likely that he was troubled by the Hastings cutoff, which he knew that others in the caravan planned to take, despite the warnings. Unable to convince Reed to change his mind, he had left, along with others who shared his concern.

Ironically, the Oregon traveler that arrived in camp brought news directly from Lansford Hastings himself. The rider's name was Wade B. Bonney. He was on his way home to Ohio, carrying hundreds of emigrant letters back east. He gladly added letters from Stanton, Virginia Reed, and others to his pack.

But he also had an open letter - addressed to any emigrants on the westbound trail - from Hastings, who was writing from the "Headwaters of the Sweetwater," a point on the trail still ahead of them. Bonney had been sharing the letter with everyone he met.

In the letter, Hastings wrote about the ongoing war between the United States and Mexico, urging the various wagon trains to "concentrate their numbers and strength" in case of attacks by Mexicans. He advised them to take the new route from Fort Bridger around the south end of Salt Lake to shorten the distance by at least 200 miles. Hastings added that he planned to meet as many emigrant parties as possible at Fort Bridger. From there, he promised to guide them across deserts and mountains along his new route to California.

Reed, the Donners, and the others who had put their faith in Hastings were encouraged by the letter, especially by his offer to act at their guide. Without taking the time to elect a new captain for their company, the Donners, Reeds, and their companions left Independence Rock. They stopped at noon about eight miles southwest at Devil's Gate, where the Sweetwater River had cut a chasm through a wall of granite that was so narrow and steep that wagons had to detour around it.

The party didn't stop again until sunset, when they caught up with the Boggs wagons, which had left the day before. Things became contentious

Lansford Hastings, later in life. He was still a young man when he wrote his guidebook to the West and lured some emigrants to their doom with his faulty shortcut.

between the two caravans over who should lead on the trail the next day, but Reed solved the issue by getting the California party up and moving early on July 14. They jumped ahead on the trail and traveled a grueling 20 miles that day, remaining always a mile ahead of the Boggs party. They made camp again along the Sweetwater.

Reed, the Donners, Stanton, and the others couldn't help but notice the chilly winds and the cold nighttime temperatures in camp. The next morning, they got their first glimpse of the "snow clad mountains" when the Wind River Range to the northwest came into view. The range contained peaks that soared more than 13,000 feet high and were dotted with lakes and glaciers. Stanton wrote, "It was now midsummer. We had been traveling for the past 10 days under a boiling sun, and it was strange thus suddenly to see this winter appearance on the distant hills."

At some point, the Boggs party had passed the caravan, but as the Donners pushed on, they cheered when they passed the Boggs

South Pass and the Continental Divide. The 28-mile summit was a disappointment to most travelers, who expected something more grandiose for the spot where rivers began running east and west.

group at one of the Sweetwater crossings shortly before stopping for the day.

On July 17, the emigrants got a late start, thanks to arguments about whether they should push on or stay in camp for a day. Those who wished to wait for a day were the younger men and some of the families who had run out of fresh meat. They wanted to spend the day hunting before leaving buffalo country. They also pointed out that the oxen and the cattle badly needed a day of rest.

The others in the group - led by Reed and the Donners - said that if they stayed in camp for another day, the other companies would get ahead of them and their livestock would eat all the grass. Reed and the Donners won the argument and the caravan rolled on.

The next day, the caravan reached another important landmark on the trail - South Pass, a 28-mile-wide summit on the Continental Divide. From this point, streams flowed east to the Mississippi River or west to the Pacific Ocean. The gentle climb to South Pass was so gradual that many emigrants did not even know they'd reached the summit. Regardless, though, all were excited. Charles Stanton wrote to his brother, "Thus the great daydream of my youth and of my riper years is accomplished. I have seen the Rocky Mountains - have crossed the Rubicon and am now on the waters that flow to the Pacific!"

After a noon stop at South Pass, the party descended along the trail and soon came to Pacific Spring, the first good water west of the Great Divide. After a brief stop, they followed the trail southwest along Pacific Creek until it merged with Dry Sandy Creek - which was true to its name. There were only a few scatters of puddles in the dry gulley and no grass for the animals.

It was nearly sundown by now, but the company continued until James Reed, who had been scouting ahead for a campsite with George Donner, returned to the wagons. There was no suitable spot ahead, Reed said, so the party returned to the bleak gulley. It was dark before suppers were cooking and Donner had still not returned. Jacob Donner and several others, fearing that George was lost, fired off guns and lit small signal fires in the surrounding hills. Finally, around midnight, George rode into camp, hungry, thirsty, and exhausted.

The emigrants packed up camp on the morning of July 19. They were eager to reach fresh water, which was at least 10 miles ahead at the Little Sandy River.

But the day got off to a terrible start.

Some of the oxen seemed to have been poisoned. It was realized that they had been drinking water out of the puddles at Dry Sandy Creek the night before. The wagon train came to a stop while the teamsters attended to the animals, but nothing could be done. The water had been tainted with alkali and three of the oxen died that morning - one belonging to Reed and two to the Donners.

They pressed on. When they reached the Big Sandy, they found that several other wagon trains going to Oregon and California were already camped there. There were several members of the original Russell party there, as well as the 16 wagons of the new Boggs party camped along the stream. Just east of South Pass, the Boggs group had merged with another small Oregon company that included Jessy and Nancy Thornton.

The groups mixed together and quietly ate their suppers. Unlike other nights spent under the stars, there was no music, little laughter, and no revelry. It was a serious and somber time for them all. In the morning, there would be one more division and a last goodbye. Some wagons would take the proven trail to Fort Hall that would lead to Oregon or continue on the standard route to California. The rest would turn left and take the road to Fort Bridger and just beyond that, to Hastings' cutoff.

James Reed, who had continued to wonder if he was making the right decision, finally felt confident that he was doing the smart thing by following his instincts and taking the new route. George and Jacob Donner fully agreed with him, as did many others. They would assemble at daybreak and head for Fort Bridger, where they expected Lansford Hastings to be waiting to guide them.

The group was tired, but before they could sleep, they decided that they needed to elect a new captain for the company. Ever since Boggs had abandoned them, Reed and George Donner had led the emigrants, but there needed to be an official election before they departed.

Some emigrants wanted Reed for the position, but most felt that he was too headstrong and arrogant. It is unknown whether he campaigned for the job or if any of the other men put their names forward for consideration. Reed did not mention the election in his journal.

The winner of the election was the likable George Donner, who was considered hardworking and reliable. He was to be the one to lead the party on the final leg of the journey, using the route that Hastings had devised. They went to bed that night eager for their adventure to continue as the Donner Party.

There was at least one person in camp, though, who while having complete faith in George Donner, was not so sure about Lansford Hastings and his shortcut.

Jessy Thornton wrote of his former traveling companions, "The Californians were generally much elated, and in fine spirits, with the prospect of a better and nearer road to the country of their destination. Mrs. George Donner was, however, an exception. She was gloomy, sad, and dispirited, in view of the fact, that her husband and others could think for a moment of leaving the old road and confide in the statement of a man of whom they knew nothing, but who was probably some selfish adventurer."

Tamzene Donner was a smart and capable woman and she had a bad feeling about the cutoff. She likely couldn't have explained that feeling if she'd been forced to, but she knew that something was wrong.

But what could she do? Perhaps she could still change her husband's mind and get him to take the well-known route. Perhaps Jacob could be swayed, she thought, or even the foolhardy Reed. She hoped there was still time to convince them not to take the cutoff before they made it to Fort Bridger.

If not, Tamzene somehow knew, terrible things were going to happen.

9. THE HASTINGS CUTOFF

The Donner Party - as it was now officially known - got back onto the trail on July 20, four months after the Donners, Reed, their friends, and employees, had left Springfield, Illinois.

As the parties in camp packed up and prepared to go their separate ways, Tamzene said a melancholic goodbye to the Thorntons - she was again losing one of her best botany companions.

Lilburn Boggs and his family said goodbye to the Donner Party at Little Sandy and then left for Fort Hall with the Boones, the Thorntons, and some of the former members of Edwin Bryant's mule caravan. Boggs had left Missouri with the intention of going to California but changed his mind after meeting James Clyman and hearing about the horrors of the Hastings route. He decided to go to Oregon with the Boones instead. But then on July 20, he changed his mind again at Fort Hall, where the standard California and Oregon Trails split and took the turn to California, as originally planned.

There were 13 members of the Murphy, Foster, and Pike families who chose to continue with the Donner Party. It became the largest group in the caravan and consisted of Levinah Murphy, a 36-year-old widow traveling with her seven children. The two oldest were married with children of their own. Levinah and the younger children traveled in two wagons and the married couples had wagons of their own. They had joined up with what was then the Russell Party in late May while waiting for the Big Blue River to subside. Levinah and her late husband, Jeremiah, were Mormons but oddly, there was no record of any conflict between the family and Lilburn Boggs during the journey.

Patrick and Margaret Breen, along with their children, were also following the Donners. Born in Ireland, Patrick had emigrated to Canada in 1828 and married Margaret - known as Peggy -- two years later. They left Canada in 1834 with two young sons and began farming near Springfield, Illinois, where they met the Donners and Reeds. In 1835, they had moved to Iowa, where they farmed and had more

Patrick and Margaret Breen would play an important role in the events at Truckee Lake.

children, finally deciding to go to California in April 1846. The family traveled in three wagons, pulled by seven yokes of oxen. They also brought along cows, horses, and their dog, Towser.

Another Irishman, Patrick Dolan, joined the Breens. One of the Breen children later described him as "red-faced, light-haired, handsome, well-built, honest, and very religious." He was a bachelor farmer, neighbor, and friend and had traded his farm for a wagon and team for the trip.

Once the Breens and Dolan got to Independence and started down the trail, they met up with the Russell Party. Early on, they decided to cross the plains alone so they would not have to compete for water and grass at the nightly campsites. When they occasionally met up with another caravan, Patrick Breen would always break out his fiddle, to the delight of the younger people, who loved to dance. They spent July 4 at Fort Laramie, some distance behind the Boggs Party, but when they caught up with them, they decided they were ready to join the Donner wagon train.

After the last of the farewells, the new Donner Party finally broke camp. With their late start, they only traveled about six miles before making camp again along the Little Sandy.

And they remained there the next day - an inauspicious beginning for the new caravan.

The poison water from Dry Sandy Creek was still taking a toll on the oxen and cattle. Several more died on July 21 and they would not be the last.

On July 22, the emigrants made it to Big Sandy Creek, where one of Patrick Dolan's steers fell dead, again from poisoned water. They found fresh water and plenty of grass at the next camp on July 23. The next morning, they pressed on toward the Green River crossing.

Over July 26 and 27, the company managed to make 36 miles, putting them almost to Bridger's Fort. They camped in a meadow with thick, lush grass near a stream of cold, clear water. There was a collective sigh of relief. The next day they would arrive at the trading post, where they would resupply, and meet the famous mountain man, Jim Bridger.

And, if they were lucky, they'd shake the hand of Lansford Hastings.

On the morning of the 28th, James Reed and George Donner rode ahead of the wagons, in a hurry to reach Fort Bridger. They were in no rush to purchase supplies and oxen, though, they wanted to find Lansford Hastings.

But they soon discovered a problem - Hastings was not at Fort Bridger as his letter to the emigrants had promised he'd be. He had been there, but he was gone. This news came as a terrible blow to Reed and Donner, but according to their hosts, Jim Bridger and his partner Louis Vasquez, Hastings had been at the fort for the sole purpose of assisting emigrant parties on their way to California. Then, earlier in July, a large number of emigrants had arrived, impatient and eager to take advantage of Hastings' offer to lead them.

On July 20, the same day the Donner Party had left Big Sandy camp, the Bryant pack train, including three new members from another party, had left Fort Bridger with Hastings' partner, mountain man James Hudspeth, as their guide. Bryant and the other former members of the Russell caravan had arrived at Fort Bridger - cold, wet,

Fort Bridger in Wyoming, founded by "King of the Mountain Men," Jim Bridger and his partner, Louis Vasquez.

and shivering after a rainstorm - four days before. Their pace had been slowed by weather and illness in the group. After arriving, they had put up their tents near the Hasting' camp and pumped the writer and Hudspeth for information.

Bryant was also excited to make the acquaintance of Bridger and Vasquez.

Pierre Luis Vasquez was a well-educated man from St. Louis. By the time he reached his twenties, he was well-known in the fur trade and had partnered with Bridger. They had built the fort on Black's Fork of the Green River in 1843.

By then, Jim Bridger had already become known as the "King of the Mountain Men." In 1822, when he was 17, he had responded to an advertisement seeking men to "ascend the Missouri River" to seek furs. Although Bridger couldn't write even his own name, he spoke several languages and had an endless supply of adventurous tales. Fort Bridger became a popular stop for mountain men and Native Americans who wanted to trade and for emigrants who began moving west around the time the fort was completed.

One of the frequent guests at the fort was a frontiersman named Joseph R. Walker, a knowledgeable guide who had led many emigrant parties to California. He had a reputation for "looking a man in the eye

Frontiersman Joseph R. Walker, photographed years after the events in this book took place.

and telling him the truth" even if it was cold and hard. Walker happened to be at Fort Bridger in July 1846 when Bryant arrived.

Bryant wrote in his journal, "Captain W. communicated to me some facts in reference to recent occurrences in California, of considerable interest. He spoke discouragingly of the new route via the south end of the Salt Lake."

Even before he had spoken to Walker about the cutoff, Bryant was already reconsidering his plan to take that route. "My impressions are unfavorable to the route, especially for wagon trains and families; but a number of emigrant parties now encamped here have decided to adopt it, with Hastings and Hudspeth as their guides; and are now waiting for some of the rear parties to come up and join them."

On July 17, several emigrant parties had arrived at Fort Bridger and others had departed, taking the proven route to Fort Hall. By midafternoon that day, rain clouds had appeared behind the mountains to the south. When the rain stopped, the clouds broke, revealing snow had fallen on the summits. In a matter of minutes, the temperature dropped from 82-degrees to 44 degrees.

The next morning, perhaps because of the extreme change in weather, Bryant and most of his party decided to take the Hastings shortcut with Hudspeth as their guide as far as the arid plain west of the Salt Lake. Bryant wrote, "Although such was my determination, I wrote several letters to friends among the emigrant parties in the rear, advising them not to take this route, but to keep to the old trail, via Fort Hall. Our situation was different from theirs. We were mounted on mules, had no families, and could afford to hazard experiments, and make explorations. They could not."

Bryant left the letters with Bridger and Vasquez for safekeeping and they promised to deliver them when the various travelers arrived.

While waiting for the wagon caravan to form, some emigrants dashed off letters while Hastings rode around the camps on horseback, assuring emigrants that his cutoff was "perfectly navigable for wagons" and would save them a lot of time. This was good news to travelers like Edwin Bryant,

The kind of troubles that Edwin Bryant and his pack mule train often had to deal with when trying to load up the stubborn animals.

who saw that the mountains surrounding Fort Bridger were "covered as deeply with snow as if it were the middle of winter."

The letters written by the emigrants were given to Captain Walker, who was traveling east. A few days later, he came upon the Donner Party making its way to Fort Bridger. He told them the same things he'd told Bryant - do not follow Hastings. When he left them, though, he knew that his advice was going to be ignored.

On July 20, Bryant's pack train left Fort Bridger. There were nine of them, plus Hudspeth and three young men from the emigrant parties.

That same day, the wagon train left Fort Bridger led by Lansford Hastings. Known as the Harlan-Young Party, it was led by an old Indian fighter named George Harlan and was made up of about 40 emigrants from four different families. Many of them had traveled with the former Russell Party earlier on the trail and were friendly with the recently formed Donner Party.

When the wagon train left on the shortcut, it's certain that they didn't know that their guide had never actually taken his own cutoff going west before. In fact, he'd never been on it at all when he published his guidebook. The first time that he set foot on it had been earlier in 1846, carrying his gear and provisions on pack mules. He had no trouble and was convinced that wagons traveling westward would have no more trouble on the route than his mules had experienced coming east.

It should come as no surprise that he was wrong.

The Harlan-Young Party ran into places on the trail that were so tight and dangerous that their wagons had to be pushed and dragged along the riverbed. The emigrants moved boulders and hacked away brush, and when the riverbed became too narrow, they were forced to hoist the wagons onto the bluffs using block and tackle. On the average, the luckless wagon train moved at a rate of a mile or less each day.

They traveled through desert regions with no water and no grass. Many of their oxen simply fell and refused to get up. Others ran about crazed with thirst and then died. Wagons had to be abandoned with no animals to pull them. At one point, in the Sierra Nevadas, the wagons had to be hauled up and down sheer cliffs.

They eventually made it to California - just as the first snows fell - but it took them three weeks longer than it would have taken using the "long way." Miraculously, only one pioneer died in the bungled effort.

The Donners would not be so fortunate.

During the days that followed, more small parties, single families, and stragglers arrived at Fort Bridger. They repaired their wagons and traded for fresh oxen. On July 26, an organized group, the Hoppe Party, left Fort Bridger on Hastings' shortcut, following the tracks of the Harlan-Young group. They met with Hastings himself that afternoon. He had left the Harlan-Young Party at a camp on Bear River and then backtracked to lead the Hoppe Party to the same location.

Things stayed busy at Fort Bridger before the Donners arrived. Bridger and Vasquez sold supplies, livestock, and whiskey, usually at outrageous prices. But their business was driven by traffic - which explains why they, unlike Captain Walker, refrained from telling the emigrants about the dangers of Hastings' cutoff. Two years earlier, a cutoff discovered east of the fort by guide Caleb Greenwood had stopped most of the traffic to Fort Bridger. This was why the two men - who certainly knew better - were pleased with Hastings' route. It was bringing them customers that they badly needed.

This was also the reason why on the morning of July 28 - when

Reed and Donner came looking for Hastings - Bridger and Vasquez strongly encouraged them to follow the Hastings cutoff after the emigrants and their animals had time to rest. This sounded like a good plan to Reed and Donner, even if they were concerned by more delays. They were given assurances that they could catch up with Hastings and the others - they could follow their wagon tracks - and, of course, these respected men would never steer them wrong.

What Bridger and Vasquez didn't share with Reed and Donner were the letters that their friend Edwin Bryant had left behind specifically warning the two of them not to take the cutoff and go on to Fort Hall instead. They knew what Bryant had written, but they refused to risk losing business.

It's my belief that Bridger and Vasquez were as much to blame for what happened to the Donner Party as Lansford Hastings was. Of course, we must add into the mix the gullibility of Reed and Donner, who believed in the cutoff, even after experienced veterans of the trail had warned them against it.

The only person that the two men might have listened to - and even then, it's unlikely - was Tamzene Donner, who was the most vocal critic of Hastings and his shortcut. But at that moment, she was busy caring for Luke Halloran, a 25-year-old Irishman who was suffering from consumption. He had left his home in St. Joseph, Missouri, bound for California, in hopes of regaining his health.

He'd never make it there.

But Tamzene was doing her best. Eliza Donner later wrote, "He was a stranger to our family, afflicted with consumption, too ill to make the journey on horseback, and the family with whom he had traveled thus far could no longer accommodate him. His forlorn condition appealed to my parents and they granted his request" to travel with the Donners. Without a moment's hesitation, Tamzene had the young man placed in one of their wagons. Halloran's trunk full of possessions and his saddle and tack were squeezed in and his horse was tied to the back in hopes that he might recover enough to ride again.

Caring for Luke was another example of George and Tamzene's capacity for helping those in need. They had given the lone bachelor Charles Stanton a place as a driver. While near Fort Laramie, George had found a spot for a young man known only as Antonio, probably from the Santa Fe area. He helped drive the wagons and herded the family's cattle.

While at Fort Bridger, Donner had his horses re-shod, purchased new oxen, and lay in supplies for the road ahead. He also recruited a new driver to replace Hiram Miller, who had left earlier in the month to join Bryant's mule group. His name was Jean-Baptiste Trudeau and the 16-year-old had been hanging around the fort, looking for work, when Donner found him. He took the job and remained with the family for the rest of their journey.

Jean Baptiste Trudeau, shown much later in life. He was only 16 when George Donner hired him at Fort Bridger. He needed work but would come to regret ever taking the job.

Another family joined up with the Donner Party at Fort Bridger - William McCutchen, his wife, Amanda, and their toddler daughter, Harriet. They were from Jackson County, Missouri, where McCutchen had farmed and was known locally as "Big Bill." He stood six-feet, six-inches tall - a towering height both then and now. They had been traveling with the Harlan-Young Party but had been delayed by wagon trouble and were left behind at the fort. They were pleased when Donner allowed them to join the last emigrant team of the season taking the Hastings cutoff.

After three days at Fort Bridger, the Donner Party prepared to leave on July 31. They wanted to catch up to the forward parties and to Lansford Hastings. That day, James Reed wrote to the Keyes family in Springfield. He shared the news of his oxen dying from the poisoned water and his enjoyment with hunting antelope and mountain sheep with his teamsters. Mostly, though, he sang the praises of Bridger and Vasquez, who he called "two very excellent and accommodating gentlemen who can be relied on for doing business honorably and fairly."

If only he had known the truth.

Finally, with 19 wagons in good repair and the stock and horses rested, the signal was given and the Donner Party - at that point numbering 74 men, women, and children - began traveling into the unknown.

The first days on the Hastings cutoff went reasonably well. Eliza Donner wrote, "The trail from the fort was all that could be desired" and James Reed noted that the company had only traveled 27 miles in two days but had been fortunate to find cold springs and plenty of grass.

And then came day three.

The emigrants got a late start when an ox went missing. After they finally got moving, they were slowed further by rough ridges and rises that Reed called "at best a tolerable rough road." After setting up camp, two 13-year-olds - Virginia Reed and Edward Breen - took their ponies out for a ride. They were galloping along when Edward's pony stepped into an animal hole and took a hard fall. Edward was knocked unconscious. Virginia ran back to the camp for help and when his father, Patrick, and others arrived, they found Edward awake but in terrible pain. He had broken his left leg between the knee and ankle. It was so bad that ragged ends of bone were protruding from his bloody leg.

There was no doctor in the camp, so a rider was sent back to Fort Bridger. He eventually returned with a "rough-looking man with long whiskers" on a mule. The mountain man - who had doubtless doctored many people with broken bones as well as victims of bear and Indian attacks - took a look at Edward's leg and then reached into his bag for a short meat saw and a long-bladed knife.

And Edward began to scream.

He'd heard about the boy who had died after having his leg amputated at the other emigrant camp on the Platte and he had no intention of that happening to him. He cried and begged his parents to let him keep his leg. The Breens couldn't bear to see their son in such a state and called off the old mountain man before he could start to cut. Breen gave him some money for this trouble and sent him back to the fort. With assistance from Patrick and perhaps from James Reed, Margaret Breen worked the broken bones back into place. She carefully cleaned and dressed Edward's leg and made splints for it from wooden strips. Eddie would be confined to the wagon, enduring every bump on the road. He'd be in pain, but at least he'd kept his leg. The Breens

Echo Canyon in the Wasatch Mountains

expected he would be back on his feet again by the time they made it to California.

It actually healed earlier than that - in about eight weeks - but not in California. He started to walk again in late September, when the company finally made it to the Humboldt River in present-day Nevada.

After the excitement, the camp calmed down for the night. They left again the next morning, followed the fresh tracks of the Harlan-Young Party, and began rolling into what is now Utah.

They rested for the night at the top of Echo Canyon in the Wasatch Mountains. This range formed the eastern wall of the Great Basin, a huge expanse that was bordered by the Sierra Nevada range on the west, the Columbia Plateau on the north, and the Mojave Desert on the south. They found the names of many mountain men, trappers, and other travelers inscribed on the walls of Cache Cave, a well-known rendezvous spot above the canyon trail.

On August 6, the Donner company entered the mouth of Weber Canyon, where they found a piece of paper secured in plain sight. It was a message from Hastings - the news was not good.

Virginia Reed wrote, "We were seven days reaching Weber Canyon, and Hastings, who was guiding a party in advance of our train, left a note by the wayside warning us that the road through Weber Canyon was impassable and advising us to select a road over the mountains, the outline of which he attempted to give on paper."

It was the first major problem. It would not be the last.

It seemed that Hastings had left the wagon train that he was leading to check on one of the smaller groups at the rear. In his absence, James Hudspeth, who had been guiding Bryant's mule team, decided to visit the Harlan-Young camp. Hudspeth advised them to take the route through Weber Canyon.

Unbelievably - or not, since both Hastings and Hudspeth seem to be a pair of clowns - they would be the first wagon train to ever attempt it.

It didn't go well.

They lost a wagon and oxen that fell from a precipice that was about 75-feet high. The remaining wagons had to be lifted through the canyon.

Weber Canyon, a main part of Hastings' "shortcut" that he urged the Donner Party not to use after discovering that it was disastrous for an earlier wagon train. Up until that point, Hastings had never traveled the canyon with wagons before.

So much for Hastings being an "expert" guide who was well-versed in the route that ran through the cutoff that had been named for him.

When members of the Donner Party read Hastings' note that explained what a terrible mistake it had been to go through the canyon, they were stunned. The note implored them not to attempt it. Hastings suggested sending a messenger ahead to him so that he could provide the party that found the note with an alternative route that would take them around the canyon and still get them to the Great Salt Lake in a timely manner.

There didn't seem to be any choice but to comply with Hastings' suggestion about the messenger. They set up camp and James Reed, Charles Stanton, and William Pike volunteered to ride in advance to Hastings and, as Virginia Reed put it, "induce him to return and guide our party."

Early on August 7, the three men rode out as quickly as they could over the rough terrain. They had not gone far before they realized why traveling through Weber Canyon would have been so dangerous - the poor route was littered with boulders and choked with brush and trees. Reed marveled at the fact that only one of the other caravans had been lost in the canyon. He wrote, "Our conclusions were that many of the wagons would be destroyed attempting to get through."

Reed and the others caught up with Hastings on the evening of August 8. He and the Harlan-Young Party had crossed the Wasatch and were camped just south of the Great Salt Lake at Adobe Rock in the Tooele Valley. Reed greeted him coolly, but Hastings apologetically assured him that he had a backup plan that Reed would find acceptable.

Both Stanton and Pike were exhausted, as were their horses, so it was decided they would stay at the camp and recover and then hurry back to the caravan. Early the next morning, Hastings and Reed, who was riding a fresh horse, started back to the Donner Party camp.

They hadn't even made it to the Wasatch before Hastings announced that he was having second thoughts. He told Reed that he was committed to leading the Harlan-Young Party - he couldn't return to the Donner camp to guide them. Instead, he would show Reed a potential route they could follow on their own.

There is no indication of how Reed felt about this - or about the man he had put so much faith in. He didn't mention it in his journal. He merely noted that they camped that night in a canyon. The next morning, Hastings took him to Big Mountain, on the great divide east of the Salt Lake. Reed recalled that they ascended to "the summit of the mountain where we could overlook a portion of the country that lay between us and the head of the canyon, where the Donner Party were camped. After he gave me the direction, Mr. Hastings and I separated."

It was the last time that anyone in the Donner Party ever saw Lansford Hastings.

Reed rode east on what he believed was an Indian trail. Thinking it might be a suitable path for the company, he used his hatchet to blaze trail markers on trees in case they decided to use the route. Reed was literally making it up as he went along. Of course, he didn't know it, but Hastings had been doing the same thing. He wasn't any more lost than he would have been under that man's leadership.

Reed arrived back in the Weber Canyon camp on the evening of

August 10. Margaret breathed a sigh of relief, but the rest of the company was disappointed to see that he had returned alone. It wasn't Stanton and Pike they were missing - it was Hastings. He had let them down again. They listened anxiously as he explained their options. They could take the difficult and risky path through Weber Canyon or could take the path that Reed had found on his return trip. Reed explained that he believed the only reason the Harland-Young Party had made it through the canyon at all was because its members were younger and fitter than those in the Donner Party. He asked them to consider using the new trail he had just marked. It would not be easy, he told them, but it would be less dangerous. After some discussion, they decided to take the route suggested by Reed.

The next day, they broke camp - even further behind schedule - and began pushing along the path that Reed had found. They were still convinced that the cutoff was going to work in their favor and get them to California in a shorter time than it would have taken by way of the route at Fort Hall.

They made it five miles that day. It wasn't much, but as they would learn over the next two weeks, all progress at all was hard to come by. Some days, the wagons never moved at all as the men hacked their way through aspen groves and ravines filled with thick brush. The trail had been easy for a man on horseback - moving all those wagons, people, and cattle through was a different story. There were large trees that had to be cut down and dragged off to the side. There were boulders so large that it took several men to move them. Some were even larger and required double- and triple-yoked oxen to clear the steep rises. The women and children stayed in the wagons. They prepared meals for the hungry work parties and helped Tamzene and Peggy Breen care for Luke Halloran and Edward with his broken leg. The long, terrible days took a toll on everyone, emigrants and animals alike.

Soon after the struggle to get through the Wasatch had started, more wagons of emigrants appeared from behind them. Leading them was a 57-year-old farmer from Marshall County, Illinois, named Franklin Graves. A native of Vermont, Graves was actually more of a hunter than a farmer. He was accompanied by his wife, Elizabeth, their daughter and son-in-law, and eight younger children. A teamster named John Snyder was with them. The Graves family had followed just behind the Donners for most of the spring and summer. They had made it to Fort Bridger just a few days after the Donners had left and had hurried to join them for the rest of the trip. They were greeted warmly - and the two men were handed shovels and axes and put to work.

With the addition of the Graves family, the Donner Party had reached its full number - 87 men, women, and children, traveling in 22 wagons.

While work continued on the trail, a search party was scouring the woods and mountains looking for Stanton and Pike, who had not yet returned from the Harlan-Young camp. They were soon found, though, just before they killed their horses for something to eat. There was a brief pause for celebration when they returned. They provided some useful trail information, ate a hot meal, and then pitched in to work on the road.

For days, the men and older boys fought to cut a road through the wilderness, only to find that the eight-mile stretch of wagon road ended abruptly at a dead end in a box canyon. Some of the party became so angry that they considered leaving and going it alone. George

Emigration Canyon, the last obstacle they faced before the Salt Lake Valley

Donner calmed everyone down, restored order, got everyone turned around, and directed onto the right path. But supplies were running out - and so was morale. The group kept moving by sheer will and determination, convinced they were close to escaping from the Wasatch.

Finally, they found themselves in what would eventually be known as Emigration Canyon, the last obstacle they faced before entering the Salt Lake Valley. The canyon was a tight passage with 19 different deep creek crossings. It required harnessing at least six or eight yokes of oxen to drag each of the wagons up the steep slope that still bears the name of Donner Hill. But as they made their slow descent to the other side, some members of the party claimed they could smell the salt from the distant lake.

On August 22, James Reed noted in his journal, "This day we passed through the mountains and encamped in Utah valley."

In all, with the delay of four days at the Weber Canyon camp, plus the 36-mile death march through the Wasatch to the Salt Lake Valley - a distance only meant to take a few days - the Donner Party was now at least 18 days behind.

And it was going to get worse.

The Donner Party descended into the valley and crossed a stream that the Mormon settlers later named the Jordan River. "Worn with travel and greatly discouraged, we reached the shore of the Great Salt Lake," Virginia Reed wrote.

The caravan had made it through the formidable tangle of the Wasatch range without any loss of life or limb. Somehow, all the oxen, horses, livestock, and dogs had come through unscathed, too. But they were all exhausted -- physically and mentally, they were utterly drained.

Their desperate struggle had been tediously slow. The delays had cost valuable time and summer was nearly over. The farmers among them knew the seasonal patterns from spending their lives outdoors. They couldn't help but notice the changing path of the sun in the sky and the shifting shadows it cast. Around the evening campfires, they no longer discussed the Hastings guidebook. They smoked their pipes and leafed through an almanac, dreading the signs that indicated the changing of the seasons.

As they began to travel across the valley, the Great Salt Lake began to be visible, glistening in the sun. Some of the emigrants in the company had crossed the Atlantic coming to America. Others from the East had also seen the ocean. But for most of them, especially the children, the Great Salt Lake was the largest body of water they had ever seen. Situated between the Wasatch Range on the east and the Great Salt Desert on the west, it was the largest salt lake in the western hemisphere. It was saltier than any ocean. James Reed noted that the water was "strong enough to brine beef."

The company, still trying to recover from their recent ordeal, was forced to move from place to place as they searched for a campsite.

They were looking for fresh water. After hours, they found a spring. It was brackish but at least it was drinkable.

By August 24, they had picked up the wagon tracks of the Harlan-Young Party and they followed them around the south end of the lake. They knew, however, that just to the west of them was the Great Salt Lake Desert - the most desolate part of the California Trail.

On August 25, death came calling at the Donner Party camp.

That afternoon, Luke Halloran, took his last breath and quietly died. He slipped away with his head in Tamzene's lap. She had cared for him as if he were one of her children. The exact place where he was buried is unknown, but wherever it was, he was laid to rest next to a man he didn't know - John Hargrave, a member of the Harlan-Young Party. While helping to get the company's wagons across the Wasatch, Hargrave had caught a cold that turned into pneumonia. He had died on August 11 and his grave was dug the next day, making him the first emigrant buried in Utah.

Although Luke's death had really been inevitable, it had been hastened by the efforts of crossing the Wasatch. Both he and John Hargrave were victims of the Hastings cutoff. Appropriately perhaps, some of the men who built Luke's coffin and dug his grave cursed Hastings and a few of them - under their breath, of course - cursed James Reed for believing it was a shortcut.

After Luke was buried, his trunk was opened. It contained his clothing, some keepsakes, and about $1,500 in gold coins. He had bequeathed it all to George and Tamzene Donner, along with his saddle, tack, and horse.

The death was the first for the members of the company since the passing of Sarah Keyes three months earlier, but the number of people in the party stayed the same. On the day that Luke had died, Philippine Keseberg, the young German woman traveling with her husband, Lewis, and three-year-old daughter, gave birth to a healthy baby boy. He was named after his father - one of the most unlikable men in the party.

Lewis Keseberg was an angry, abusive man who was known to beat his wife. He was also believed to have defiled a Native American burial site on the journey. He was not a popular man. Still, most of the emigrants came to call on the newborn and his mother.

After Luke's funeral, the company moved on. The next stop was

Twenty Wells, a pleasant resting place named for the 20 sweet water springs found there. They didn't stay long, though. There were no more days of rest and leisure. They had to keep moving. They were now in a race with the coming winter and losing that race could be fatal.

From Twenty Wells, they rounded Stansbury Mountain and camped at Burnt Spring in the north end of what Hastings called Spring Valley. It soon became better known - thanks to the ancient human and bison bones found there - as Skull Valley.

On the evening of August 28, the emigrants arrived at what Reed described as "delightful freshwater wells" at a place that was aptly called Hope Springs.

But it would not be "hope" that they found there.

While quenching their thirsts at the well, they found something that Eliza Donner would never forget. She later wrote, "Close by the largest well stood a rueful spectacle - a bewildering guide board, flecked with bits of white paper, showing that the notice or message which had recently been pasted and tacked thereon had since been stripped off in irregular bits. In surprise and consternation, the emigrants gazed at its blank face, then toward the dreary waste beyond. Presently, my mother knelt before it and began searching for fragments of paper, which she believed crows had wantonly pecked off and dropped to the ground."

Many of the others dropped to their knees and helped her search in the grass and loose soil. When they found anything, they brought it to Tamzene. When they had gathered all they could find, she laid the guide board across her lap and began fitting the pieces of ragged paper together like a puzzle, matching the scraps to marks on the board. It had been written by Hastings - the handwriting was the same as on the earlier message at Weber Canyon - and it spelled out the following:

2 days - 2 nights - hard driving -

cross - desert - reach water.

The group tried to make sense of the message at first - and then it slowly began to sink in. Just like Hastings' earlier message, this one also caused emotions that ranged from anger to shock, disbelief, and fear. In his guidebook, Hastings had claimed that the upcoming desert crossing was flat and easy. He had said it was only 35 or 40 miles and could be crossed in a day and a night with a few brief rests. But now this warning indicated that the journey would be at least twice as long as he had claimed.

And there would be no water.

George Donner called a quick meeting with the men from each family. But they all knew they had no choice but to go on. They cut as much grass as they could and bundled it up for livestock feed. Every cask, jar, and bottle that could hold any water at all was filled to the brim. It had to be enough for man and beast to cross the desert in two days and two nights.

There were many prayers said on August 30 when the wagon train moved on. The company paused to top off the water supply at Redlum Spring, but the water was brackish. They climbed to Hastings Pass through the Cedar Mountains, the range that formed the western edge of Skull Valley, and then crossed the Grayback Hills. They were now in the Great Salt Lake Desert and on the edge of an 83-mile stretch of trail with no grass and no water.

It was more than twice the distance reported by Hastings in his book.

On that same day, the quick-moving Bryant mule party had already crossed the Sierra Nevadas and were less than one-day's journey from a fort that belonged to Captain John Sutter in California. They spent that night at John Calhoun Johnson's Six Mile Ranch - a place where many emigrants stayed the winter -- and were treated to "piles of small cheeses and numerous pans of milk with thick cream upon them."

Hastings and the Harlan-Young Party were far west of the desert crossing on that day. They were making their way through the Ruby Valley in what is now Nevada. They would soon reach the Humboldt River and return to the original California Trail.

Far behind, and mostly forgotten, the members of the Donner Party could not be concerned about the companies that were ahead of them. There was no time. They were alone - the last wagons on the California Trail for the season. As Reed wrote in his journal, "We started to cross the desert traveling day and night, only stopping to feed and water our teams as long as water and grass lasted."

His daughter, Virginia, also wrote of the start of their desert trek. "It was a dreary, desolate, alkali waste; not a living thing could be seen;

it seemed as though the hand of death had been laid upon the country. We started in the evening, traveled all night, and the following day and night - two nights and one day suffering from thirst and heat by day and piercing cold by night."

By September 1, the emigrants had separated. The Eddy and Graves families had healthier and faster oxen teams and they surged ahead, crossing the salt flats toward Pilot Peak, the landmark they'd

After more than 90 years, the tracks left by the Donner Party wagons were still visible across the Great Salt Lake desert.

Below - Discarded artifacts from the wagon train were still being discovered in the 1930s.

aimed for when starting across the desert. The nine heavily-loaded wagons of the Donners and Reeds fell behind from the start. They soon ended up at the rear of the caravan, which stretched out for a mile.

The group, with very few exceptions, plodded along next to the wagons, hoping to lighten the strain on the oxen. They walked by day under a relentless sun and at night under a canopy of stars. They wrapped themselves in blankets after darkness fell, trying to ward off the chill. During both day and night, the desert was silent and empty. Nothing, they believed, could live there. The only sounds they heard were their own muffled steps and the hoofbeats of the stumbling livestock.

Farther across the desert, the hard, dusty flats became a shallow lake with a thin crust. When the wagons and herds tramped into this stretch of the trail, the alkali collapsed into loose, sticky sand and slowed the wagons even more. The emigrants described it as "walking through deep oatmeal mixed with glue." People and animals became mired and the wagon wheels had to be constantly scraped off.

As a change from usual, James Reed was at the back of the caravan, devoting all his attention to his struggling family, teamsters, horses, and livestock. All were showing signs of stress, particularly the oxen. By September 2, the company's third day in the desert, the supply of food and water was almost gone. The oxen would soon stop moving and, likely, lay down and die. If that happened, they would be stranded, and then everyone else would soon die, too.

Reed decided that he needed to take action - he would ride out alone and find water. After he saddled Glaucus, he told his teamster Milt Elliott to wait until the oxen became so exhausted that they could go no more before removing them from the wagons and driving them up the trail until they found water. He also instructed his workers, Walter Herron and Baylis Williams, to remain with the wagons and watch over his family. Reed then rode off toward Pilot Peak.

Other families also had to take drastic actions when their oxen refused to go on or fell dead in their tracks. The Donners left their families in their wagons, released the oxen, and herded them down the trail. The Eddys, who had been far ahead of the others, were also forced to abandon their wagon before reaching Pilot Peak. Carrying their two small children, they drove their cattle ahead of them by the light of the moon.

By nightfall, James Reed had ridden the 20 miles to Pilot Peak, where he found a freshwater spring. He left Glaucus there to rest and started back on a borrowed horse to bring water to his stranded family. Along the way, he met up with teamsters herding cattle and horses. He warned them to be careful as they approached Pilot Peak. If the cattle caught the scent of water, they could stampede and become lost. Reed rode on toward the wagons and, just as he predicted, the cattle he'd just passed escaped from their handlers and ran toward the distant water.

When he made it back to his three wagons, Reed made sure that

Margaret, the children, and the workers all had plenty to drink. Walt Herron then left on the borrowed horse to return to Pilot Peak and wait for the family to catch up. The rest waited for the teamsters to return with fresh oxen, but by the end of the day, there was no sign of them. The water that Reed had brought back with him was almost gone.

The Reeds were in trouble.

Pilot Peak, the landmark used by the Donner Party as they traveled across the desert.

Virginia later wrote about their predicament: "Towards night, the situation became desperate and we had only a few drops of water left; another night there meant death. We must set out on foot and try and reach some of the wagons. Can I ever forget that night in the desert, when we walked mile after mile in the darkness, every step seeming to be the last we could take? Suddenly all fatigue was vanquished by fear; through the night came a swift rushing sound of one of the young steers crazed by thirst and apparently bent on our destruction. My father, holding his youngest child in his arms and keeping us all close behind him, drew his pistol, but finally the maddened beast turned and dashed off into the darkness. Dragging ourselves along about ten miles, we reached the wagon of Jacob Donner. The family were all asleep, so we children lay down on the ground. A bitter wind swept over the desert, chilling us through and through. We crept closer together, and, when we complained of the cold, papa placed all five of our dogs around us, and only for the warmth of these faithful creatures we should doubtless have perished.

"At daylight papa was off to learn the fate of his cattle, and was told that all were lost, except for one cow and an ox. The stock, scenting water, had rushed in ahead of the men, and had probably been stolen by Indians, and driven into the mountains, where all traces of them were lost."

It took nearly a week for the entire company to make it to Pilot

Peak and the freshwater spring that would someday be renamed for the Donners. All the emigrants had survived the hellish days and nights in the desert, including the newborn Keseberg baby, but it had taken a terrible toll on the oxen, cattle, and horses. Many of them were either dead or missing. Reed lost 18 animals and other members of the company were unable to account for 20 more. Several wagons - filled with the start of a new life in California - were abandoned on the salt flats.

The party spent days and time they could not afford trying to find missing livestock, culling through belongings from the wagons left in the desert, and transferring what little food and supplies remained into wagons that were still trail worthy.

Many animals were still alive but were so weakened by the ordeal that they were abandoned and left to fend for themselves. Several had to be put out of their misery by a bullet to the head. Some of the teamsters and families cared for the animals so much that they could not kill them. They simply walked away and never looked back.

This was likely when Virginia Reed lost her beloved pony, Billy. In her writings, she does not say exactly when it happened. She only wrote, "A day came that I had no pony to ride, the poor little fellow gave out. He could not endure the hardships of ceaseless travel. When I was forced to part with him, I cried until I was ill, and sat in the back of the wagon watching him become smaller and smaller as we drove on, until I could see him no more.

James Reed, and most of the other men, returned to the desert to retrieve things from the marooned wagons. They returned with essentials, valuables, and documents, but most of the furniture, clothing, and luxury items were left behind. They hid them as best they could in the desert sands with the intention of returning for them someday - plans that were likely forgotten.

Sadly, the children were expected to part with their personal things, like toys and books. Patty Reed, just eight-years-old, could not bear to leave her prized possessions buried in the sand. Without anyone else knowing it, she carefully hid the wooden doll that had been given to her by her grandmother, Sarah Keyes, in the hem of her apron. She also kept the lock of her grandmother's hair she had been given, Sarah's pincushion, and a few other keepsakes.

Patty Reed - shown on the right as an adult - refused to leave a doll that had been made for her by her grandmother in their abandoned wagon. She kept it hidden during their ordeal and kept it throughout her life.

George Donner left a wagon behind and so did Lewis Keseberg. Only one of the three Reed wagons could be salvaged and was brought back to the camp at Pilot Peak. Reed placed what goods and belongings the family kept in the large family wagon, where Sarah had ridden in her featherbed until her death. The bed and cookstove were left in the desert. Others in the company loaned the Reeds a yoke of cattle. His remaining cow and ox made up the second yoke.

By September 10, they had determined that all the strays that were going to be found had been retrieved - it was time to move on. The emigrants and the livestock were rested and, at last, the trip to California resumed.

They were desperately behind schedule.

And nature proved that to them that morning, as the wagons moved out, by sending a snowstorm down on them as they traveled around the base of Pilot Peak. They passed through it, but it made an impression.

Years later, Patrick Breen's son, John, recalled that snowstorm and the apprehension they all felt from the delay in the desert.

It had, he recalled, "made the mothers tremble."

10. BLOOD ON THE TRAIL

On September 11, the Donner Party was back on the trail, now in what would someday be Nevada. The "mothers" that John Breen had described as "trembling" were not shaking because of the cold - it was from anger and fear. The women knew what lay ahead of them, even if the men were determined not to admit it. A simple glance at the almanac calendar confirmed for them what most had suspected for a while now - they were running out of time.

Hope was in short supply and so was food. Everyone in the party was hungry. There was little to sustain them. The many delays that had occurred during the Hastings "shortcut" had badly depleted their supplies. They had seen no game in the desert and what little they found after crossing would not last long.

At camp that evening, James Reed was asked to take an inventory of the entire party's remaining provisions. It was quickly apparent that there wasn't nearly enough food to get them to California. Someone was going to have to go for help.

Years later, Reed recounted, "After receiving an estimate of each family, on paper, I then suggested that if two gentlemen of the company would volunteer to go to Captain Sutter, in California, I would write a letter to him for the whole amount of provisions that we wanted, and also stating that I would personally become responsible to him for the amount. I suggested that from the generous nature of Captain Sutter he would send them. Mr. McCutchen came forward and proposed that if I would take care of his family, he would go. This the company agreed to. Mr. Stanton, a single man, volunteered, if they would furnish him a horse. Mr. McCutchen, having a horse and a mule, generously gave the mule."

That McCutchen volunteered to make the trip was no surprise. He was a decent man, but he also had no wagon, only the horse and mule. By leaving his wife and little girl with the Reeds, they would travel in greater comfort.

William "Big Bill" McCutchen, shown here more than 30 years after the events in the book. McCutchen would risk his life several times for fellow members of the Donner Party and for his wife and child.

Charles Stanton had no family in the caravan, but was well-liked with many friends. He chose to go out of a sense of duty. He joined McCutchen and the two men, with blankets and meager rations, started for California.

With Amanda McCutchen and baby Harriet safely with the Reeds, the Donner Party pressed forward. They had to follow Hastings' route for several days on a detour around the Ruby Mountains. When they reached the Humboldt River, they could once again pick up the true California Trail.

On September 13, they camped at a place that Reed dubbed "Mad Woman Camp." As he put it in his journal, "all the women in camp were mad with anger." He didn't need to explain any further because there was much to be angry about.

Or perhaps there was something in the water at that particular camp. More than five weeks before the Donners arrived, Bryant's mule team had also camped there. During the evening around the fire, an argument over "a very trivial matter" started an altercation between two members of the party who leveled guns at each other. Luckily,

Bryant, always cool-headed, stepped between them and kept them from killing each other.

No one pointed a rifle at James Reed, but he undoubtedly was getting a lot of angry stares. He had been the one, of course, who had convinced everyone to take the Hastings cutoff and now, had put everyone's life in danger. The women seemed much more inclined to blame Reed for their delays.

And things kept getting worse.

On September 16, while camped on the east side of the Ruby Mountains, two of George Donner's horses vanished. They had presumably been stolen by Shoshone Indians during the night.

They moved on. They would soon reach the Humboldt River and get back on course. By then, hopefully, McCutchen and Stanton would be back from California with enough supplies to get the wagons over the Sierras.

After the wagons made the turn around the south end of the mountains, the days still dragged on. The emigrants tried with all the energy they could muster to make as many miles each day as possible. As far as they were concerned, the adventure was long over - they just wanted to reach their destination.

They stopped at several springs, including some hot springs, where they bathed and washed their clothes, improving morale in the group. They also found fresh game. The hunters went out and returned with prairie dogs, antelope, sage hens, and Rocky Mountain sheep. The meat, roasted on open fires, helped to subdue the gnawing pain in their bellies.

On September 24, the company camped near the entrance to the canyon of the South Fork of the Humboldt River. The next evening, they found shelter in a narrow, winding gorge.

They could finally feel a little better. After what must have seemed like a lifetime, they had reached the Humboldt River. It had taken them 68 days to complete the Hastings cutoff and rejoin the established California Trail.

Scouts were sent out to investigate the river they would follow until it emptied into the Humboldt Sink. The sink was a body of water in the spring when the snow melted, but by late summer, it turned into a wide and sandy low spot where what little water that remained was soaked up by the sand. The Donner Party had heard many stories about the Humboldt - about the lack of shade, the turbulent waters, twisting bends, and the stagnant areas that could trap animals and emigrants alike.

The river had already gone by many names and would not officially become the Humboldt until 1848, when the name appeared on a map published by John C. Fremont. But no matter what it was called, most travelers hated it. Unlike the native Shoshone and Paiute, who used the river and surrounding marshes for food, emigrants wrote terrible things about it. They filled their journals with notes about how the Humboldt was "not good for man nor beast" and added, "there is not timber enough in 300 miles of its desolate valley to make a snuff-box, or sufficient vegetation along its banks to shade a rabbit, while its waters contain the alkali to make soap for a nation."

When the Donners arrived at the river, they found it low, with little grass along its banks. After a brief discussion, they decided to break the company up into two groups. The Donner brothers would take the lead - their livestock was faring better than the others - and the slower-moving wagons, like the Reeds and the Eddys, would follow.

On the surface, the division of the group seemed to be because of the lack of forage for the animals, but in truth, the company had been in the process of splitting up since the crossing of the salt flats. They had been on the trail together for so long that as nerves frayed, disagreements that would normally be considered petty had turned into grudges.

Another concern was the growing number of Native Americans that the travelers had encountered since entering the tribal lands of the Shoshone and the Paiute along the Humboldt. To these people, the strangers in wagons were a curiosity. At first, they were willing to offer advice and answer questions. The Shoshone - even though they had little to share - were even generous with their food.

But as more wagon trains passed through, leaving less grass, scarce game, and more polluted land and water, the mood of the natives had changed. It had become evident to them that the white men took whatever they wanted from the land and rivers without a thought for the people who lived on the land they were passing through. So, in return, the Indians decided to retaliate by stealing everything they could from the emigrants. The white emigrants, of course, considered all Indians the same - as has been obvious by the stereotypes described throughout the journey of the Donner Party - and this led to antagonism from both sides.

The Donner Party had seen large gatherings of Indians, including one sizable group near the Humboldt. They stayed nearby but did not enter the camp. Everyone was tense and on alert.

A few days after this encounter, the last group of the company - made up of the Reed, Graves, Murphy, Eddy, and Breen families - was greeted by a friendly Paiute who spoke English that he had learned from previous emigrant companies. They dubbed him "Thursday" in homage to Robinson Crusoe's companion, Friday. Soon, another Paiute who spoke English joined them. The two men traveled with the party and camped with them that night at Gravelly Ford, named for the shallow river crossing nearby.

During the night, the campfire ignited some dry brush and all hands, including the two Paiute, turned out to fight the fire. After it was extinguished, they all ate a small supper, and went back to bed. When they woke in the morning, the Paiute were gone --- along with a yoke of oxen and a shirt that belonged to Franklin Graves.

There was no time to look for the missing oxen - and everyone assumed they were long gone anyway. They crossed the river and continued along the trail. Two nights later, on October 1, one of Graves' horses was stolen. Again, there was nothing they could do but keep going.

Over the next couple of days, they traveled another 22 miles. By then, the honking of geese heading south was heard almost every day. They looked for game along the river and even in the sagebrush, but Eddy and the other hunters found nothing.

There was still no sign of Stanton and McCutchen with provisions.

The religious among them - mostly the Breens and a few others - prayed constantly. They beseeched God for food, for game, for safety, and for at least things not to get any worse.

But the next day, things got worse.

It all happened in a moment - and there was a lot of blood.

The morning of October 5 started quietly for the Reed, Graves, Keseberg, and Breen families, who were following the lead caravan headed by George Donner. A small breakfast was eaten, rationed by the women who wanted to stretch what food they had as far as possible.

The night before, camp had been set up where the trail left the south bank of the Humboldt River and now, they followed the trail over some bluffs. After a noon stop, they approached a steep and sandy slope that was called Pauta Pass. The caravan had to stop before attempting to ascend the hill. Because of the grade, they were forced to double-team the oxen and pull the wagons up the hill one at a time.

The wagons were lined up at the bottom of the slope and two of the Graves family wagons, with double teams of oxen straining against the yoke, were pulled to a stop.

Next in line was the family's third wagon, driven by teamster John Snyder, who decided that he could make the climb with just two oxen. He knew what he was doing. He was too impatient to wait around for another Graves team to be brought down the hill and hitched to the wagon. Snyder cracked his whip and pushed the oxen forward, although it quickly became painfully obvious that the steep grade was too much for just two animals. Behind Snyder, Milt Eliot was driving the large family wagon shared by the Reeds and the Eddys. He had already hitched another yoke of oxen to the wagon, borrowed from William Pike, and he was ready to go.

Tempers were already short, and nerves were on edge from the pressure of knowing that time was running out to get across the Sierra Nevada range before the first heavy snow. On this day, tempers boiled over.

Becoming impatient because of Snyder's incompetence, Elliot went around Snyder's wagon to go up the hill. Snyder was angered by this and tried to block Elliot's ascent. The two men exchanged words and curses when the teams of oxen became tangled together. Now, everything was at a standstill. Snyder, furious at the other man, lost control and began to beat his oxen with the heavy wooden handle of his whip. As Snyder was beating the helpless beasts, James Reed rode up to the scene.

Virginia Reed recounted the scene that followed: "Snyder, having taken offense at something Elliot had said, declared that his team could pull up alone and kept on using abusive language. Father tried to quiet the enraged man."

Reed tried to reason with Snyder, mostly to keep him from beating the oxen, which they were dependent on. If the animals were too injured to pull the wagons, they would all be stranded. He calmly offered the use of the Reed's oxen to help with the wagon, but Snyder refused and now began to curse Reed, too.

"We can settle this, John, when we get up the hill," Reed told the teamster.

"No," Snyder replied and swore at Reed again, "we can settle it now."

Snyder jumped down onto the tongue of the wagon and swung the whip handle at Reed, striking him hard in the side of the head. Then, he swung it and hit him again.

Reed went down, stunned, and blinded by the blood that was now streaming into his eyes from the wounds on his head. Snyder swung again and would have struck Reed, perhaps fatally, but suddenly, Margaret Reed rushed between them.

Reed saw the uplifted whip but only had time to call out Snyder's name before it came down and struck Margaret.

In a flash, Reed's hunting knife was in his hand and he stabbed Snyder just below the collarbone, puncturing his left lung.

Despite the wound, Snyder drove Reed to his knees with two more vicious blows to the head before collapsing backwards into the arms of Billy Graves, who laid him on the ground. When John Breen rushed forward to help the young teamster, who had become his friend, it was said that Snyder whispered just before he died, "Uncle Patrick, I am dead."

Reed managed to get to his feet, nearly falling down again. He staggered blindly, with blood still running into his eyes and down his face. He flung the knife that had killed Snyder into the river. Margaret and the girls rushed to his side to try and stop the bleeding, but Reed broke away and went to see Snyder. Some of the emigrants who were present later said that Snyder mumbled, "I am to blame," just before he died. Reed was overwhelmed with grief and guilt, even though he had acted in self-defense and to protect his wife.

Travel was over for the day. Camp was made at the top of the hill and the Graves family took Snyder's body to wash and prepare for burial. Reed volunteered boards from his wagon to be used for the coffin, but Franklin Graves rejected the offer.

Reed returned to the wagon and found Margaret stricken with a migraine and badly bruised from the blow she'd sustained from the whip handle. He asked Virginia to help him after she finished tending to her mother in the family tent. Once Margaret was settled, Virginia brought a wash basin and sponge to the wagon, washed away the caked blood, and dressed her father's head wounds.

Virginia later recalled, "When my work was finished at last, I burst out crying. Papa clasped me in his arms, saying: 'I should not have asked so much of you,' and talked to me about my feelings, so that we could go to the tent where mama was lying down. We then learned that trouble was brewing in the camp where Snyder's body lay."

Virginia was right - trouble was brewing.

That evening around the fire, there was a general consensus that Snyder's death could not be ignored. The emigrants who had witnessed the mayhem on the slope were mostly in agreement about what had happened - to a point. But the same eyewitnesses came up with different scenarios. If the person didn't like Reed– and there were quite a few after the Hastings cutoff fiasco - then he was portrayed as the aggressor who had challenged Snyder and then attacked him with his knife.

The issue of what to do about James Reed caused a lot of debate and a range of solutions was offered. One suggestion was that everyone's written statements be taken and then used against Reed in court when they reached California. But that did not suit those who were eager to avenge Snyder's death. One of those was Lewis Keseberg, who hated Reed from past conflicts on the trail about the treatment and abuse of Keseberg's wife. He raised a wagon tongue into the air and demanded that Reed be hanged from it. The Graves family and some of the others probably would have gone along with this, but Milt Elliot and William Eddy - armed and dangerous men - made it clear they wouldn't allow that to happen to a man who had acted in self-defense.

Late in the evening, the standoff ended when all agreed that Reed's punishment would be his banishment from the party. At first, it was stated that he would be forced out on foot, but after pleas from his friends, a compromise was reached. He would still have to go alone, but he could take his horse. He could leave with the clothes on his back, but nothing more. With no food or weapons, his chance of survival was extremely low. Most of the emigrants considered Reed's banishment to be a death sentence.

At first, so did Reed and he refused to accept the punishment. While he did not intend to take another's man life, he had acted to protect his own life and that of his wife - he had done nothing wrong. He would not, he said, desert his wife and children. But his few friends convinced him that it would be best to leave. They promised to look after his family. They also pointed out that Stanton and McCutchen had not returned with food - and perhaps they never would. But if Reed successfully made it over the Sierras, he could bring back provisions and win over those who wanted to force him to leave.

Reed was still hesitant, but Margaret changed his mind. Virginia wrote, "Knowing only too well what her life would be without him, yet fearing that if he remained he would meet with violence at the hands of his enemies, she implored him to go, but to no avail until she urged him to remember the destitution of the company, saying that if he remained and escaped violence at their hands, he might nevertheless see his children starving and be helpless to aid them, while if he went on he could return and meet them with food. It was a tearful struggle; at last, he consented, but not before he had secured a promise for the company to care for his wife and little ones."

In the morning, the entire group - including Reed with his head wrapped in bloody bandages - gathered for Snyder's burial. There was no coffin. The body had been wrapped in a sheet and placed in a hole between two boards. While some of the men and boys shoveled sand over the corpse, Reed embracing his sobbing wife and children and promised he would return.

He then climbed onto Glaucus and rode away. Margaret and the girls watched him until he was out of sight.

Despite Reed's stubborn belief in the Hastings route, his departure was a great loss and had a shattering impact on the company. They had banished one of the most loyal, capable, and resourceful men in the wagon train. It was often said that if steady and stable George Donner had been there, instead of miles ahead with his own group, the verdict against Reed would have been a very different one.

Margaret Reed had convinced her husband to leave the party for his own good - and for the good of everyone else if he could return with supplies - but she was not going to let James leave empty-handed. That night, Virginia and Milt Elliott slipped out of the camp into the darkness.

They followed Virginia's father through the darkness. Virginia later wrote, "I carried him his rifle, pistols, ammunition, and some food.

I had determined to stay with him, and begged him to let me stay, but he would listen to no argument, saying that it was impossible. Finally, unclasping my arms from around him, he placed me in charge of Elliott, who started back to camp with me - and papa was left alone. I had cried until I hardly had strength to walk, but when he reached camp and I saw the distress of my mother, with the little ones clinging around her and no arm to lean upon, it seemed suddenly to make a woman of me. I realized that I must be strong and help mama bear her sorrows."

With no wagons, no livestock, and no family to care for, Reed rode long and hard. After two days, he caught up with the Donners and gave them an abbreviated version of his story, suggesting that he was going after the supplies that had still not been delivered by Stanton and McCutchen.

He stayed in the Donner camp that night and in the morning after breakfast, Walter Herron, Reed's former teamster now traveling with the Donners, volunteered to go with Reed to California and bring back provisions. Reed welcomed the company. Although Herron had no horse, Reed suggested they share riding time. He wanted to move at a slow and steady pace so that he didn't wear out Glaucus and splitting the time would do that. One could walk while the other rode and they'd still make good time.

They left camp, taking rations for a few days and a letter to John Sutter from George Donner asking for enough oxen teams and supplies to get the company to California. In the letter, Donner gave his personal pledge that Sutter would be paid in full when he arrived at his fort.

After a few days, the food the two men had with them was gone. They tried to hunt but had little luck. Reed later wrote, "There was no game to be seen; hunger began to be felt, and for days we traveled without hope or help."

While Reed and Herron were trying to get to California, the emigrants at the second camp at the Humboldt River were struggling to rally their spirts and move on. They were now bitterly divided and lacked the leadership and the strength to reunite and work together. Only individuals and families mattered - all sense of community had gone with James Reed. Many of them were starting to regret their hasty decision.

Virginia Reed wrote, "We traveled on, but all life seemed to have

William Eddy was one of the most resourceful members of the Donner Party. He hunted frequented and, when possible, kept the party fed with wild game. He would eventually become the leader of the "Forlorn Hope."

left the party, and the hours dragged slowly on. Every day we would search for some sign of papa, who would leave a letter by the wayside in the top of a bush or in a split stick, and when he succeeded in killing geese or birds would scatter the feathers about so that we knew he was not suffering for food. When possible, our fire would be kindled on the spot where his had been. But a time came when we found no letter, and no trace of him. Had he starved by the wayside, or been murdered by Indians?"

As usual, hostile Indians were on the minds of all the emigrants, not just Virginia. On October 7, William Eddy and William Pike were in the brush hunting for badly-needed game and were attacked by a band of Paiutes. They escaped the assault but returned to camp empty-handed.

When they arrived back, though, they learned that one of the emigrants was missing.

The missing man was Hardcoop, the driver for the Kesebergs. He was about 60-years-old and his health was fragile. When Keseberg was questioned about the missing man, he claimed that he had no idea where he was but acknowledged that something might be wrong. A rider backtracked the trail and found Hardcoop five miles behind them. He was returned to the camp and told the others that Keseberg had forced him out of the family wagon. Keseberg had started the journey with two wagons but had abandoned one in the Utah desert. He decided he had no more use for the driver and since he was too worn out to walk, he had to leave. There wasn't room for him in the wagon. But Keseberg was told to make room for him - he had hired Hardcoop and the man was his responsibility.

One can imagine how well this went over with the angry and

bitter German.

The next morning, it was decided to leave behind the last Reed wagon, the large one that had been outfitted for Sarah Keyes. Some of the Eddys' clothing and tools were also left behind to lighten the load. A smaller wagon was obtained from Franklin Graves for the Eddys and Reeds and the party continued their march along the Humboldt.

About an hour into the day's journey, Hardcoop managed to catch up with Eddy and told him that Keseberg had once again forced him out of his wagon. The old man said that it was impossible for him to travel on foot and he begged Eddy to let him ride in his wagon. Eddy agreed, but because the wagons were moving through deep, loose sand, he could not stop then but would do so as soon as he could. Hardcoop said that he would try his best to keep up until then.

But, as it turned out, the caravan did not stop again until early evening. When they made camp, Eddy looked around but Hardcoop was not there. Some of the boys who had been driving livestock far behind the wagons said they had last seen him earlier in the day. He had been sitting shoeless in the shade of a clump of sagebrush. His feet were black and so swollen that the skin had split open.

A signal fire was lit on a hillside, hoping that Hardcoop might see it and find his way to camp. The night guards and Baylis Williams kept the fire going until morning but saw no sign of the old man.

Margaret Reed, Milt Elliott, and William Eddy tried to convince Keseberg to go back and look for the man, but he refused. Patrick Breen and William Graves wouldn't even lend a horse to anyone who offered to search. It wasn't worth the risk, they said, to man or horse to go look for an old man who was unfit to travel and had probably already been killed by Indians. When Pike, Eddy, and Elliott proposed to go look for Hardcoop on foot, the others said they wouldn't wait and would leave without them. There was no time, they stated.

Every ounce of kindness and charity had been drained from the emigrant party. The few people who cared about the old man could only hope that his death was swift. The rest of them simply forgot about the kindly old Belgian man whose first name they never bothered to learn.

The next day - in what some might say was retribution for the abandonment of the old man on the trail - the group stumbled into a long stretch of exceptionally deep, loose sand that took them more than

12 hours to cross.

Then, at 4:00 in the morning, October 10, they arrived at the camp of the other part of the Donner Party. It had an ominous feeling about it.

A month earlier, another emigrant caravan, including several people known to the Donner Party, had attacked a band of Paiute that had stolen some of the party's cattle. One of the emigrants had been wounded and lingered for three days before dying.

Andrew Grayson, whose family had once traveled with the Russell Party, had been part of the attack but came away unscathed. Another former Russell Party member, Benjamin S. Lippincott, had been hit with an arrow that had been dipped in rattlesnake venom, but survived.

Traveling across Paiute land, wagon trains were frequently harassed and attacked by the natives. On occasion, the confrontations became bloody.

The dead man was William Sallee, who had been buried in a shallow grave in the middle of the trail. The emigrants drove their wagons over the grave to conceal it, but the Paiute found it anyway and dug up his remains. They stole his clothing, scalped him, and mutilated the corpse. Wolves had then picked over his rotting remains. They were still on display for the Donner Party, next to a board that had been stuck in the sand, bearing a warning about hostile Indians, and telling the story of the assault and Sallee's death.

The scattered bones and stark warning were seen by everyone in party.

At camp that evening, the second group passed on the details - both true and false - about the death of Snyder and the abandonment of Hardcoop. More accusations and finger-pointing followed, causing bitterness in the ranks of both factions of the party.

During the bickering, Paiute raiders slipped into camp and stole all the Graves family's horses. Of course, this gave the emigrants who had wanted to go back for Hardcoop a chance to gloat, because the horses Graves had refused to let them borrow. were now gone.

The party now consolidated, abandoned another wagon, and moved on. The next day at the company's camp in a marshy area known as Big Meadows, they were raided again by the Paiute. They stole - or killed with poisoned arrows - 18 head of cattle belonging to the Donner brothers and stole a milk cow from Graves. The Donners now had no more oxen and had to yoke cows to their wagons.

That night, they camped in a boggy area that had little edible grass for the livestock. There was water that was difficult to get to and which turned out to be bad. When one of Patrick Breen's horses got mired in a sinkhole, he asked William Eddy for help. But Eddy reminded Breen about how he had been unwilling to lend a horse to look for Hardcoop and walked away. Breen struggled alone but couldn't free the horse - it smothered in a pool of thick mud.

The entire party - even the most generous and stout among them - were coming apart.

Near midnight on October 12, the party finally reached the Humboldt Sink. In the final push that night, one of Eddy's oxen collapsed and it was left next to the trail. The emigrants were barely out of sight before Paiutes appeared and quickly killed and butchered the animal.

Camp was made and extra guards stayed with the remaining livestock throughout the night. Things stayed quiet, but in the morning, when the guards came in for breakfast, Paiutes attacked and killed 21 cattle with poisoned arrows. Most of the animals didn't die right away. They bellowed and screamed in pain, so badly wounded that they had to be killed and butchered for the little meat that remained on their bones. There was no time to dry and preserve the meat either, so it had to be cooked and consumed on the spot. Between the Indian attacks and the brutality of the trail, the emigrants had very few livestock left. The Eddys and the Wolfingers had only one ox each so both families had to leave their wagons behind.

William Eddy buried his family's last possessions, unsure if he would ever be able to return and retrieve them. The family now had to travel on foot. Eleanor had to carry the baby, Margaret, and William carried their son, James, and the only food they had left - a small amount of tea and three pounds of loaf sugar.

Fortunately for the Wolfingers, they were traveling without children. Jacob Wolfinger had been a prosperous merchant and was thought to be carrying gold coins and other valuables. This might explain why he decided to wait until everyone else left camp before he buried his wagon - with his possessions inside - for safekeeping.

The caravan trudged on. They were tired, and worse, they were starving. It had been a month since Stanton and McCutchen had gone for help. They had not returned and hope that they would come back was now gone. The emigrants still faced a 40-mile march over a horrific alkali desert. They would not wait for Wolfinger to catch up - no one even wished him luck.

At the last minute, Joseph Reinhardt and Augustus Spitzer - both men hired by Wolfinger - volunteered to stay with him and help bury the wagon. They would get the work finished and then catch up with the company while Wolfinger's wife continued on with those who were leaving. The couple embraced and then she walked away with the ragtag party. Dorthea Wolfinger had started the journey with fine gowns and sparkling jewelry and now she was walking through the desert empty-handed with a group of dirty women and children.

Worse, she would never see her husband again.

The company's wagons, pulled by teams of scrawny cows and oxen, reached a fork, and took the right branch, called the Truckee Route. It was named for a friendly Paiute chief who was known for guiding emigrants along the edge of the desert and through the Sierras. There was no grass on the route, no water, and no shade. There was only mile after mile of crusty salt and dirt. They traveled by night to stay out of the brutal sun. Along the trail, they saw furniture, clothing, and books that had been thrown out, along with dead horses, mules, and oxen that had simply gone no farther. If there was no moon at night, the emigrants set fire to the broken-down wagons on the path to light their way.

About halfway across the desert, they reached Boiling Springs, a hot spring that would have been appreciated under better circumstances. William Eddy took some coffee that had been given to him by one of the Donner women and mixed it with the hot water. He didn't drink any of it, but gave it to his wife and the two children. The bitter brew revived them, but they had gone without water for so long that Eddy feared the children would die. Knowing that the Breen family had at least 10 gallons of fresh water, Eddy asked for a small amount for the children.

He should have known better.

Patrick Breen first denied having any water at all but when Eddy pressed him, he admitted that he did but was saving it for his own family.

But the trail had pushed Eddy to the limit. He looked Breen in the eye and told him that he'd have water, or he'd die trying to get it. He pushed past him, took a small amount of water, and returned to his family with it.

The final 10 miles through the desert turned out to be the worst. They marched along a ridge of deep sand that drained them of the strength they had left. Six more oxen died. The party pushed on, knowing that just ahead, on the banks of the Truckee River, there was lush grass, shade trees, and good clean water. And then they arrived. It was not a mirage of the desert. They had reached the green banks of the river and soon they were lined with emigrants and animals drinking water until they could stand no more.

But water wasn't food. Some of them had a few supplies left, but the others had little, or nothing. William and Margaret Eddy had not eaten in two days. All their children had tasted were lumps of sugar that they sucked on. Eddy swallowed his pride again and he begged Elizabeth Graves for some meat for his children, but she coldly refused his plea. He went to Peggy Breen with the same request, but like her husband, told him they had nothing to spare.

But then they heard the sound of geese squawking, and some were seen on the wing above the river. Eddy's gun had been broken on the trail, so he borrowed a weapon from Keseberg. He returned to camp a short time later with nine plump geese. A story that circulated later said that despite their rude behavior, Mrs. Graves and Mrs. Breen were given two geese each to feed their families, while Keseberg was given one for the loan of his rifle. True or not, at least the Eddys ate well that night.

As the company was traveling up Truckee Canyon, two riders approached fast from the rear - Reinhardt and Spitzer, who had remained behind with Wolfinger. They had a terrible story to tell. They explained to the distraught Dorthea Wolfinger that Paiutes had attacked them, and her husband had been killed. They had barely escaped with their lives.

It was a sad end for the young German immigrant - or so it seemed. There were several members of the party who raised doubts about their story and the strange way the men acted after returning to the group seemed to justify their suspicions. They refused to offer many details about the attack and both men made sure their belongings were always kept close to them, leading some to wonder what they were hiding.

Philippine Keseberg, who also spoke German, did her best to comfort the grieving widow, as did the other women in the party. Wolfinger was the third member of the Donner Party to die that October.

The company continued to travel along the south side of the Truckee. The canyon was often so narrow that they were forced to cross the winding river 27 times. Their thirst was quenched by its waters, but they still needed food. There was still no sign of Stanton and McCutchen.

Finally, on October 20, the Donner Party reached the wide valley known as Truckee Meadows. They were only 40 miles from California and the Sierra Nevadas - a name that translated meant "snow-covered mountain range."

11. SNOWBOUND

The Donner Party had been strung out for some distance by the time the leaders arrived at Truckee Meadows. Stragglers continued to drag themselves there for the next several hours. They were the last emigrants still on the California Trail, a full month behind Edwin Bryant's mule train. Even the children were aware by now that they were in desperate straits. Time - or rather, the serious lack of it - was against them. Even so, the emigrants were sharply divided about when to proceed.

The weather had already turned cold. The heavy clouds that hung over the mountains loomed, foreshadowing the winter. Some of the members of the party - fearing that snowstorms might block their passage through the mountains - wanted to push on as soon as possible. But others were relieved to find the inviting meadow. They wanted to rest and give the animals time to recover.

In what was now a rare show of compromise, it was decided that it would be best for the company to stay in camp for a few days. The emigrants and the animals needed rest before tackling the Sierra Nevadas, the most difficult obstacle of the entire journey.

Whether this was a wise decision on the part of the emigrants was soon to be learned.

While the party was reaching Truckee Meadows, James Reed and Walter Herron were on the other side of the mountains, still struggling to reach Sutter's Fort. Both men were in desperate need of food. For an entire week, they had eaten nothing but wild onions. They had to keep moving, which made hunting difficult. Herron was so ravenous that he suggested they kill Glaucus for food. The mare was worn down and could no longer bear the weight of the saddle. Reed assured Herron that if they did not find food soon, he would kill the beloved horse himself.

Reed wrote later, "Soon after this, he became delirious." They moved on and Reed spotted a single bean along the trail. He picked it up and gave it to Herron and the two of them got down on their hands and knees to look for more. "We found five beans in all," Reed recalled. "Herron's share was three of them." It wasn't a meal, but at least it gave them a little hope.

Reed added to the story: "The next morning, after traveling a few miles, we saw some wagons. We soon reached and ransacked the wagons, hoping to find something to eat, but we found nothing. Taking the tar bucket that was hanging under one of the wagons, I scraped the tar off and found a streak of rancid tallow at the bottom. I handed the tar bucket to him, having some of the tallow about the size of a walnut in it. This he swallowed without giving it a smell. I then took a piece myself, but it was very repulsive."

Herron, apparently having a much stronger stomach than Reed, wolfed down more of the grease. He would have eaten more but Reed convinced him to stop. After walking a short distance, Reed experienced a wave of nausea and a moment of blindness - common with victims of poison. He purged what little was in his stomach and collapsed onto the grass to rest. He soon recovered. Herron, apparently, had not been affected by eating the tallow at all.

Reed managed to get to his feet and he and Herron, leading a stumbling Glaucus, descended a steep slope into Bear Valley, where they found a group of emigrants with their wagons circling a campsite. Those who greeted them had more than putrid grease to offer their guests. Sitting by the fire, wrapped in blankets, Reed and Herron ate hunks of fresh bread and drank down sugared tea. Glaucus was fed and watered.

And then a figure emerged from the shadows - Charles Stanton.

He was on his way back to the Donner Party. At first, he didn't recognize the hollow-eyed Reed and Herron. Both men were dirty, thin, and drawn. But when they spoke, he knew them immediately, hugged

Sutter's Fort in California was the end of the California Trail and the spot that every emigrant wanted to see before the snow started to fall in the mountains. Most of them made it - but not the Donner Party.

them, and greeted them joyfully. They sat together by the fire and spoke for hours.

Stanton explained that in early October, after a hard and furious ride, he and William McCutchen had made it to Sutter's Fort on the Sacramento River. Sutter lived up to his reputation of offering generous assistance to emigrants in need. His fort was located at the end of the California Trail and he had been welcoming travelers since the first significant parties arrived in the region in 1841.

Sutter was an excellent host, but he was also a shrewd businessman with an enterprise that he needed to

John Sutter

finance and manage. Those who accepted his generosity eventually had to pay for the services and goods that were rendered. He was open to giving credit, but with the understanding that the debt would be paid as soon as possible. Once he had reviewed the letter that was given to him, signed by James Reed with promise of payment in full, Sutter gladly supplied seven mules and what he thought would be enough provisions to allow the Donner Party to complete their journey.

Sutter also sent along two Miwok Indian guides - Salvador and Luis. The Miwok, indigenous to Northern California, had endured many cruelties from the Spanish, from the diseases they brought with them to the swords and crosses used to try and subjugate them and force their religion upon them. When the Mexicans came, they kidnapped the natives to work as slaves on large ranches along the coast. The Miwoks soon found that the white settlers who followed were different than the Spanish and the Mexicans - in some ways, they were worse. One of those who consistently took advantage of the Miwok was John Sutter.

When Sutter presented Luis and Salvador to Stanton and McCutchen, he called them "my vaqueros," the Spanish word for cowboy, because they were skilled horsemen. In truth, they were little more than slaves. The native labor force had become essential to Sutter's operations and he supplemented his income by selling Indians to rancheros and used slaves as payment for overdue debts. He kept Indian women for his personal pleasure and was known to have given a young girl as a gift to one of his friends.

Despite his place in California history, he was a despicable person. The 600 to 800 slaves that he worked at his fort were treated like animals. He even went as far as to feed them out of troughs, as if they were pigs.

If Stanton or McCutchen witnessed the conditions at the fort, they never mentioned it. Stanton did tell Reed and Herron that after arriving at the fort, McCutchen had become so ill that it was going to take him at least two weeks to recover. But Stanton was so anxious to get back to the company that he left him behind. By October 18, he was on the return trail with the mule train and the two Miwoks.

The two guides were indispensable to Stanton - they had to be. If they caused trouble or escaped, they knew Sutter would have them hunted down and punished. But Stanton treated them well and grew to like the two young men as they traveled together.

The mule team left the emigrant camp in Bear Valley early the next morning but before he left, Stanton gave Reed and Herron enough meat and flour to tide them over until they could make it to Sutter's Fort.

Back in Truckee Meadows, the emigrants had given up on seeing Stanton and McCutchen ever again. They scrounged what they could and hoped they could survive the trek ahead of them with what little food they had.

The men used the time in camp to repair their wagons and to care of the livestock that had been wounded by Paiute arrows and survived.

And then, misfortune struck again.

Brother-in-laws William Pike and William Foster, two of the 13 members of the Murphy-Pike-Foster family group, decided that, instead of waiting for Stanton and McCutchen to return, they would try to get to California themselves and bring back supplies.

William Foster, photographed many years after accidentally killing his best friend and brother-in-law, William Pike.

The two men had been close friends for many years. They had been shipmates on a Mississippi River steamer, *LaSalle*, when it departed from Warsaw, Illinois, in the winter of 1842 and became icebound while traveling to St. Louis. Among the passengers had been Levinah Murphy, a widow with seven children, including her oldest daughters, Sarah and Harriet. While the boat was stuck in the ice, romance bloomed between the two sisters and the two friends. Shortly after Christmas, Sarah married Foster and Harriet married Pike in a double ceremony. Now with children of their own, the two couples were sharing a great adventure to California, where Levinah Murphy wanted to live with her children and grandchildren.

The two young men began preparing for the trip. They loaded their saddlebags, trying to take nothing that would slow them down, but making sure they had all the essentials. Foster checked his weapons, loading a small multi-barreled pistol that he had called a pepperbox because it resembled a household pepper grinder. Apparently, while he was loading it, the gun went off and sent a bullet into Pike's back.

The wound - at such close range - turned out to be fatal, but not immediately so. Pike fell down in pain, gasping for breath while Foster,

Harriet, and the rest of the family tried to help him. One of the Murphy children, Mary, later wrote, "He died in about one-half hour and in that time, he suffered more than tongue can tell."

Harriet, only 18-years-old, was left a widow with two daughters. One was an infant and the other, a toddler.

Death had called once again at the emigrant camp.

By the time William Pike was in his grave, many members of the company were ready to leave. They were no longer a functioning wagon train but for the purposes of traveling, they were split into three factions. The Breen family took the lead, with their friend Patrick Dolan out front. They had lost fewer cattle and had generally fared better than the others. They were also the most insistent about pushing on to make the steep mountain crossings before the snow became too deep. The Eddys and the Kesebergs went with them.

The second faction consisted of the Murphys, Margaret Reed and her children, and the extended Graves family. They were the largest group, but also had the fewest wagons.

Bringing up the rear and traveling at a slower pace were the Donner brothers, their families and teamsters, and Dorthea Wolfinger.

The Donner Party had not been a unified group for some time and even within the three factions, the only allegiance that anyone felt was to their own family members. Survival was all that mattered to them - but only their own survival. They cared nothing for the others in the party, which is why they consistently failed. Each time they had faced danger, struggles always erupted between people and within families. They failed to learn that survival didn't depend on being fearless - it was about making decisions, even if the decisions turned out to be wrong. The party had no leader after James Reed had been banished. George Donner had been elected as captain, but he traveled at the rear of the company and was too amicable to make the harsh decisions that sometimes needed to be made. It was that lack of leadership - and having someone to make decisions to help them all work together - that caused the Donner Party to meet with disaster.

On the day they left Truckee Meadows, they traveled upriver beneath heavy clouds, strung out in three separate groups, too far apart to help anyone who encountered trouble. The temperature dropped that morning. It was already cold, but now it had become bitter.

It was late October when the Breen faction moved to higher

ground. Pat Dolan, riding out ahead of the others, saw what appeared to be another party coming toward them. He strained his eyes to look closer and then let out a whoop and a shout - it was Charles Stanton with his two Miwok escorts. They had seven mules with them, packed with flour, jerked beef, tea, coffee, sugar, beans, and other kinds of food.

The emigrants broke into a cheer and the men waved their hats as the mule train came to a atop. Stanton and the Miwoks opened the packs and doled out food to emigrants who had not had a decent meal in weeks.

They all could have learned something from Charles Stanton. He had no family in the company and yet had sacrificed his life to help his companions. He could have easily ridden off and never returned but he felt a duty to try and save those he'd traveled with. It was a brave and heroic moment for a member of the Donner Party - there would be more to come.

After the Breen group was resupplied, Stanton continued to ride east to the next party of the emigrants. There was another celebration when he arrived. The Graves and Murphy families crowded around the three men and called them heroes as they were handed sacks of flour and sugar, bags of beans, and packages of dried meat.

Virginia Reed was one of those who greeted Stanton. She later wrote, "Hungry as we were, Stanton brought us something better than food - news that my father was alive. Stanton had met him not far from Sutter's Fort; he had been three days without food and his horse was not able to carry on. Stanton had given him a horse and some provisions, and he had gone on."

The news that her husband was alive brought tears to the eyes of Margaret Reed. She made a fire and baked a batch of biscuits for the trail. Virginia handed out the warm bread to each of her siblings. Later, after Stanton had made the rounds with the mule train and the supplies had all been distributed, he and the Indians returned to see the Reeds. He was determined to make sure they no longer had to walk to California.

Virginia wrote, "We now packed what little we had left on one mule and started with Stanton. My mother rode on a mule, carrying Tommy in her lap; Patty and Jim rode behind the two Indians, and I behind Mr. Stanton, and in this way, we journeyed on through the rain, looking up with fear towards the mountains, where snow was already falling, although it was only the last week of October. Winter had set in a month earlier than usual. All trails and roads were covered; and our only guide was the summit which it seemed we would never reach. Despair drove many frantic."

The Dolans and the Breens in the lead group left the Truckee River after numerous crossings and worked their way northwest through a narrow canyon. They crossed over a range that was partially covered by ponderosa pines and through what would become known as Dog Valley, thanks to the packs of feral dogs that roamed it.

At camp that evening, just north of Crystal Peak, William Eddy took guard duty using a borrowed rifle. It would be put to good use. At some point that night, an Indian attacked the camp, firing arrows into 19 cows. Luckily, none of the wounds were fatal - but the shot fired by Eddy was. The ball struck the Indian in the back, between the shoulders, and exited his chest. The dead man fell down an incline into some willow trees.

On this same evening, the five wagons of the Donner family and Dorthea Wolfinger, were slowly closing the gap between themselves and the other groups. Even so, they were still some distance behind. George and Jacob figured that if they could get in a good day or two of travel along the Truckee, they might catch up with the others.

They were making good time until an axle on George's wagon snapped while climbing a steep rise. The wagon overturned with his daughters Eliza and Georgia inside. Four-year-old Georgia was pulled free, but her younger sister could not be found at first. They searched frantically through a pile of quilts and clothing in the wagon box and then Jacob found the little girl. While she was fussed over by Tamzene, George and Jacob cut down a tree and went to work hewing a new axle. They were in a hurry to get the wagons rolling again.

Jacob was giving the finishing touches to the axle when the chisel that he was using slipped out of his hands and slashed George's hand, opening up a serious wound. He had been steadying the log as Jacob smoothed it into shape. Jacob was able to stop the bleeding from his brother's hand and then Tamzene carefully washed and dressed it with strips of clean cloth.

It seemed that if something could go wrong, it would.

Jacob fitted the new axle and with George's hand bandaged, they

Truckee Lake, the shores of which would become the home for most of
the Donner Party during the brutal winter of 1846-1847.

were ready to move on.

Jacob felt terrible about the accident, but George did what he could to ease his guilt. He joked that it was only a scratch and said they had better things to worry about. He was only partly correct with that statement.

Years later, Eliza Donner wrote, "The consequences of the accident, however, were far more wide-reaching than could have been anticipated."

It was almost November when the first two factions of the party approached Truckee Lake - later re-named Donner Lake - a narrow, three-mile-long body of water that had been carved thousands of years earlier by a glacier.

Past the lake, the emigrants had to ascend more than 7,000 feet to Fremont Pass. Sutter's Fort was less than 90 miles away.

But it had started to snow.

A storm that began in the Gulf of Alaska moved south along the jet stream, following the coastline. Clouds filled with moisture rolled over the sea and shore. The storm turned east, flowing over the coastal ranges. It climbed the High Sierras and the moist air inside the clouds turned cold. The temperature was below freezing, changing the water to icy crystals, and then to snowflakes, which began to fall across the region.

Normally a storm like this would make crossing the Sierra Nevadas difficult, but possible. But that was not the case in the fall of 1846. Starting on October 16, earlier than normal, the first heavy snow had fallen. Another big storm soon followed, bringing even more snow.

When it began snowing again on the emigrants, they dismissed the danger. The remnants of an early snowfall remained, but they were confident it would not last. The emigrants had experienced plenty of snowstorms - even blizzards - in the Midwest. They knew that after a few days, the snow and ice always melted, and the sky cleared until the next storm came along. But this was not Illinois or Missouri - this was the High Sierras, where terrible storms often came one after another, with the next one fiercer than the last.

The storm that began when the emigrants arrived at Truckee Lake continued for two weeks, with only a few breaks.

On the day they arrived at the lake, the lead party skirted the north shore and headed toward the looming mountain range ahead. The grass was covered with snow and was difficult to get to, so the men cut pine boughs to feed the hungry cattle, which were exhausted from moving through the snow. They also came across an abandoned cabin that looked like promising shelter if they needed to turn back.

John Breen, the oldest son in the family, later wrote: "In the morning it was very cold, with about an inch of snow on the ground. This made us hurry our cattle more, if possible, than before. We traveled on, and, at last, the clouds cleared, leaving the towering peaks in full view, covered as far as the eye could reach with snow. This sight made us despair of even entering the long sought valley of the Sacramento; but we pushed on as fast as our failing cattle could haul our almost empty wagons. At last, we reached the front of the main ridge, near Truckee Lake. It was sundown."

That night, John and his father were pleased when the wind died down and the sky cleared. But that happiness didn't last. There was a bright, full moon in the sky. A halo was formed around it, which all farmers knew signaled an approaching storm.

The arrival of daylight confirmed their fears. They could see snow falling heavily on the summit that they had yet to cross. They set out early, hoping to get through, and traveled one or two miles, with the snow getting deeper with every step. Eventually, it was as high was the wagon axles. A poor decision was made - they'd abandon the wagons, pack the oxen, and keep going.

John Breen wrote, "By the time we got the oxen packed, it was impossible to advance; first, because of the depth of the snow, and next, because we could not find the road; so, we hitched to the wagons and returned to the valley again, where we found it raining in torrents."

John Breen was only a young boy during the events in this book. This photograph was taken years later.

The emigrants took shelter in the abandoned cabin they'd seen and built a fire to stay warm - only to find that the roof leaked so badly that it would have been just as dry outside. They ended up sheltering under their wagons for the night.

It had cleared off by morning, which gave them some hope. But as John wrote, "We were so little acquainted with the country as to believe that rain in the valley was rain on the mountain also, and that it would beat down the snow so that we might possibly go over. In this, we were fatally mistaken."

By morning, the second group of emigrants had arrived, and discussions took place about what to do next. They were all determined to reach the pass, but it began raining again. Everyone stayed in camp and watched the downpour. Some of the new arrivals assured the Breens that rain at the lake meant snow at the pass, but they weren't convinced.

It rained all day and through the night, but when the skies brightened, the Breens and their party yoked up their oxen and prepared to conquer the trail ahead. The snow at the lake was three feet deep - and had been rained on - making it hard for anyone,

The famous illustration of the emigrants as they attempted to reach the summit and get through the pass to California.

including the oxen, to move around. The animals, weakened by a diet of pine boughs, were unlikely to make it very far from the lake, let alone through the pass, but they had to try.

"We set out that morning to make a last struggle," John Breen recalled, "but did not advance more than two miles before the road became so completely blocked that we were forced to retrace our steps in despair. When we reached the valley, we commenced repairing the house; we killed our cattle and covered it with their hides."

As the Breens stored the butchered meat in the growing snowdrifts and repaired the roof of the cabin with animal hides, Charles Stanton and the two Miwoks, Luis and Salvador, arrived with the rest of the second group, who were determined to make their own attempt to reach the pass. They were confident that with the mules in the lead, a trail could be broken.

The group with Stanton included the Reed, Graves, and Eddy families. Lewis Keseberg also decided to go with them, even though he could barely walk. While hunting a short time before, he had stepped on a willow stub that tore through the bottom of his buckskin moccasin and pierced the ball of this foot. His wife had washed and dressed the wound, but his foot became so swollen that he was unable to walk for several days. He got some relief after another emigrant lanced his foot and extracted a small piece of the willow stub. Determined to go over the pass, Keseberg asked for help getting onto his horse. Once seated, his foot was tied into a sling that was attached to his saddle.

There was one thing stopping the expedition - aside from the snow, that is - and that was the wagons. They were too burdensome, it was decided, and needed to be left behind. The remaining oxen and cattle would be turned into pack animals to follow Stanton's mules. This decision caused a panic in the party - what would they leave behind? Franklin Graves' main concern was what he should do with his hoard of silver coins. Some of the women wanted to bring along bolts of calico and a few men insisted that crates of tobacco had to be packed.

This photograph was taken in the pass in the 1920s, long after it had been turned into a road. Needless to say, the Donners did not have access to automobiles but I included this image to give the reader and idea of the depth of snow they had to face.

The clearheaded among them knew that carrying such things over the mountains was ridiculous. In fact, some suggested that the wagons, overloaded with things no one really needed, had helped put them in the predicament they were in. William Eddy tried to convince everyone that all they needed was enough food to support them for six days, by which time they would have reached the Bear River and safety.

Unfortunately, Eddy and the other realistic emigrants did not win the argument. That became evident when a few members of the group, unable to decide what to leave behind, chose to bring their wagons. A few others backed out, frightened of trying to tackle the Sierras in the snow. They believed wintering at the lake was a better idea.

Those who continued soon found that turning oxen - some of the dumbest animals alive - into pack animals with unfamiliar loads on their backs was not an easy task. They bucked and bellowed and wallowed in the snow, rubbing against pine trees to try and tear off the packs. Finally, with prodding from the teamsters, the oxen accepted their fate and began trudging up the trail.

It was near midday when the party approached the pass. The snow was now waist deep and it was difficult to walk through, especially if carrying provisions or a child. It was impossible to find any trace of the trail. One of the Indians, with Patty Reed clinging to him, rode a mule that kept its head down and plowed through the snowdrifts, clearing a path for the others. The emigrants who insisted on bringing wagons now had no choice but to abandon them. They unyoked the oxen and stomped through the snow with the others. As they climbed higher, the snow got deeper and finally, the exhausted travelers could go no further.

Stanton told everyone to rest and he and the Miwoks went on to scout the area ahead. They pushed through snow as deep as their chests to see how far it was to the summit. As he stood and looked beyond, he knew that he would live if he just kept going. Behind him, he also knew, was a chance that he might die. He had left the company once to bring back supplies and now he had the opportunity to do it again.

Many men might have considered saving themselves and just kept going, but those men were not Charles Stanton. Not only did he have a group of shivering people who were waiting for him, but he also had borrowed mules that he had promised to return to Sutter's Fort. His honor would not allow him to fail in this.

And as it turned out, the Miwoks were just as loyal to Stanton as he was to the rest of the company. Several times, other emigrants tried to convince the Indians to leave Stanton and the mules and guide them over the mountains to safety. They refused, even though they knew the danger of each hour's delay. There are some who say that Stanton had convinced the two men that Sutter would hang them if they returned to the fort without the mules, but I think there was more to it than that. I don't believe the Miwoks were as simple as contemporary writings - rooted in the casual racism of the era - would have us believe. These men had to have known that Sutter's reach was not as great as he claimed. If they had wanted to leave, they could have gone east, and would never have been seen again.

They chose to stay with the man they now called their friend.

Stanton, Luis, and Salvador made their way back through the drifting snow to where the emigrants waited. As they neared the temporary campsite, they saw what appeared to be a roaring tower of flames. In their absence, the others decided they could go no further and would stay there for the night. Someone had set fire to a tall pine that was oozing with resin. The emigrants used it to stay warm while they dug out places to sleep.

But Stanton urged them to stop. The summit was only three miles ahead and they could still get across it before more snow fell and made the journey more difficult.

No one listened to Stanton, except for Lewis Keseberg, who hobbled around on one foot and tried to persuade the others to keep going.

But it was no use. The idea of a "forced march," as Virginia Reed called it, held no appeal for anyone. As the tree was consumed in flames, the emigrants basked in the warmth and at that point, Stanton knew there was nothing he could say that would change their minds.

If he ever second-guessed going back to the party, it was probably then.

One of the Miwoks wrapped himself in a blanket and spent the night on watch, leaning against a tree. The camp fell silent, aside from the cracking and popping of the burning tree.

And it began to snow again.

The white powder fell throughout the night, covering the sleeping emigrants. It was Keseberg who woke first. He felt like he had a heavy weight resting on him and he jerked up into a sitting position with a cry. When he looked around, he at first thought he was alone, but when he called out, he started to see heads popping up all around him in the snow. "The scene was not unlike what one might imagine at the resurrection, when people rise out of the earth," he said later.

The expedition had turned into a disaster overnight. The mules were lost, the cattle had strayed away, and another foot of snow had fallen in the darkness. There were now snowdrifts around them that were 10 feet high. The big pine tree had turned into a charred, smoldering stump. They shook the snow off their clothing and blankets and managed to start a new fire, but it was painfully clear they couldn't continue to the summit. The pass was completely blocked.

If only they had listened the night before.

The group retreated to Truckee Lake, but even going downhill was now a struggle. They didn't reach the lake until late afternoon. The Breens were now snugly ensconced in the cabin and, not surprisingly, refused to let anyone else in. The rest of the emigrants made a makeshift camp for the night. They would begin building their own shelters in the morning.

Meanwhile, further back on the trail, the Donners were still struggling. Their progress had been slowed by the wagon accident and the injury to George Donner's hand. The only people at the lake camp that had seen them were two riders who had gone back to warn them that the pass above the lake was blocked with snow.

Although George didn't complain about his injury and tried to help with the work, he was unable to use his hand and was in constant pain. The deep cut turned out to be more serious than anyone first thought. Tamzene cleaned the wound every day and wrapped it with the cleanest cloth she could find, but it did not seem to be healing. It was swollen and painful to even Tamzene's most gentle touch. She knew it needed proper medical attention - as soon as possible - so she did all she could to try and keep the party moving. Even if the pass was blocked now, Tamzene, like all the others, believed the snow would stop and they could press on.

Tamzene also believed there was strength in numbers, and it would be in all their best interests to catch up to the others. But George and Jacob disagreed. They decided that before continuing, they would cache everything but the essentials and then take the wagons apart to build carts that could be pushed and pulled on the trail. They spent several days trying to work out the logistics of how to do this - and then scrapped the idea altogether. More time had been lost.

The next plan was to pack the oxen to carry their belongings, but they didn't even fare as well with this as the second party had. The animals jumped and kicked, scattering everything, so this plan was also scrapped. They ended up reloading the wagons and moved on.

They didn't stop until they reached the junction of Alder and Prosser Creeks, about six miles northeast of Truckee Lake. Concerned about the storm clouds above the mountains ahead, George thought they had found a suitable winter camp in a valley that was, at that point, free of snow. They would unpack and build a cabin where they could wait out the winter and make the final crossing to California in the spring.

Work began. George tried to help despite his injured hand, but he couldn't do much. Jacob was sick and so most of the work was done by the teamsters, the women, and the children who were old enough to

A photograph taken many years after the events at the Alder Creek Camp, used by the Donners. The tree stumps in the image were from trees cut down by the Donner family and their workers.

assist them. Some cut down trees, while others trimmed off the branches, while the teamsters used the oxen to drag the logs into place.

The cabin walls were only four logs high when work stopped. Snow started to fall. The emigrants were able to see it coming, like a great curtain of white that swept over them. It was the same storm that had forced the two groups to dig in at the lake. By the time it reached the Donners at Alder Creek, the storm had been whipped into a frenzy by the wind. It came down in a blinding fury and they were forced to throw together shelters from branches and discarded logs until the skies cleared.

Jean-Baptiste Trudeau, the young teamster hired by the Donners at Fort Bridger, would later refer to the site as "that camp of snow and suffering."

Leanna Donner, only 12 at the time, wrote about what she recalled 30 years later: "We had no time to build a cabin. The snow came on so suddenly that we barely had time to pitch our tent, and put up a brush shed, as it were, one side of which was open. It was covered in

Leanna Donner was only 12 when the family made camp at Alder Creek. This photograph was taken many years later.

pine boughs, and then covered with rubber coats, quilts, etc. My uncle, Jacob Donner, and family, also had a tent, and camped near us."

George Donner's camp, made up of a tent and a lean-to, was on the north side of the creek, somewhat sheltered by a large pine. A shallow hole was dug near the tree's trunk for cooking and the tent was used as sleeping quarters. They managed to fashion crude beds from poles and pine boughs. It was a tight squeeze for George and Tamzene, the five Donner daughters, and the widow Wolfinger.

Jacob Donner's camp was about 300 yards up the creek in a clearing with no trees nearby. It was recalled later that as the snow continued to fall, Jacob's camp could not be seen from George's camp because of the high snowdrifts. When they wanted to visit, they had to look for smoke rising from the snow to show them the way.

George's hand continued to get worse, although he didn't complain. Even so, his children could see the pain in the features of his face. He spoke little and spent most of his time staring into the fire with lifeless eyes. Their grand journey had fallen apart. Both George and Jacob now knew they would never make it to California in time to obtain land for the spring planting season.

At this point, they had to have wondered if they would ever make it to California at all.

The snow fell for the next eight days. Eliza Donner later wrote of the conditions under which they lived: "There was nothing to break the monotony of torturing, inactive endurance, except the necessity of gathering wood, keeping the fires, and cutting anew the steps which led upward, as the snow increased in depth. Hope nigh-well died with us. Axes were dull, green wood was hard to cut, and harder to carry, whether through loose, dry snow, or over crusts made slippery by sleet and frost. Cattle tracks were covered over. Some of the poor creatures had perished under bushes where they sought shelter. A few had become bewildered and strayed; others were found under trees in snow pits, which they themselves had made by walking round and round the trunks to keep from being snowed under. These starvelings were shot to end their sufferings, and also with the hope that their hides and fleshless bones might save the life of a snow-beleaguered party. Every part of the animal was saved for food. The locations of the carcasses were marked so that they could be brought back piece by piece into camp; and even the green hides were spread against the huts to serve in case of need."

The emigrants at the Truckee Lake camp had no time to worry about those in the Donner camp, several miles away. They needed food and shelter if they wanted to survive the winter. Keseberg's injured foot kept him from building a proper cabin for his wife and two children. Instead, he and fellow Germans Augustus Spitzer and Charles Burger put together a lean-to from cut poles and pine branches. They constructed it on the west end of the cabin that had been taken over by the Breens.

Besides the nine members of the Breen family, the cabin also sheltered their friend, Patrick Dolan, and the teamster known only as Antonio.

The other emigrants built sturdy cabins. About 200 yards south of the Breen cabin, William Eddy, with help from William Foster and some of the Murphys, constructed a cabin of unpeeled pine logs against the flat side of a huge boulder. The rock was used as a hearth, allowing smoke to rise through a gap between the boulder and the roof. When completed, it was used to shelter 16 people - the Eddy, Murphy, Foster, and Pike families.

Franklin Graves selected a site for a cabin for his family, the Reeds, and several others about a half-mile downstream from the other cabins. There was no clear explanation for why he moved so far away from the rest of the group. His daughter, Mary, later said that she believed it was because it was more sheltered from the wind and storm, but Patty Reed believed he'd done it just to be contrary of the "minds and wills" of the others.

It was a large double cabin - two rooms, each with its own

Mary Graves, photographed many years after the events in this book. Her father, Franklin, constructed a shelter for his family apart from the other cabins at Truckee Lake.

fireplace - separated by a log wall. The Graves family and Amanda McCutchen, whose husband was ailing at Sutter's Fort, and her infant daughter lived in one of the rooms, while Margaret Reed and her five children and their employees lived in the other. They were joined by Stanton and the two Miwok guides. There were no windows, but each side had a separate door. This reduced the tension between the Graves family and the Reeds, which still lingered from the death of the Graves' teamster, John Snyder.

Although some of the emigrants still hoped they might make it through the pass before spring, the realists among them knew they were stuck for the winter. Of the 87 members of the Donner Party - plus the addition of the Miwoks, Luis and Salvador - 81 people were trapped in two camps in the Sierra Nevadas. There were 59 at the lake camp and 21 dug in at the Alder Creek camp. More than half were under 18, and many of those were small children and infants.

They were all - some better than others - sheltered against the ice and cold but the provisions that Stanton had brought from Sutter's Fort were starting to run out. They had started to kill their cattle, but once the livestock was gone, there was no way to get wagons over the summit.

Even more serious - some of the emigrants still had cattle and oxen to kill, but others did not. Would any of them share their food with others? How far would they go to feed hungry children?

Ironically, being trapped in the snow could have been avoided if the party had taken advice from what was a very unlikely source - Lansford Hastings. Although most of them would have gladly killed the man on site, he had included a tip that might have saved the Donner Party within the six pages that he wrote about the cutoff they had followed.

It was short and to the point:

"Unless you pass over the mountains early in the fall, you are liable to be detained by impassable mountains of snow, until spring, or, perhaps, forever."

12. THE "FORLORN HOPE"

They were trapped.

Buried in deep snow that never seemed to stop falling, the emigrants of the Donner Party were constantly cold, hungry, and afraid. There seemed no way to get warm in their flimsy shelters or in the cabins that continually let in drafts. Blankets and cow hides were hung over the doors, but they did little to keep out the frigid air. The only warmth came from huddling around the fires, but as they burned down, trips into the nightmarish outdoors were needed to replenish the wood, which was getting hard to find close to the camps.

The hope that they might survive was starting to fade.

But for some, a small amount of hope remained. They knew they had not been forgotten. Somewhere, on the other side of the mountains, James Reed was still alive. He would do anything to save his wife and children and by rescuing them, he would also save the lives of the people who had banished him from their company.

And they were right. James Reed was alive. On October 28, 1846, the emaciated and haggard man, dragging Walter Herron with him, stumbled into Sutter's Fort. Reed found himself in good company. Not only was John Sutter there to greet him, but so were many old friends - friends who had been smart enough not to take Hastings cutoff. Among them were Edwin Bryant, William Russell, George McKinstry,

Benjamin Lippincott, and Andrew Grayson. That same day, Lilburn Boggs and his family arrived at the fort and joined in the reunion. In the evening, after having the meal he had dreamed about for weeks, Reed caught up on news of the war between the United States and Mexico.

William Todd's original Bear Flag, which became the symbol of the revolt in Alta California.

A short-lived rebellion had recently occurred in Alta California and rumors were circulating that the Mexican authorities were going to exile all foreign settlers who were not citizens. This news was important to Reed because the leader of what was called the Bear Flag Revolt was William Ide, a former Springfield farmer and schoolteacher who had emigrated to California in 1845 with Robert Keyes, Reed's brother-in-law. Robert being in California was the reason that his elderly mother, Sarah, had insisted on traveling with the Reeds in 1846.

Reed was told that another acquaintance from Springfield, William Todd - nephew of Mary Todd Lincoln - had also had an active part in the revolt. Todd had designed the distinctive California Bear Republic flag, which depicted a lone red star, a grizzly bear, and the words "California Republic." Although the revolt only lasted 22 days, Todd and his men then joined the forces of John C. Fremont to try and take California away from Mexico. Fremont was in command of the California Battalion, a combined force of members of his surveying crew and volunteers from the Bear Flag Republic.

Just that night at Sutter's Fort, news had arrived from Fremont at his headquarters in Monterey. According to the dispatch, a large number of Mexican troops had driven off a force of Americans. He needed more men and was sending out a call for volunteers to join a new regiment of men to engage the enemy.

Edwin Bryant wrote, "On receipt of this intelligence, I immediately drew up a paper which was signed by myself, Messrs.

Reed, Jacob, Lippincott, and Grayson, offering our services as volunteers, and our exertions to raise a force of emigrants and Indians which should be sufficient reinforcement to Colonel Fremont."

The letter was addressed to U.S. Navy Lieutenant Edward M. Kern, who was the commander at Sutter's Fort - officially Fort Sacramento. The next morning, Kern accepted the proposal and work was started to engage volunteers, uniform the men, and purchase supplies.

James Reed had signed the document that committed him to serve with the volunteer army, but he had a caveat - he needed to first be allowed to take provisions back to the Donner Party. If allowed, he promised to enlist all the men he could between the fort and Bear Valley.

William McCutchen stepped forward as a volunteer to go with him. He was recovered from his illness and was worried about his wife and daughter. Reed happily agreed to his help.

Sutter was just as eager to equip Reed, especially when cash collateral was offered until his animals were safely returned and a promise was made to pay off the balance. Reed, who had traveled to California because of bankruptcy, had managed to squirrel away a substantial amount of cash, likely with the help of his shrewd attorney, Abraham Lincoln.

Sutter allotted Reed and McCutchen 30 horses, a mule, a hindquarter of beef, and an ample supply of flour and beans. He also assigned two more Miwok Indians to help drive the pack train through the snow.

In early November, Reed, McCutchen, and the two Miwoks left Sutter's Fort with a long string of horses. They rode east for four consecutive days of rain before reaching the head of the Bear River, where the rain had turned into 18 inches of snow. Reed hoped that by the time they reached the valley, they would discover the Donner Party, but the emigrants were nowhere to be found.

Reed and McCutchen mistakenly believed that the party had made it through the pass and were still moving in the direction of Sutter's Fort. They had no idea, at that point, that their families were stranded in the mountains.

On the evening of November 5, the rain turned to sleet and continued all night. The men were cold and miserable. Reed later wrote,

"We drove on until a late hour before halting. We secured the flour and horses, the rain preventing us from kindling a fire."

The next morning, the snow was more than two feet deep at the foot of Emigrant Gap and they came upon the camp of Jotham Curtis and his wife. They were emigrants from Missouri who had left their wagon train after a disagreement. Because of the threatening weather, they chose to take their chances in a winter camp - but it seemed to Reed they had used up their last chances. Their oxen had run off and they were out of food.

According to Reed, "They hailed us as angels sent for their delivery, stating that they would have perished had it not been for our arrival."

Mrs. Curtis told them that they had killed their dog for food and, at the time of their arrival, had the last piece of it in the Dutch oven baking. Reed insisted they had plenty of food with them and were happy to offer them some, likely not interested in eating anyone's family pet. But Mrs. Curtis insisted, and the two men were too courteous to refuse.

"I cut out a rib, smelling and tasting, and found it to be good," Reed recalled, "and handed the rib over to Mr. McCutchen, who, after smelling it some time, tasted it and pronounced it good dog."

And that, I suppose, is how you make friends along the trail.

Before leaving the Curtis camp the next morning, Reed promised to retrieve the couple on his return trip to Sutter's Fort. He also left some flour and beef to tide them over until that time. Since they were out of dog, he didn't want them to go hungry.

Reed, McCutchen, and the Miwoks - who, unlike Luis and Salvador, were not named in anyone's writings - slogged through deep snow all day before making camp on the mountain. During the night, Reed and McCutchen heard what sounded like horses moving down the trail and discovered that the Indians had run away, taking several of the horses with them. McCutchen quickly saddled his horse and went after them, but it was too late. The men had vanished into the night.

Early the next morning, they pressed on, but soon, were unable to find the trail because of the snow. The horses, carrying heavy packs, struggled to keep moving. Reed later wrote, "We pushed them on until they would rear upon their hind feet to breast in the snow, and when they would alight, they would sink in until nothing was seen of them but the nose and a portion of the head. We found it utterly impossible to proceed with the horses. Leaving them, we proceeded further on foot, thinking we could get in to the people, but found that impossible, the snow being soft and deep."

They were only 10 miles from the summit - which the party was snowbound on the other side of - but could go no farther. Even if they had made it on foot, it would have been pointless since the packs of food had been left behind. Reluctantly, they turned back to the horses, dug them out of the snow, and backtracked to the Curtis encampment. There they hung the dried meat in trees to keep away animals, cached the flour and other provisions in a wagon, and waited for Curtis and his wife to pack a horse for a trip to Fort Sutter. In the valley, where there was little snow, there was plenty of underbrush for the horses to forage on.

"As soon as we arrived at Captain Sutter's, I made a statement of all the circumstance attending our attempt to get into the mountains," Reed wrote. "He was not surprised by our defeat. I also gave the captain the number of head of cattle the company had when I left them. He made an estimate and stated that if the emigrants would kill the cattle, and place the meat in snow for preservation, there was no fear of starvation until relief could reach them. He further stated there were no able-bodied men in the vicinity, all having gone down the country with and after Fremont, to fight the Mexicans. He advised me to proceed to Yerba Bueno and make my case known to the naval officer in command."

Reed was disappointed and now could only ponder what to do next to save his family. There was no way that Reed could have known that he and Sutter's estimates about the cattle were wrong. The settlers had lost many of the cattle and oxen they had after Reed left. There wasn't nearly enough meat to last them through even part of the winter, let alone until spring, when help would be able to reach them.

Meanwhile, Margaret Reed, stranded with the rest of the party on the other side of the Sierras, was trying to figure out how to keep her children alive. If she had even a little of the money that her husband had hidden from his creditors, her worries would have been over.

The Breen and Graves families - who, as you might have gathered from this author's tone, were not among my favorites in the party -

still had about six oxen each. Margaret, of course, didn't have any. She was in a desperate situation, just like all the teamsters who had to trust in the goodwill of their employers to stay alive. Despite her migraines, Margaret - who knew that no one would be willing to just give her food - managed to find the courage to approach Franklin Graves to see about buying an ox.

Graves was still angry at the Reeds because of the killing of Snyder and he had taken out that anger on Margaret and her children after her husband was banished. Even so, he could not let a woman and her children starve to death. He sold Margaret two of his oxen on credit. But Graves being the man he was, told her that the money had to be paid back double when they made it across the mountains. He also sold William Eddy a dead ox for $25. Margaret bought two oxen from the Breens with the same deal. The Breens also traded two oxen to Levinah Murphy's son-in-law, Jay Fosdick, for a gold watch.

The families began the task of slaughtering the half-starved oxen. They decided to spare the mules for as long as they could, knowing they had to be accounted for at Sutter's Fort. The farmers among them were used to killing and butchering, but even they had a difficult time with the job. Most of the beasts had served the company faithfully for many months and had shared in their journey. Almost treated like pets and given names, the oxen were now simply sustenance.

After the animals were killed, their throats were quickly cut and as much blood as possible was captured in containers. The deep snow forced them to be butchered on the ground rather than being hung by their hind legs, which made the work even harder. Large cuts of meat were stacked in the snow and froze quickly, and the blood was consumed while it was still warm or was used for cooking. The ox's brains and organs were also harvested, as were the tongues. The tail was sliced into sections for soup. Bones were cracked open to retrieve the marrow and the hides were used for shelter covers. Like the Native Americans on the plains who used every bit of the buffalo for their daily needs, the emigrants learned to do the same with their oxen.

But the emigrants weren't just depending on their slaughtered work animals. Each day, William Eddy - the best shot in the company - borrowed a rifle and went hunting. All the deer had retreated to lower elevations for the winter so there wasn't much to shoot at, but he tried.

He did succeed in bagging a coyote that made a good supper for his family and on another day, he shot an owl. The stringy meat didn't go far, though, especially after he gave half of it to William Foster for letting him borrow his rifle.

Finally, on November 12, it stopped snowing. The skies cleared, inspiring some of the emigrants to make another attempt to climb the mountain, get through the pass, and go for help for those left behind. The party was made up of 13 men, led by Graves and Charles Stanton, and two women, Mary Graves and Sarah Foster. They left with good intentions, bundled up against the cold and each with a piece of meat for their rations. They managed to get through many high snowdrifts and up the steep ravines, but when they encountered soft snow, they found it was at least 10 feet deep. They called a halt to the expedition, well short of the pass. They made it back to the camp around midnight, just missing a dinner of some ducks that Eddy had killed that afternoon.

The following day, Eddy went out hunting again, hoping to return with something larger than ducks. He found some tracks in the snow that he believed were made by a bear, possibly a grizzly. He was right. It wasn't long before he found the bear digging in the snow to get to some roots. Eddy took aim and fired. The bear immediately roared, stood up on its hind legs, and charged at Eddy, who was behind a tree. By the time the bear reached him, Eddy had already reloaded - no easy feat using a muzzle loading rifle while an angry bear is coming your way - and he fired again. This shot brought the bear down. He used a tree branch to finish it off and then went for help.

Franklin Graves returned with him and the two of them chained the bear to an ox and dragged the carcass back to camp. Eddy gave Foster half the meat for the use of his gun and gave a portion of it to Graves for the loan of the ox. He also gave a share to the Reed family. Meat from the bear, estimated to have weighed at least 800 pounds, and oxen meat sustained the emigrants for a time as they secured their shelters and worried how they would make it to the spring thaw.

On November 20, Patrick Breen began keeping a journal. It is the only daily chronicle of events at the Donner Party camps during that terrible winter. It was written on eight small sheets of paper, folded into a 32-page book. His writing was straightforward and often understated - and he knew nothing about punctuation -- but it kept track of most things that occurred.

The first entry, the longest in the journal, summarized the emigrant's situation from the time of their arrival at what became their winter camp. He wrote:

Friday, Nov. 20th, 1846.
Came to this place on the 31st of last month that it snowed we went on to the pass the snow so deep we were unable to find the road, when within 3 miles of the summit then turned back to this shanty on the lake, Stanton came one day after we arrived here we again took our teams & wagons & made another unsuccessful attempt to cross in company of Stanton we returned to shanty it continuing to snow all the time we were here we now have killed most part of our cattle having to stay here until next spring & live on poor beef without bread or salt it snowed during the space of eight days with little intermission, after our arrival here, the remainder of time up to this day was clear & pleasant freezing at night the snow nearly gone from the valleys.

As mentioned in the journal, there was melting snow in the valleys and this encouraged some of the emigrants to again make an effort to cross the mountains on foot. This new party consisted of 22 of the travelers - including Stanton and the two Miwoks. On the morning of November 21, they set off with only a few supplies in their packs and with seven mules.

Most of the men and all the women in the party came from the lake camp. Lewis Keseberg, still nursing his injured foot, stayed behind. So did Patrick Breen, who was suffering from painful "gravels" - kidney stones. The only one from the Donner camp at Alder Creek to join them was Jean-Baptiste Trudeau.

On the first day, they made good time. Much of the snow had melted and that which remained was covered by a thick crust. They made it through the pass, where Eddy measured the snow and found it to be 25-feet deep. That evening, they camped in a valley on the west side of the Sierras. It was brutally cold, and the high winds made it difficult to get a fire going. They had to dig out a camp from six feet of snow.

As it turned out, this is as far as the party would make it.

An argument started between Stanton and some of the others about the mules. Although the crusted snow made it easier for the people to walk, the mules were too heavy and broke through the crust. They were exhausted and slowing the progress of the expedition. When it was suggested that the mules be left behind so the emigrants could make a quicker descent to the valley, Stanton disagreed. As things tended to do among the company, the disagreement got heated. Stanton argued that the mules were John Sutter's property and neither Stanton nor the Miwoks were going to leave the animals to die.

Without the three men most familiar with the trail to guide them, the rest of the party knew they could go no farther. Eddy tried to change Stanton's mind, but it was useless. The next day, the dispirited party - along with all seven mules - marched back against the cold wind to the pass and arrived in the dark and silent camp after midnight.

At that same time, another storm was brewing in the north. It would soon become another blizzard in the Sierra Nevadas.

Things were more dire at the Alder Creek camp of the Donners, although George held out hope that relief would come, or someone would get over the mountains and find help. He had encouraged Jean-Baptiste to make the last attempt with the others. The young man was the fittest in the group and Donner believed he had a good chance of making it. He was disappointed when the young man returned but did not give up on a future expedition.

In fact, even though his wounded hand had still not healed, he managed to scribble a note that Trudeau, Elliott, or one of the other men could take with them on the next attempt. It read:

Donners Camp Nov. 28, 1846
This is to certify that I authorize Milford Elliott and make him my agent to purchase and buy whatever property he may deem necessary for my distress in the mountains for which my arrival in California I will pay Cash or goods or both.

2 Gallons Salt
$3 worth Sugar
150# Flour
3 Bus Beans

50# Cake Tallow
5 pack mules and two horses - purchase or hire.

During the first months of that winter, other emigrants, like Jacob Donner and William Foster, wrote similar authorization notes - none of which were fulfilled.

There was nothing certain about their days, except that more snow would fall, they would be cold, and they would be hungry.

For days, Breen's journal told the same story - "continues to snow," "Snowing fast," "deep soft wet snow," "still snowing," "killed my last oxen today," "hard to get wood," and as December arrived, the grim note: "Snowing fast wind W about four or five feet deep, no drifts, looks as likely to continue as when it commenced no living thing without wings can get about."

That first week of December brought more snow. When it cleared briefly, the emigrants emerged from shelter to find that the remaining cattle and horses were dead, buried under the snow. Sutter's mules were also gone. They were likely buried under the snow or had been stolen by Washoe Indians who wintered in the area and traveled using snowshoes. But really, it made no difference what had happened to them - they were gone. There would be no way to use them to escape and they could not be eaten for food. The men probed the snow with long poles, hoping to at least find a cow to be butchered, but had no luck.

The deep snow made gathering firewood even more difficult. The wood they did find was wet. The tops of pines were poking up out of snowbanks and they cut them off for firewood, but the green wood made so much smoke in the shelters that the occupants were forced to go outside. Some of the more desperate emigrants began chipping away at the walls of their cabins for tinder. Eventually, the stranded wagons were taken apart and burned to stay warm.

At the lake camp, there was still meat, but not much of anything else. A few cups of flour were hoarded to make a thin gruel for the infants and a little sugar, tea, and coffee remained, but no salt. The trout in the lake had burrowed in for the winter and refused to bite. Eddy's hunting expeditions failed to turn up game.

Augustus Spitzer was so sick and weak from hunger that he could no longer sit upright. The Breens took pity on him and moved

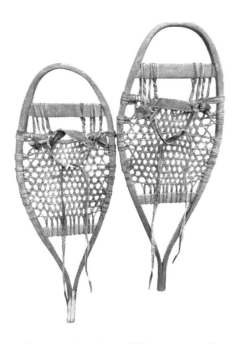

Long strips of rawhide were used to make bindings for the snowshoes. In a pinch, those bindings were also consumed as a meager amount of food.

him from the crowded Keseberg lean-to into their cabin. Margaret Reed was spending her time rationing out food to her children and helping Eliza Williams nurse her half-brother, Baylis, as he slowly died from malnutrition.

Meanwhile, the stronger emigrants were looking for other ways to stay alive. By mid-December, Franklin Graves and Charles Stanton had put their practical knowledge of snowshoes to good use. No one else in the party had ever used snowshoes but the two men assured them that if they knew how to walk, they could use snowshoes. They were designed to distribute a person's weight into a larger area, so they didn't sink down into the snow. To make them, they dug down into the snow and salvaged the discarded wooden oxbows from the wagons and turned them into snowshoe frames. The women were enlisted to cut long strips of rawhide from cattle skins for the bindings. The plan was to make at least 15 pair, wait for a clear day, and then cross the deep snow to freedom. As work was being done, Graves made the rounds of the camp to recruit candidates for the snowshoe party.

In preparation for this expedition, Stanton wrote a note to Tamzene Donner at the Alder Creek camp and asked her to send him a pound of their "best tobacco" and the loan of a pocket compass that they could use on the trek. Tamzene complied, but these things were the last things on her mind. George's arm was now badly infected, and his general health was getting worse - much worse. Her brother-in-law, Jacob, was on his deathbed, and three of the party's younger men

- Sam Shoemaker, Joseph Reinhardt, and James Smith - were nearing death themselves.

Eliza Donner later wrote, "Three of our men became dispirited, said that they were too weak and hungry to gather wood, and did not care how soon death should put an end to their miseries. The out-of-door duties would have fallen wholly upon my Aunt Betsy's two sons and on Jean-Baptiste and on my crippled father, had the women lost their fortitude. They, however, hid their fears from their children, even from each other, and helped to gather fuel, hunt cattle, and keep camp."

But as the cold December days passed at the Alder Creek camp, there were simply no more cattle to be hunted. Wood became hard to find. The only things to eat were roasted mice and a broth of the glue that formed in cooking pots when cattle hides were boiled. It was repulsive, but it did help to ease the gnawing pangs of hunger.

For now.

As the calendar ticked closer to Christmas, emigrants began to die. At the lake camp, the first to perish was Baylis Williams, the Reeds' albino hired man who, because of his sensitive eyes, had slept in the wagons by day and tended the fires at night. He had been poorly throughout the entire long journey, and by the time the company became trapped in the two camps, he was suffering from fevers, diarrhea, and what seemed to be pneumonia. Bayliss had stayed beneath a blanket in the Reeds' half of the cabin. His sister, Eliza, and Margaret Reed had tended to him, but there was little food, and he had no interest in eating. Near the end, malnutrition caused delirium and when he died on December 15, he was crazed with fever and was crying out in pain. He was only 25-years-old.

Virginia Reed later described it, "Baylis Williams, who had been in delicate health before we left Springfield, was the first to die; he passed away before starvation had really set in."

William Graves, Franklin Graves' 17-year-old son, and John Denton were given the chore of cleaning and clothing the corpse. Baylis was wrapped in a sheet and buried with little ceremony in a snowdrift not far from the cabin.

At almost the same time the emigrants at the lake were burying Baylis Williams, four people died at the Alder Creek camp. The first was Jacob Donner, a kind man who had lived in his older brother's shadow for most of his life. He was 56 and described as a "slight man of delicate constitution." He had long seemed older than his years, causing many to assume that he was the oldest brother, even though he was four years younger than George.

Even his niece didn't realize how old he was. Eliza later wrote, "Uncle Jacob, the first to die, was older than my father, and had been in miserable health before we left Illinois. He had gained surprisingly on the journey, yet quickly felt the influence of impending fate, foreshadowed by the first storm at camp. His courage failed. Complete prostration followed."

Neither his wife, Betsy, nor his children could revive Jacob. Even George failed. The journey had sapped his strength and despair had exhausted what energy he had left. He simply gave up and waited to die.

His family gathered around him at the end. He died while sitting at a table in his shelter, with his head in his hands. George, racked with pain, rallied to be by his brother's side, just as he had been his whole life. The two men had moved from North Carolina to Kentucky, Indiana, Illinois, and finally across the plains and mountains to a snowbound camp next to a river and had never been far apart.

"My father and mother watched him during the last night and the following afternoon, helped to lay his body in a cave dug in the mountain side, beneath the snow," Eliza remembered.

George Donner, who had buried two wives before marrying his beloved Tamzene, tried to use his one good arm to carve his brother's icy tomb. But before the snow had covered Jacob's body, three of the young men in the camp - Sam Shoemaker, James Smith, and Joseph Reinhardt - died one after another.

Eliza wrote, "The snow had scarcely resettled when Samuel Shoemaker's life ebbed away in happy delirium."

Like most of the hired hands and teamsters in the company, little is known about Shoemaker. He was about 25-years-old and had come to Illinois from Ohio. In September, Shoemaker had pitched in and helped William Eddy repair one of the Reed family's wagons. At the end of his life, Eliza later reported, he imagined that he was a boy again in his father's house and believed that his mother had built a fire and offered him his favorite foods. He spoke of those visions and then died at peace with a smile on his face.

James Smith, a Reed teamster, was also about 25 and died peacefully. Eliza said that his death was like "a tired child falling asleep."

Joseph Reinhardt, though, did not die peacefully at all. For days before his death, the 30-year-old mumbled and wept - sometimes in English and sometimes in German - about his life. Members of George Donner's family remembered the man's passing, especially his final words about the death of Jacob Wolfinger at the Humboldt Sink.

In a letter that she wrote 30 years later, Leanna Donner said, "Joseph Reinhardt was taken sick in our tent, when death was approaching and he knew there was no escape, he made a confession in the presence of Mrs. Wolfinger that he shot her husband; what the object was I do not know."

Eliza also recalled the man's death. "When Joseph Reinhardt's end drew near, his mind wandered, and his whitening lips confessed a part in Mr. Wolfinger's death; and my father, listening, knew not how to comfort that troubled soul. He could not judge whether the self-condemning words were the promptings of a guilty conscience, or the ravings of an unbalanced mind."

But the dying declaration from a guilty conscience was soon accepted as the truth. Dorthea Wolfinger was present when Reinhardt confessed and, finally, she knew what had happened to her husband. He had not been killed by Indians - as Reinhardt and Augustus Spitzer claimed - he had been killed for his gold. George Donner assured the young widow that once the emigrants were rescued, there would be an inquiry to ensure that Spitzer was held accountable for his part in the murder.

At this point, however, it had become more a question of if the emigrants were rescued, rather than when.

Even George Donner was not optimistic. He was the last adult male in camp and with a wound that would not heal that prevented him from doing any work, he was worried. Some days, he could barely stay on his feet. Tamzene and his recently widowed sister-in-law, Betsy, were almost single-handedly keeping everyone alive.

Luckily, Milt Elliott and Noah James, two teamsters from the Truckee Lake camp, had arrived at the Donners' camp just before Jacob and the others had died. They helped to bury the four men, gathered firewood, and showed Jean-Baptiste how to probe the deep snow and look for the carcasses of cattle. It was Elliot who had brought the letter to Tamzene from Charles Stanton, asking for tobacco and her compass. They also told the Donners about the planned snowshoe expedition and invited anyone who felt strong enough to come with them to the lake camp.

None of them could make the trip.

The two men had planned to return to the other camp as soon as they could, but a blizzard began the day they arrived, followed by another wave of storms. Finally, there was a break between storms and Elliott, eager to join the snowshoe party before they departed, left the Donner camp. James, who had been one of George Donner's drivers, stayed behind to help them search for food.

It was no easy task, as Eliza wrote, "It was weary work, for the snow was higher than the level of the guide marks, and at times they searched day after day and found no trace of hoof or horn. The little field mice that crept into camp were caught and then used to ease the pangs of hunger. Also pieces of beef hide were cut into strips, singed, scraped, and boiled to the consistency of glue, and swallowed with an effort; for no degree of hunger could make the saltless, sticky substance palatable. Marrowless bones which had already been boiled and scraped were now burned and eaten, even the bark and twigs of pine were chewed in a vain effort to soothe the gnawings which made one cry for bread and meat."

There were no pleasant memories to be made in this snow-covered prison that the Donners found themselves in. It was only about survival. The children who did survive would carry the trauma of that winter with them their entire lives. Never again would winter be a time of snowball flights, sleigh rides, and building snowmen. It would always be a menacing and loathsome season and one anticipated each year with dread.

And, of course, those who did not survive that brutal winter went to their graves with their last moments being those of pain, cold, isolation, and starvation.

Milt Elliott made his way back through the deep snow to the lake camp, only to find that the snowshoe party had left without him.

The snow had finally stopped - at least for a few days - and the brave emigrants recruited by Franklin Graves and Charles Stanton were eager to leave while the sky was clear. As much as they had wanted that compass from Tamzene Donner, they believed they could rely on their own sense of direction to get them over the mountains and into the Sacramento Valley. Believing that Elliott and James had been delayed by the recent storms, they left before the men returned.

The party that left Truckee Lake on the morning of December 16 was made up of 17 emigrants - ten men, five women, and two children. The youngest were brothers Lemuel Murphy, 13, and William Murphy, 10. The others were all in their twenties and thirties. The evidence of how desperate they had all become is proven by the fact that four of these men were fathers, leaving behind their families, and three of the women were mothers, who entrusted their small children and babies to other women in the camp.

The party included Franklin Graves, his two oldest daughters, Mary Ann and Sarah, and Sarah's husband, Jay Fosdick. Amanda McCutchen, whose husband, William, had left the company in September and hadn't returned from Sutter's Fort, left her baby, Harriet, behind to be cared for by Elizabeth Graves, who stayed in camp with her seven youngest children. Besides the two young Murphy boys, there were others from the Murphy family in the group, including their older sister, Harriet, the widow of William Pike, and Sarah, with her husband, William Foster, who had accidentally killed Pike. Harriet's baby son and the Fosters' two toddlers had been left with their grandmother, Levinah Murphy. William Eddy was also part of the group, although he had a difficult time leaving behind his wife, Eleanor, and his young son and daughter. But Eddy knew, perhaps better than anyone, that the trip was necessary. In addition to getting help, it also meant there were less people in camp who needed to be fed.

Sarah Graves Fosdick, who joined the snowshoe party with her husband, Jay, was only 18-years-old when her expedition to California began.

There was also a half dozen of the single men in the party - Patrick Dolan, Charles "Dutch Charley" Burger, Charles Stanton, the two Miwoks Luis and Salvador, and Antonio, the teamster who had been hired at Fort Laramie.

When they left camp on that cold morning, each of them was dressed as warmly as possible in layers of linen shirts, wool coats, pants, cloaks, socks, and hats. The women pulled on flannel undergarments beneath loose trousers that had been made from their dresses. Scarves and wraps covered their necks and the lower parts of their faces, a hopefully protection against the wind. Each also had a makeshift backpack and a blanket.

Divided among them were an ax, a rifle, a few pistols, three horns of gunpowder, ammunition, and all the tobacco they had left. Chewing on a plug of it - man or woman alike - helped ease stress and hunger pangs. The rations for each person consisted of some tea or coffee, a bit of sugar, and about eight pounds of stringy dried meat. It was meant to be food for six days - the time they believed it would take them to cross the mountains and reach the foothills on the other side.

Between the 17 members of the party, there were only 14 pairs of snowshoes. Milt Elliott had one pair and he had used them to get to the Donner camp. The two young Murphy brothers and Dutch Charley, without snowshoes, brought up the rear so they could walk in the footprints left by the others - which turned out to be much harder than they thought it would be.

After tearful goodbyes, the party trudged away through the snow around the north side of the lake. They left camp with great determination, but likely had no idea if the daring plan would succeed. They only knew that danger - and perhaps death - awaited them on the snow-clogged trail ahead. Far from the camps they had been calling home and far from their families, they walked off into the wild.

More than 33 years after that fateful winter, Charles McGlashan wrote a book about the Donner Party and in it, he coined the name that the snowshoe party would always be remembered by - the "Forlorn Hope."

He named them from the German phrase *verloren hoop*, which means "lost troop." It referred to a group of soldiers who are sent out on a deadly mission with little chance of success.

It turned out to be the perfect description.

The party made little progress the first day. It soon became apparent that for every step an adult took on snowshoes, the Murphy boys had to take two steps. The short and stocky Dutch Charley also found walking tough. His thick legs pushed deep in the snow and buried him to his hips. He was soon gasping for breath and, like the two boys, falling behind. The rest of the party had to stop several times and wait for them to catch up. They were only halfway around the lake and had to stop for the fourth time. This time, William Foster agreed to lead 10-year-old William Murphy and Dutch Charley back to the lake camp.

William Murphy was a young boy when he ventured out with the Forlorn Hope but was unable to keep up without snowshoes. He was taken back to the lake and it turned out that his inability to walk in deep snow likely saved his life.

He'd catch up to the others when they made camp. Lemuel Murphy wanted to keep going and he promised to keep up.

The first night's camp was made just beyond the head of the lake. They could practically see the camp they'd left behind. At that rate of travel, they knew their meager rations would never hold out, so they were determined to get farther the next day. William Forster easily caught up with them, surprised they had not traveled a greater distance. He joined the others at the fire, where Franklin Graves was improvising a smaller pair of snowshoes for Lemuel Murphy from some packsaddles they'd found on the trail.

The next morning, the group - now with 15 members - walked on, serious about traveling more than the four miles they had managed the previous day. They made it - pushing on for six miles over a snowpack that was often between 12 and 16 feet deep - and made camp west of the summit.

Mary Ann Graves would later recall the party's second day of travel: "We had a slavish day's travel, climbing the divide. Nothing of interest occurred until reaching the summit. The scenery was too grand for me to pass without notice, the changes being too great; walking now on loose snow, and stepping on hard, slick rock a number of hundred yards in length. Being a little in the rear of the party, I had a chance to observe the company ahead, trudging along with packs on their backs. It reminded me of some Norwegian fur company among the icebergs. Well do I remember a remark one of the company made here, that we were about as near to heaven as we could get."

And perhaps that was true, but they were still a long way from where they needed to be.

They camped that night, too exhausted to go any further. The snow at their campsite was 12 feet deep but they made a fire by cutting down two green saplings and placing them parallel on the snow a few feet apart. More green wood was placed across them to make a platform and then the fire was built on top of this. So long as the fire was kept going through the night, the emigrants would stay warm, even with only one paltry blanket each.

The emigrants returned to their snowshoes at first light, reaching the open, downward slope on the other side of the summit. Most of them had frostbitten hands and feet. The high altitude often had them panting for air. The rising sun felt good on their faces, but as the day passed, the sun became just as dangerous as the bitter cold, wind, and snow. They traveled only short distances at a time, blinded by the glare of the sun on the snow. Franklin Graves became snow-blind, but his daughters and son-in-law helped him to stay on track, and he quickly recovered.

Charles Stanton, though, did not. He was in far worse shape. At first, his eyes turned red and watery, followed by an uncontrollable twitching before swelling shut. The pain was almost unbearable, and he began to fall behind. He would often wander into the camp each night after sunset. Since he was the one among them who knew the trail best, his misfortune affected all of them. They were fortunate to have the two Miwok guides along with them.

They pressed on, trudging over and through snow that was at least 11 feet deep. It had started to snow on and off, adding to the difficulty of the journey. Since leaving the lake, they had seen no game and their rations were almost gone. They were also starting to doubt the route now that Stanton was unable to see. They feared they were

An illustration of the Forlorn Hope snowshoe expedition, attempting to get help for those stranded in the Sierra Nevadas.

lost and wished that Milt Elliott had returned in time with the compass.

There was hunger, there was fear and, finally, terror. They began to hallucinate as they dragged themselves through the snow, hearing strange sounds, eerie cries in the woods, and seeing drifting shapes that appeared and then disappeared before their eyes. They began to believe that the ghosts of those who had died on the expedition were calling to them. As they made camp each night, they built the fires high so the flames would keep away the spirits, whether they were real or hallucinations.

On December 21, William Eddy was digging in his backpack and discovered a package that his wife had concealed there before the party left camp. He unwrapped a half-pound of bear meat from the grizzly he'd killed earlier in the month. There was a note with the package that said the meat might save his life. It was signed, "Your own dear Eleanor." In the past, Eddy had always shared the game he shot with others in exchange for borrowing a weapon or for the loan of an ox to drag a carcass back to camp. This time, though, he couldn't do it - not unless he absolutely had to. Eddy planned to keep the meat to himself and make it last as long as possible.

On that morning - the sixth day, the last for which the party had food - Mary Graves noticed Charles Stanton sitting near the smoldering fire. He was smoking his pipe and staring into the flames with blinded eyes. They were preparing to move on, and she asked him if he was coming with them.

He turned toward her voice. "Yes, I am coming soon," he replied. They were the last words that the emigrants ever heard Stanton speak.

When they left, Stanton, with the smoke from his pipe swirling upward, seemed lost in thought.

The Forlorn Hope started away, guided rather uncertainly by the two Indians, who had only been on the trail once and then there had been no snow on the ground. As it turned out, the Indians took them in the wrong direction, which would cost them many painful days and miles. They didn't realize just how lost they were for more than a week.

Later that night, in camp, the emigrants used up the last of the beef strips and wanted expectantly for Stanton to show up and warm himself around the fire - but he never came.

The next day, they had traveled only about a mile before a heavy snow began to fall. They stopped and made camp and spent the day with no food, again waiting for Stanton. They watched for him, but the small man still did not come staggering in through the snow.

By nightfall, they gave him up for dead.

The courageous man, who had performed acts of kindness and made heroic attempts to save his starving fellow travelers, was never seen again. He was a gentleman and a hero to the very end, sacrificing his own life rather than endanger the lives of his friends by holding them back.

Two years later, Phillip Stanton, one of Charles' brothers, wrote, "He was always noble and generous, even to a fault - always ready and willing to share his last cent with his less fortunate brothers and sisters. This characteristic he bore from his earliest childhood. He was ever ready to sacrifice his own interest and means to the welfare of others, and hence it is not so surprising that he should be found willing to yield up his life in endeavoring to relieve his perishing companions."

The following day, December 23, they climbed the barren, rocky surface of Cisco Butte, the highest point in the area, and tried to get their bearings. Without Stanton to guide them, they had to plot their own route. The easiest way appeared to be toward the south, where the mountains looked less fierce than in other directions.

It turned out to be the wrong direction.

Back at the lake, where the last of the livestock had been eaten, the miserable families gnawed on boiled hides and bones seasoned with pepper.

They were doing anything they had to do to stay alive. For some, it was only a matter of saving themselves. They were prepared to do whatever they had to so they could live, no matter the cost to others. For others, they also fought for the lives of their families, rallying repeatedly to make certain their children, husbands, wives, brothers, and sisters were saved.

But with each passing day, survival became more difficult.

Time itself seemed to have frozen solid for the stranded emigrants. Days and nights were simply light and darkness. With each hour that passed, they became a little more tired, a little more cold, and a little more hungry. There was only so much more they could take.

Patrick Breen was the only one at the lake camp who knew what day it was, thanks to his journal. He wrote about ordinary events each day. He faithfully scratched notes about everything that happened, from Dutch Charley's failure to keep up with the snowshoe party to Milt Elliott's return with the compass that had been so urgently needed. He also wrote of Elliott's news about the death of Jacob Donner and the other three men at the Alder Creek camp.

The emigrants were stunned by the deaths of four men from their company, but were not surprised to learn about Reinhardt's deathbed confession to murdering Jacob Wolfinger. There was no rush to punish Reinhardt's accomplice - Augustus Spitzer was lingering near death in the Breen cabin.

Patrick Breen continued to make careful notes in the days that passed - about the weather, the snow, his kidney stones, and about all the time he had spent in prayer.

If there was ever a time to pray, this was it.

There were plenty of prayers being sent to the heavens out on the west flank of the Sierras from the Forlorn Hope - but it didn't seem that anyone was listening.

They prayed as they trudged through the snow. They prayed around the fire at night, hoping for sleep. They had prayed for Stanton's return. They prayed for the snow and rain to end. They prayed that the Miwoks would find their way. They prayed that some game would cross their path so they could eat. None of their prayers were answered.

Desperation was starting to set in. Surrounded by snow, they were chilled to the bone and starving. They shivered constantly, which generated heat, but also caused fatigue that lowered their body temperatures.

Any exposed skin was in danger of frostbite in the cold mountain air. At first, the skin became dullish white and went numb. If the frostbite went deeper, the soft tissues hardened and became immovable. To treat frostbite, the accepted remedy of the day was to rub fingers and hands with snow. In truth, though, this was the worst thing they could have done because it could cause permanent damage. Drinking plenty of water was a much better treatment because it increased the blood's volume, which helped to prevent frostbite to start with.

But that was another problem. Humans can only survive a few days without water, but can go weeks without food. They had to have water and, luckily, the snow provided a vast water supply. By checking the color of their urine in the snow, they could determine if they were becoming dehydrated. The darker it was, the more water they needed. They consumed cups of melted snow, unaware that eating snow instead of melting it to liquid lowered the body's core temperature and caused further dehydration.

The party struggled on, limping aimlessly through a series of snowstorms that fell on them like heavy curtains of lead. For several days, they were totally without food, and shortly after, a series of gruesome events began -- events that would earn the Donner party a unique place in the annals of the West.

The painful journey continued on Christmas Eve, when another foot of snow fell. They struggled along for two or three miles before finally sitting down to hold a meeting.

All the men, except for William Eddy and the two Indians, wanted to give up and return to the camp at Truckee Lake. Eddy exploded. This was a foolish and suicidal plan, he told them, and in their weakened state, they would die before they made it back. The women were all vehemently opposed to this idea. They would, they said, go through with the mission or die.

Mary Graves wrote in a letter in 1874, "Some of those who had children and families wished to go back but the two Indians said they would go on to Captain Sutter's. I told them I would go, too, for to go back and hear the cries of hunger from my little brothers and sisters was more than I could stand. I would go as far as I could, let the consequences be what they might."

By then, the Forlorn Hope had gone without any food for three days. Eddy had his secret stash of bear meat, but it was almost gone. It had been more than two months since any of them had eaten a full meal and were now showing the classic signs of starvation. They grew weaker and often felt dizzy as their fat reserves and muscles became more depleted. The simplest tasks became difficult. Their hands and feet were swelling because their circulation had slowed. With continued weight loss, the emigrants would experience painful constipation, followed by diaherrea, and then their immune systems would collapse.

They were already experiencing irregular heartbeats, muscle pain, insomnia, and hallucinations. When they did sleep, they dreamed of consuming massive quantities of food. They were miserable and knew that death was coming - a death marked by cardiac arrest and a loss of all bodily functions.

They needed a way to survive. It's unclear how many of the emigrants reached the solution that was proposed next, but we do know that Patrick Dolan, the formerly carefree bachelor, put the unthinkable into words.

He proposed that one of them might die to save the rest. It was unthinkable - the ultimate taboo - and yet, it made sense.

Members of the Forlorn Hope fell silent. How would the decision be made? Dolan proposed that they draw lots to determine who might be killed so that the others could eat, but William Foster opposed this plan, not wanting to take the risk that he might draw the bad lot.

Eddy offered a compromise, suggesting that two of the men take revolvers and shoot it out until one of them died. This sporting proposition was also voted down. Eddy then spoke up again and suggested that perhaps they should let nature take its course and continue walking until someone died. After some argument, the others agreed, and they staggered on into the storm for another few miles.

Weary and disturbed, they slowly marched on. They were all so exhausted that they found it difficult to keep their balance. They took a step at a time, floundering in the snow and trying to catch their breath. There was little or no talking - there was nothing left to say.

Their only purpose now was to walk until one of the weaker ones fell dead. Staggering through the snow, shielding their faces from the fierce wind, they must have been hoping that one of them would fall soon.

They didn't go far before stopping for the night. They were simply too tired and too cold to go any farther. The snow and wind made it almost impossible to get a fire started. When the flame at last caught, the travelers piled on enough wood to make a blazing bonfire. Even though they had nothing to cook at least they could be warm.

But one of them did not enjoy the fire for long.

Antonio, the cattle herder, lay in an exhausted slumber near the fire and in his sleep, he flung out an arm and his hand landed in the hot coals. Eddy saw it happen but was too tired to move and help the sleeping man. He thought sure that the heat from the burns would rouse Antonio, but he didn't wake up. He was so bone-weary and in such bad shape that he continued to sleep. His flesh began to burn, and this was more than Eddy could bear. He dragged himself forward to pull the unconscious man from danger. When Antonio flung out his arm again, Eddy realized that it was no use to try and help him. Antonio died without ever awakening from what, under normal circumstances, would have been excruciating pain.

The first of the Forlorn Hope was dead.

Less than an hour after the young man's death, another storm of wind, snow, and hail swept down upon the camp. More wood was piled onto the fire and it became so hot that it began to eat its way down into the snow, devouring the blazing logs and the platform of green wood that had supported it. When the fire disappeared, it became apparent to all of them that they would die before morning without heat.

A new fire was started but it was difficult to keep going because the supply of dry wood had run out. One of the men took the party's lone hatchet and went to cut more wood. But as he chopped at a log, the head of the hatchet flew off and was lost to the depths of the snow. It was impossible to find in the darkness of the storm, even if he had managed to summon the strength to dig for it.

This left the emigrants no choice but to wade out into the snow and tear off any dead branches or green boughs that could be used for fuel. Without a log platform for the fire to rest on, the fire melted the snow and sank beneath the surface.

The emigrants were forced to crouch around it with their feet in ice-cold melted snow. They knew that the fire would soon sputter out in the water so a few of them stood the half-burned foundation logs on end and rebuilt the fire on top of it. At this point, one of the Indians stood up to get closer to the warmth, and clumsy with cold and weariness, lurched against the new platform. The rickety structure fell over and the fire hissed out in the icy pool of water in which the party was standing.

This was the end, they thought. This was how they would all die. Despair set in and most began to pray for a merciful death - except for William Eddy and the women.

Eddy, always resourceful, persuaded his companions to try a trick that he had heard about from someone on the trail. He prodded them all out of the pit made by the fire and made them spread their blankets on the surface of the snow. They then sat on their blankets in a tight circle with their feet in the center while Eddy dragged himself across the circle and spread other blankets over them. He then slipped into the circle himself, and the blankets, with the snow that fell on top of them, formed a snug, insulating tent that held in their body heat and kept them warm. It was simple enough to do, but some of the emigrants were so apathetic that it took Eddy nearly an hour to bully them into position.

Franklin Graves, the oldest member of the party, had been growing weaker throughout the evening and he now told Eddy that he was dying. His two daughters, Sarah and Mary Ann, were by his side and with his last words, he told them that he was prepared to die and asked them to tell their mother and the other children how much he loved them. He also urged his daughters to eat his body when he was gone. He knew that it was the only way that they could survive.

His corpse was laid in the snow next to the frozen body of Antonio. The shrieking wind drowned out the cries of the two young women who had just watched their father die a terrible death.

The emigrants remained beneath the blanket tent for the rest of the night, protected from the storm and the cold. The sun rose the next day, Christmas morning, but the storm didn't stop and neither did the dying.

The emigrants who managed to doze off were awakened by the

deranged screaming of Patrick Dolan. He had become delirious from hypothermia and starvation and began to cry and babble incoherently. As he raved, he thrashed about beneath the blankets. Eddy and the others tried to calm him down, but then he pulled off his boots and most of his clothing and shouted to Eddy to follow him down to the settlements --- they would be there in just a few hours, he promised. The other emigrants were frightened, unaware of the compulsion of people in the final stages of hypothermia to strip off their clothing as they are overwhelmed by the sensation of extreme heat against their skin.

With great difficulty, the others managed to overpower Patrick and subdue him. He thrashed about as they held him down until eventually, his energy exhausted, he became quiet. He drifted into death, his companions later said, looking as he was enjoying a calm and pleasant sleep.

In the morning, the party finally emerged from the makeshift tent. Except to relieve themselves or help move a body, they had been trapped in the shelter for nearly 36 hours. The snow was still falling outside.

Eddy tried to start a fire using gunpowder as tinder, but his cold hands were clumsy, and a spark caused his powder horn to explode, burning his face and hands. Amanda McCutchen and Sarah Foster were also burned, but not seriously. The burns did not stop Eddy from creeping out from under the tent later that afternoon. The storm had passed and as he looked around, he discovered a huge, dead pine tree standing nearby. Using some scraps from the cotton lining of Harriet Pike's coat as tinder, he started a small fire with sparks from flint and steel and soon was able to set fire to the pine tree. The emigrants lay down around the burning tree to enjoy the warmth and were too weak and uncaring to dodge the big, burning limbs that began falling in their midst. Luckily, no one was injured.

As the day wore on, the survivors huddled under their blankets close to the fire, half-crazed with hunger, but unable to take that final step toward cannibalism.

Finally, late that afternoon, they gave in. The body of Patrick Dolan, who had no familial ties to anyone else in the party, was butchered. Their knives cut strips of flesh from his arms and legs and the meat was skewered on sharpened sticks. Unable to look one another in the eye, they began to roast and eat strips of flesh from Dolan's body.

Only Eddy and the two Indians, overcome by guilt and grief, refused to take part in the feast. The others dried what they did not eat and saved it for later. Within days, Eddy and the Indians, now almost mad from a lack of food, surrendered and ate some of the meat.

Those members of the Donner Party were not the first or the last people to resort to cannibalism to avoid death. It was considered "savage behavior," but it occurred more than society wanted to admit. The brutal winter of 1609 at the Jamestown colony of Virginia came to be known as the "Starving Time." When hundreds of the colonists perished, the survivors were forced into cannibalism. Long before the Donner Party became stranded in the mountains, officers and crews of ships practiced the "custom of the sea," that was separate from maritime law. It allowed the practice of cannibalism among shipwrecked survivors, by the drawing of lots to see who is to be killed and eaten so that the others might survive.

The Forlorn Hope did not resort to cannibalism because they wanted to - it was either eat the dead or die.

The depleted survivors stayed at this site for the next four days and more death followed. Sarah Murphy Foster and Harriet Murphy Pike tried to feed a little of Dolan's flesh to their little brother, Lemuel, but he could not eat. Just the day before, he had been just as desperate for food as the others. When a mouse had run out of its winter hole and scurried across the snow, several of them tried to catch it, but it was Lemuel who snatched it up. He stuffed the squirming mouse into his mouth and ate it alive.

He was no longer the young boy who tried to share his food with others at the lake camp. As he became more delirious, he thrashed about and even tried to bite the arms of his sisters, screaming, "Give me my bone!" But as night fell, he grew quiet. His pulse weakened and his breathing became shallow. He grew steadily weaker and then died in the early morning hours with his head in Sarah's lap.

Sarah would remember that moment for the rest of her life and would think of her little brother who died at what the emigrants would come to call the "Camp of Death."

13. STARVATION CAMP

The survivors of the Forlorn Hope - now five men and five women - spent the final days of 1846 regaining their strength at the Camp of Death. One after another, the bodies of Patrick Dolan, William Graves, Antonio, and Lemuel Murphy were dismembered with knives and either roasted or dried to save for later. Smaller pieces of flesh were cooked immediately, while livers, hearts, and lungs were extracted, dried over the fire, and packed away for safekeeping.

Those who did the butchering made every effort to make sure that no one ate the flesh of a family member. Everyone ate the meat from the single men, Antonio, and Dolan. The Graves daughters refused to go near their father's corpse, just as Lemuel's sisters and brother-in-law avoided his body.

But this did nothing to save them from mental anguish.

One evening, Sarah Foster was sitting by the fire, grieving the loss of her little brother, and looked up to see others across the fire roasting meat on sticks. Sarah suddenly realized that she was watching her friends eating her beloved Lemuel's heart. She became hysterical. Her husband gathered her in his arms and led her away.

Many years later, the survivors seldom spoke of their forced cannibalism - some denied vehemently that it ever occurred at all - but there was no denying that, for the members of the Forlorn Hope, the deaths of their companions had quite literally saved their lives.

They left the Camp of Death on December 30, and although rested by the layover and fortified by the first food they'd had in a long time, they were shadows of their former selves. The emigrants looked like living skeletons and were also in great pain as they tried to walk. Their frostbitten feet were so swollen that the skin cracked and burst. They wrapped strips of blankets and rags around their bloody feet, but the pain was nearly unbearable. They made it only four miles that first day.

They walked as if they were resigned to dying. When William Eddy, hiding his own fear and pain, tried to cheer them up, they responded only with sighs, tears, and moans. The women regained some of their spirit, but the other men continued to sulk.

At least they had food when they made camp that night. They removed a dried piece of meat carved from the dead and roasted it over the fire.

The next day, December 31, the party managed to make six miles. Somehow, they had accidentally blundered back onto the trail that Charles Stanton had started them on. The Indians had confessed to Eddy a few days earlier that they were lost, but he chose not to tell the others, believing they had no choice but to continue. But while the party was back on the right track, it was the most terrifying portion of the journey so far. They walked along the edges of icy, rock-strewn cliffs and crossed ravines on fragile bridges of snow. They teetered precariously on their clumsy snowshoes, but their luck held out. After what seemed like an eternity of picking their way along, they reached a high point on the ridge and paused to take in the view. In the distance, to the west, they could see the vast, green plain of the Sacramento Valley. The sight gave them hope, but their joy was dampened by the mountains and canyons that still lay in their path. Subdued, but not broken, they continued.

When they made camp that night, they left a trail of blood in the snow behind them. Still cursing the loss of their hatchet, they set fire to a pine tree again. Basking in the warmth, they ate the last pieces of their lost companions. No one spoke. There was nothing to say - they knew what had been done to stay alive.

There was still a long march ahead of them before they reached the end of the trail.

Back at the camp at Truckee Lake, many of the emigrants had given up on the snowshoe party. There had been so many other attempts to reach safety, why would they believe this one would work when the others had failed? They had been gone for two weeks. That was enough time to get help, they believed. The snowshoers had also perished.

There was no open talk of cannibalism at the lake camp - not yet anyway. However, the possibility of it was weighing on many of their minds. Patrick Breen noted in his journal, "The prospect is appalling but hope is in God."

Since the departure of the Forlorn Hope, life had only become worse at the Truckee Lake and Alder Creek camps. They were still trying to survive on the boiled down animals hides and leather. The marrow had been picked clean from the slaughtered animal bones and they had been boiled so many times for soup that they were soft enough to be chewed. Only a few families at the lake still had scraps of meat. The Donners, dug in at Alder Creek, had none. They relied on field mice for nourishment.

Eliza Donner had grim memories of the holiday season that year. "Snowy Christmas brought us no glad tidings, and New Year's Day no happiness. Yet, each bright day that followed a storm was one of Thanksgiving, on which we all crept up the flight of snow steps and huddled about on the surface in the blessed sunshine, but with our eyes closed against its painful and blinding glare."

At Truckee Lake, after a night of rain, another snowstorm began on Christmas Day. Patrick Breen was again suffering unbearable pain from his kidney stones but was able to lead his family in Christmas prayers. When finished, he sent his sons, John and Edward, out in the storm to bring back wood for the pile. It was becoming increasingly difficult to find. The snow outside was nearly nine feet deep. Trees that were cut down in the snow had to be dug out before they could be used. This was exhausting to those still capable of working, draining what little energy they had left.

Most of the emigrants in camp were eating broth made from boiled hides and bones on Christmas Day, but Levinah Murphy surprised everyone in her cabin by adding an oxtail to the cookpot that she had been saving for the occasion.

After supper, Levinah put all the babies left in her charge to bed. Later, young William, who had tried to go with the snowshoe party but had to return to camp, was reading to Levinah when she suddenly became ill. This was the start of her decline, although she continued to care for the children. She also prayed each day for her family members with the snowshoe party, unaware, of course, that Lemuel had died, and his body had been used for food.

The most memorable Christmas dinner took place in the Reeds' half-cabin. Virginia described the meal. "The misery endured during those four months in our little dark cabin under the snow would fill pages and make the coldest heart ache," she wrote. "Christmas was near, but to the starving its memory gave no comfort. It came and passed without observance, but my mother had determined weeks before that her children should have a treat this one day. She had laid away a few dried apples, some beans, a bit of tripe, and a small piece of bacon. When this hoarded store was brought out, the delight of the little ones knew no bounds. The cooked was watched carefully, and when we sat down to our Christmas dinner mother said, 'Children, eat slowly, for this one day you can have all you wish.' So bitter was the misery relieved by that one bright day that I have never sat down to a Christmas dinner without my thoughts going back to Donner Lake."

Two additional feet of snow fell on Christmas night and put a damper on what little cheer had been conjured up. On December 28, Dutch Charley Burger died in Lewis Keseberg's lean-to shelter. He had not been well since he had dropped out of the snowshoe party. His health had deteriorated after his return to camp and he died at the age of only 30. After putting his body out in the snow, Keseberg and Augustus Spitzer, not far from death himself, divided up the dead man's personal possessions - something that likely does not surprise the reader.

Spitzer took his coat and rain slicker and Keseberg pocketed $1.50 in cash, along with a gold pin, two silver watches, three boxes of percussion caps for guns, and a straight razor.

Burger was the first person to die at Truckee Lake since Baylis Williams, the Reeds' hired man. Patrick Breen made a brief note about the death in his journal, right after the weather report.

The following day, another monstrous storm swept over the mountains and hit the camp. Virginia Reed wrote, "The storms would often last for ten days at a time, and we would have to cut chips from the logs inside which formed our cabins, in order to start a fire. We could scarcely walk, and the men had hardly the strength to procure wood. We would drag ourselves through the snow from one cabin to another, and some mornings snow would have to be shoveled out of the fireplace before a fire could be made. Poor little children were crying with hunger, and mothers were crying because they had so little to give their children. We seldom thought of bread, we had been without it so long. Four months of such suffering would fill the bravest hearts with despair."

On New Year's Day 1847, Margaret Reed was forced to do something that those who knew her would never have thought her capable of doing. The last real food her children had eaten had been the surprise Christmas "dinner," which it was hard to call an actual meal. Margaret had done her best to find food and had even traded her husband's watch and a Masonic medal for some meat. She refused to give up now. She put on a coat, slipped a knife into her pocket, and told the children she was going to take the family's beloved dog, Cash, for a walk. He dutifully followed Margaret out the door. She let him run in the snow and then she picked him up and stroked his fur - and then sliced his throat with the knife. Margaret wept as she cut up his body.

The children cried for hours. Margaret did her best to make them understand why she'd done it and Virginia, who had loved Cash almost as much as she'd loved her pony Billy, tried to help her mother. She gently explained to the younger children that Cash had to die so that they could keep living. And they did live on Cash, for nearly a week. They ate his flesh, his entrails, head, paws, and tail. Spare pieces were used to make soup.

When Cash was gone, though, Margaret had no idea what the family would eat next. They had nothing but hides and a few hidden pieces of dried meat. Their chances of survival - without help from somewhere - were slim.

And that's when this remarkable woman - who had once suffered from debilitating stress migraines, had buried an infant son before leaving Springfield, and had encouraged her husband to leave the wagon train to save his life and now had no idea if he was alive at all - devised a daring plan. Margaret refused to sink into lethargy like others in the camp. She would protect her family by sheer force of will and would form her own rescue party to find a way over the Sierras. Others in the camp were critical of her plan, but Margaret's mind was made up. She believed the risk was worth taking.

As her daughter Virginia wrote, "Time dragged slowly along on short allowance of food, but we were simply starving. My mother determined to make an effort to cross the mountains. She could not see her children die without trying to get them food."

Margaret knew that her three youngest children would not be able to keep up on the trail. She went from cabin to cabin asking other emigrants to look after her children until rescue parties arrived at the lake. In a rare show of cooperation among those in this party, she found some who were willing to help. Patty, who was 8, went to stay with the Kesebergs. James, 5, went to the Graves family and Thomas, 3, was left with the Breens. Margaret's party would be made up of Virginia, the faithful friend and teamster, Milt Elliott, and Eliza Williams.

On January 4, the party left camp with only a small ration of dried meat. The three children being left behind cried and begged Margaret to take them with her. Virginia would later write about how difficult it was for her mother to say goodbye to them. "It was hard to leave them, but she felt it must be done. She told them she would bring them bread, so they were willing to stay, and with no guide but a compass we started - my mother, Eliza, Milt Elliott, and myself. Milt wore snowshoes and we followed in his tracks."

Unfortunately, Margaret's expedition only lasted five days - and most of that was time being spent to get back to the lake camp. Eliza managed to make it through the first day before freezing temperatures and snow convinced her to go back. The others went on, but when Elliott's compass began to behave erratically, they became lost. By then, they had frostbite and knew going on would likely kill them.

Virginia painted a vivid picture of the horrible excursion. "Often, I would have to crawl up the mountains, being too tired to walk. The nights were made hideous by the screams of wild beasts heard in the distance. Again, we would be lulled to sleep by the moan of the pine trees, which seemed to sympathize with our loneliness. One morning, we awoke to find ourselves in a well of snow. During the night, while in the sleep of exhaustion, the heat of the fire had melted the snow and our little camp had gradually sunk many feet below the surface until we were literally buried in a well of snow. The danger was that any attempt to get out might bring an avalanche upon us, but finally steps were carefully made, and we reached the surface. My foot was badly frozen, so we were compelled to return, and just in time, for that night a storm came on, the most fearful of the winter, and we should have perished had we not been in the cabins."

By the time the weary trio returned to Truckee Lake, they were exhausted by four nights in the snow. They were also homeless. Assuming they would not be back, other families had taken the hides from the roof of their cabin and used them for food. Elliott took Eliza with him and headed to the Donner camp on Alder Creek, Virginia moved in with the Breens, and Margaret found a place with the Kesebergs.

The arrangement didn't last long, though. Soon the Breens invited Margaret and all the Reed children to move in with their family, merging 15 people into one cramped space. There wasn't much room to move around, but it was warm. And, as Virginia had written, it was just in time. The next great storm dumped so much snow on the camp that the cabins were completely buried.

The final days of the year brought the Forlorn Hope no more cheer than Christmas had. They continued plodding through canyon country but were soon out of food. All the meat they had brought with them from the Camp of Death was gone. The only good news was that there were no new storms, and no one had died.

They spent the next day negotiating a canyon. They worked their way down the slope by squatting on their snowshoes and sliding down to the bottom, usually ending up in a snowdrift. The fierce cold had frozen the water below, the Bear River, and they were able to cross without difficulty. Climbing up the other side of the canyon was a nightmarish task. For the first 50 feet or so, the hunger-weakened men and women had to cling to cracks in the rock to keep from tumbling back down the steep slope. As it became less vertical, they dug their snowshoes into the snow and stair-stepped upwards, moving slowly and carefully as they climbed.

They spent the next two days crossing a broad plateau over mostly level ground. The snow was firm enough that they could walk on it without their snowshoes.

Things began to look more encouraging on January 3. The snow remained firm and it looked like they were coming down from the upper elevations as oaks could now be seen among the conifer trees. When they camped that night, the snow was only three feet deep, which was a cause for celebration. Believing that they would no longer need their snowshoes, they toasted the rawhide strings that held them together and ate them for dinner. Eddy also cooked a pair of worn-out moccasins and shared them with the group. There was no nutritional value to the "meal," but the act of chewing and filling their stomachs eased their hunger pangs a little.

With their boots nearly worn out - and, in some cases, turned into makeshift meals -- they wrapped more strips of cloth around their feet. Frostbite had already taken a toll. When they walked, they left bloody footprints behind them in the snow. The Miwok, Luis, was in such poor condition that one of his blackened toes simply fell off.

Jay Fosdick was also falling apart. He moved slowly and was unsteady on his feet. When he started to fall behind, his wife, Sarah, slowed to walk with him. The others often had to wait for them to catch up. Eddy and Foster realized that before long, Fosdick would be able to go no farther and they would have fresh meat again.

Before that could happen, though, William Foster began acting strangely. He was starving and starting to show signs of delirium. Instead of waiting for Fosdick to die, he proposed killing the two Miwoks and eating them. As far as he was concerned - like far too many Anglo settlers - the Indians weren't important, and their lives didn't count.

But William Eddy was violently opposed to this. The two men were his friends. When others voiced agreement with Foster's suggestion, Eddy argued with them, but finally realizing that he could not change their minds, he warned Luis and later that night, the two Miwoks slipped out of camp and wisely disappeared into the night.

The next morning, Eddy devised a new plan to get food for the group. They still had their flintlock rifle and a meager supply of ammunition, so Eddy became determined to take the gun and go hunting. If he had some luck, he knew he could save the lives of his remaining companions, but if not, they would be no worse off. The party was now out of the snow and on bare ground and he had seen signs of game.

When he mentioned his plan to the women, however, they wept

A photograph of Forlorn Hope
survivor Sarah Foster, taken
many years after the events of
this book.

and begged him to stay with them, perhaps believing that he planned to abandon them in the wild. But Eddy's mind was made up. Harriet Pike threw her arms around his neck and implored him not to go. The others joined in, convinced that he was not coming back. The once-beautiful and now-emaciated Mary Ann Graves decided to accompany Eddy; she was the only one left who was strong enough to keep up with him.

The others - William and Sarah Foster, Amanda McCutchen, Harriet Pike, and Jay and Sarah Fosdick - waited and prayed they would return for them.

William and Mary Ann walked through the forest for more than two miles, keeping an eye out for signs of deer. Eddy was an experienced hunter and when he eventually found a place where an animal had laid for the night, he burst into tears. When he explained what he had found to Mary Ann, she also began to weep.

They continued prowling through the forest and, not much farther into the woods, they saw a large buck. Eddy raised the gun but found to his dismay that he was too weak to aim it. As much as he tried to hold it still, the gun wavered back and forth and dipped too low to fire. He changed his grip and tried again but failed once more. He heard Mary Ann sobbing behind him. Eddy whispered for her to be quiet and she explained, "Oh, I am afraid that you will not kill it." Then, she fell silent.

Once more, Eddy lifted the rifle to his shoulder and raised the muzzle above the deer. As his weak arms started to let it fall, he pulled the trigger with the deer in his sights. The rifle thundered and the deer leaped three feet into the air and stood still. Although Mary feared that he had missed it, Eddy knew that his aim had been true. The deer dropped its tail between its legs, a sign that it was wounded, and began to run. Eddy and Mary limped after it until it crashed to the ground about 200 yards away. The animal was still alive when Eddy reached it and he cut its throat. Mary fell to Eddy's side and the two famished survivors drank as the animal's warm blood gushed out.

They rested a bit and then rolled the carcass to a spot where they could butcher it. They built a fire, and with their faces still covered with blood, ate part of the deer's liver and some of its other organs for supper. They gorged themselves on the heavy meat and that night, for the first time in many days, they enjoyed sleep without dreaming of food.

During the night, Eddy fired his gun several times to alert their companions. At the camp, Fosdick heard the first crack and knew what it meant. "Eddy has killed a deer!" he weakly cried. "Now, if only I can get to him, I shall live."

But Fosdick's hopes were not meant to be. He died during the night and Sarah, his wife for less than a year, wept as she wrapped his body in their one remaining blanket and lay down on the bare ground to die next to her husband.

But death did not claim her.

She survived the frigid night, and, in the morning, she felt better. To her horror, though, she saw two of her traveling companions -- likely William and Sarah Foster, although no records ever stated for sure -- approach her campsite, convinced that she and her husband had both died during the night. They planned to help themselves to not only their flesh, but to their jewelry, money, and watches, too. Embarrassed at finding Sarah still alive, they turned back to their own campsite and there they met Mary Ann and Eddy, who had emerged from the forest with venison for everyone.

As Eddy dried the remaining meat on the fire, Sarah and the two Fosters returned to Jay Fosdick's body. Sarah gave him one last kiss and retrieved a few keepsakes from his coat.

The Fosters had other plans.

Despite Sarah's entreaties, the Fosters, now numb to the atrocities they were committing, cut out Jay's heart and liver before her eyes and took his arms and legs, the meatiest parts of the body. Sarah, now a young widow and only 22 years old, made a little bundle of her valuables and returned to the campfire with the two people who had just callously butchered her husband. Uncaring, they skewered Jay's heart on a stick and began to roast it in the fire as Sarah looked on. When she could stand it no more, she fled to Eddy's campsite a short distance away.

William Eddy had just arrived in camp with as much meat as he and Mary Ann could carry and yet the Fosters chose to dine on human flesh. This act went beyond cannibalism for survival and became eating human flesh by choice.

Some would argue that the Fosters had lost their minds on the tortuous trail. And it would get worse.

Over the next couple of days, the survivors made it to the north branch of the American River and crossed. They had to climb another steep canyon wall on the other side, but when they made camp that night, they were cheered by the fact that the weather was good and sat down peacefully to eat the last of the venison. Eddy made a speech mourning their lost companions -- tactfully avoiding any mention of cannibalism.

After supper, William Foster took Eddy aside. From the time of the first hardships experienced by the group, Foster had been strangely unhelpful and weak, unable to make decisions on his own and totally dependent on Eddy. He had also continued to behave strangely, depressed, and mentally unbalanced. He asked for Eddy's approval to kill and eat Amanda McCutchen. His excuse was that she was a nuisance and could not keep up, bu, in truth, he had acquired a taste for human flesh and deep down, his guilt over it had likely driven him mad.

Eddy was shocked and revolted by the suggestion. He told Foster that Amanda had a husband and children and besides, she was one of their companions and depended on them for protection. Foster continued to argue until Eddy told him sternly that he was not going to kill her. Foster than turned to the sisters, Sarah Fosdick and Mary Ann Graves. He pointed out that neither of them had children and Sarah no longer had a husband. At that, Eddy walked away in disgust and returned to the fire. He loudly warned Sarah and Mary Ann of Foster's plans for them in front of the rest of the group.

At that, Foster became angry and said that he did not care what Eddy said -- he could do whatever he wanted. Eddy, losing patience, challenged Foster to settle their differences on the spot. He grabbed a large stick, banged it on a log to see that it was solid and then tossed it to Foster, ordering him to defend himself. Sarah Fosdick gave Eddy her late husband's knife, and he went for Foster as quickly as his weakened condition would permit. Eddy was ready to kill him when all the women except for Sarah --two of whom Foster had just proposed to kill and eat -- seized Eddy and dragged him to the ground. They took his knife away, but luckily, Foster just stood there in a daze.

When Eddy recovered, he warned Foster once more that he would kill him if he ever again showed the slightest inclination to take the life of any member of the expedition. If anyone were to die, it would either be Foster or himself, he said. And they would settle the question in a fight to the death, since Foster had never been willing to draw lots, which Eddy had once believed was the only fair way of selecting a victim.

On January 8, they left the campsite and continued their journey. They had walked about two miles before coming on the bloody tracks of the Indian guides who had wisely deserted them some time back. Foster, now obviously deranged, vowed that he would track down the Indians and kill them. Another mile or two farther, they found the two men on the trail, near death. Eddy wanted to let them die in peace, for they could not last more than an hour or two, but Foster, now in an almost manic state, refused to wait. He shot the two Indians in the head and then butchered their bodies. Then he cut the flesh from their bones and dried it over the fire.

That night, Eddy ate only dried grass, refusing to eat the flesh of the Indians. And from that night on, only Foster's wife would camp with him. The others kept a safe distance away, with one of them always remaining on watch, afraid of what the man might do next.

As they continued and passed through the forests, they saw numerous deer, but Eddy was so weak that he could no longer aim and fire the rifle. He was still living on nothing but handfuls of grass, as he refused to touch the meat taken from the Miwoks. They all staggered as they walked and were so weakened and weary that they could only travel for a quarter mile or so before they had to stop and rest. The slightest obstacles would cause them to stumble and fall. A cold rain began to fall on the wretched wraith-like figures, and it did not stop.

At last, on January 12, they found an Indian trail through the forest and decided to follow it. That afternoon, they reached a Miwok village in the foothills. When the ragged and gaunt party first came into view, the Miwok were terrified and believed they were ghosts. Then they heard their pleas for help and burst into tears of pity when they saw the skeletal figures.

They hurried to bring the survivors their winter food of acorn bread and soup, but the emigrants' stomachs were unable to handle much. The Indians knew the starving survivors could die from eating too much so they kept the portions small, even when the emigrants begged for more. Eddy was unable to stomach the bitter acorns and was forced to go back to eating grass.

The next day, the village chief sent runners ahead to a nearby encampment and told them to take care of the travelers and to have food ready for them. An escort accompanied them as they continued their journey. Two Miwoks were assigned to each member of the party so they could be supported and helped along. In this way, they passed from village to village toward the white settlements.

On January 17, they reached a village. One of the men there had collected a large handful of pine nuts for them. For some reason, after eating them, Eddy felt miraculously restored and with this new energy, he pushed his comrades on. But the others gave out after a mile and collapsed on the ground, ready to die. The Indians were greatly distressed but were unable to get them to continue.

All Eddy could think about was his wife and children starving in the mountains and he resolved to make it through or die trying. One of the Miwoks agreed to accompany him to the closest white settlement but after five miles, Eddy's strength gave out. Luckily, another Indian passed by and with the promise of tobacco, agreed to help Eddy continue. They managed to make it another five miles before Eddy collapsed again, this time for good. His strength had completely failed, but the Indians half-carried him along, dragging his bleeding feet on the ground.

At about a half hour before sunset, Eddy, starved beyond the point of recognition, came upon the home of a settler named Matthew D. Ritchie, who had arrived late in the fall of 1846 and had built a cabin in which to spend the winter. Several other emigrants, who planned to claim their own spreads in the spring, lived in other winter quarters nearby. Ritchie's daughter, Harriet, heard a noise outside of the house and went to the door. There, she saw two Indians supporting a hideous-looking bundle between them. The shape lifted its head and, speaking in English, asked her for some bread. Harriet burst into tears and let the Miwoks bring Eddy into the house. Her family put him to bed, fed him, and heard his story. He remained in bed for four days, too exhausted to even turn over.

Harriet Ritchie ran immediately to the neighbors with the news of starving travelers on the trail behind Eddy. The women collected all the bread they could spare and added sugar, tea, and coffee to go with the beef that had been recently butchered. The men rode back and forth between the cabins bearing messages and collecting food. Four men took backpacks loaded with as much food as they could carry and set off on foot, for they did not want to risk their horses by riding at night. They were guided by the Indians and found the remaining members of the Forlorn Hope around midnight. One man stayed up all night cooking for them. Eddy had warned the rescue party not to give them too much to eat, but the survivors wept and begged for food so pathetically that they could not deny them. As a result, gorging caused all of them to vomit.

In the morning, more men came with food, this time on horseback. They had no trouble following the trail for the last six miles were marked by Eddy's bloody footprints. The rescuers could not believe that he had covered such a distance, amazed at what had to have been a superhuman effort. By this time, the party had been on the trail for 33 days.

That night, the rest of the Forlorn Party was brought down to the settlements. The ordeal was now over for what was once a party of 17 men and women. Eight of them - all men - had died in the mountain snow. Only Eddy, Foster, and five of the women had made it out alive.

They now told the harrowing story of the Donner Party, a company that had been the source of rumors for weeks, and that story began to spread across the country.

While the outside world was learning about the fate of the snowbound Donner Party, nothing was changing for those still trapped in the two miserable camps in the Sierra Nevadas.

Daily life had become both tedium and horror. They no longer had any idea of the passage of days or what might be happening in other places. They knew nothing outside of their day-to-day existence, the nerve-shattering cold, and the always-present ravenous hunger.

Probably more than the other emigrants, the mothers at the lake camp felt a complete disconnection from everything but the basic needs of their children. Their families received all the compassion they had left. There was nothing left for anyone else. Like wounded animals, these women were only concerned with their children's survival.

There were exceptions to this, however. At the Breen cabin, which was overflowing with the Breen and Reed families, Peggy Breen ruled the home. She was especially frugal when it came to handing out the precious dried oxen meat that she kept hidden away. Fixated on keeping her own children alive, she could not afford to be passing out meat to others. Several of the emigrants who tried to coax her into giving them a little of the meat found that out. Still, she did have a softer side. She loved the Reed children, especially Virginia. When Peggy noticed that Virginia could not tolerate eating animal hides, she slipped the girl a few pieces of meat. Patrick Breen was also a comfort to Virginia, who missed her father desperately. She and James had always been very close and now Patrick filled his role as her protector and spiritual guide.

Virginia later wrote, "I often went to Catholic church before leaving home, but it was at Donner Lake that I made a vow to be Catholic. The Breens were the only Catholic family in the Donner Party and prayers were said aloud regularly in that cabin, night and morning. Our only light was from little pine sticks split up like kindling wood and kept constantly in the hearth. I was very fond of kneeling by the side of Mr. Breen and holding those little torches so that he might see to read."

Patrick, still urinating blood and enduring the nausea and pain from his kidney stones, found comfort in reading his Bible and praying - even though his prayers always seemed to go unanswered.

There were few other books in the lake camp besides Breen's well-worn Bible. Many of the emigrants had left their books in the desert to lighten the load, but some held on to favorite titles. Virginia read and reread a thick book about the life of Daniel Boone that winter, likely taking the girl's mind off her own misfortunes.

Little Patty Reed was often comforted by the tiny wooden doll that she could not bear to part with when the emigrants left most of their personal possessions behind. She had kept the doll hidden in her clothing ever since. She and the other children were expected to devote some part of each day studying the only schoolbook they had, *English Grammar in Familiar Lectures* by Samuel Kirkham, but they also loved to hear Virginia, or their mother, read to them in the evening.

These were the few bright spots the emigrants managed to embrace. Occasionally, Patrick Breen would note in his journal, "very pleasant today sun shining brilliantly renovates our spirits praise be to God." But overall, there was not enough food, the weather was terrible, and the sun that Patrick praised was usually swallowed by clouds before noon. There was no way of knowing if James Reed, William McCutchen, or the snowshoe party were still alive or had ever made it to Sutter's Fort.

It was the dark lining on the occasional silver cloud that chewed apart any hope or optimism that might be struggling to bring peace to the emigrants in the camps.

Levinah Murphy - a family matriarch at only 37 - was dying. She had been in decline since falling ill over the Christmas supper of boiled bones. She still tried her best to care for the little ones, including three granddaughters left in her care when her own daughters went to find help, but she had lost her vision from snow blindness and was becoming mentally unstable from the stress and strain of keeping her remaining family alive. Her moods swung wildly in every direction, causing her to laugh one moment and weep the next. It was all she could manage to make a thin soup from snowmelt and some coarsely ground wheat flour, which she spoon-fed to the nursing baby, Catherine Pike.

Levinah became even more distraught when her son, John, who had turned 17 in camp, also started to fail from malnutrition. At one time he had been a strapping young man and now he could no longer eat hides and had become delirious and difficult to control, just as his brother Lemuel had been just before he died with the Forlorn Hope party.

At the camp along Alder Creek, the Donners and the others kept watch, always hoping that a relief party was on the way. Sometimes, Jean-Baptiste would climb a tall pine tree to scan the snowfields for any sign of movement. There was no food left in the camp except for beef hides and field mice. Jean-Baptiste and Noah James continued to search for the cattle they knew were buried somewhere nearby. Eliza

Donner later wrote, "They made excavations, then forced their hand poles deep, deeper into the snow, but in vain their efforts - the nail and hook at the points brought up no sign of blood, hair, or hide."

George Donner, not completely incapacitated by his infection, was still hanging on, thanks to Tamzene's constant care.

Occasionally, some of them - usually the young, single men - made trips back and forth between the two camps, checking on everyone's well-being and hoping to find some morsel of food. That search was rarely successful. One January morning, Jean-Baptiste, along with John Denton and Eliza Williams, the Reeds' servant girl who had been brought to Alder Creek by Milt Elliott, made a trip to the lake. Eliza was getting desperate because she was unable to digest the boiled hides. She begged Margaret Reed for food, but there was nothing to give her. They were all in desperate straits. As Patrick Breen noted in his journal, Margaret had to send the girl back to Alder Creek "to live or die on them."

On January 22, snow began to fall just after sunrise. It increased in strength and ferocity all the next day and into the night. It had become a full-blown blizzard. Breen declared it "the most severe storm we have experienced this winter." Over the next few days, snow occasionally stopped, raising everyone's hopes, but then it started again, as fiercely as ever.

During a break in the storm on January 27, a spectral Philippine Keseberg came to the Breen cabin with tragic news. Three days before, as the wind was howling outside the Murphy cabin where the Breens were now living, Philippine's baby boy had died. Born on the trail, the infant was less than six months old. The boy's father, still hampered by his infected foot, was shattered by the loss, but was unable to walk to help his wife place the little corpse into a snowbank.

According to Philippine, conditions at the Murphy cabin had badly deteriorated. Levinah seemed to be going insane and needed all the help she could get to take care of the babies that had been left with her. Three of the Murphy boys - Landrum, Bill, and Simon - were seriously ill, although Landrum was the worst. Philippine did not believe he would last much longer.

She was right. Just a few days later, Landrum was lying on the floor of the cold cabin next to his two sick brothers and not far from Lewis Keseberg, also sick and in mourning. Levinah managed to pull herself together enough to go and beg the Breens for a small bit of food to revive her son. But no one at the lake was feeling charitable. That same day, Elizabeth Graves had called in the Reeds' loan from many weeks before and took some of the family's hides as payment. But Peggy Breen would not turn away a grieving mother. She graciously gave Levinah a small piece of meat.

Years later, William Murphy would recall, "I remember the little piece of meat; my mother gave half of it to my dying brother, and he ate it, fell off to sleep, with hollow death-gurgling snore, and when I went to him, he was dead - starved to death in my presence."

Three months had now passed since the emigrants had been trapped in the snow. There was no relief in sight as February began. In fact, things were going to get worse.

On February 2, another day of snow and cold, Harriet McCutchen, the one-year-old child of William and Amanda McCutchen, died without her parents. Her father had gone for help long before and her mother was with the snowshoe party. Lovina Graves had promised to care for Harriet, along with some of the other children, but when Elizabeth began a rapid physical and mental decline, the children suffered along with her.

As if the cold and hunger were not bad enough, Harriet's entire body had become infested with lice. As they crawled all over the child, feeding on her blood, their bites caused such intense, painful itching that her agonizing cries could be heard all over camp. Many years later, Patty Reed would still believe she could hear "the terrible screams of that poor little one." Near the end, Lovina tied the baby's arms to her sides to keep her from continually scratching her arms and legs until they bled. The screaming got louder and then suddenly stopped.

Harriet's death was a mercy.

Two days later, on February 4, another toddler died. There was nothing left of little Margaret Eddy but skin and bones. Her mother, Eleanor, like the other young nursing mothers, was so sick and starving that she just had no more milk to give. When the baby died, Eleanor died with her. She lingered for a few days and then she was also gone. John Breen later buried the mother and daughter together in the snow.

The next day, Augustus Spitzer - one of the killers of Jacob Wolfinger - died after weeks of suffering. He had become an outcast who probably would have been hanged if the men had enough strength left to do it. Instead, he was ignored by everyone, but Lewis Keseberg and he died on his own. Later, some of the emigrants would recall that just before he died in the dark morning hours, he pleaded with Peggy Breen to put a morsel of meat in his mouth so that he could die in peace. She ignored him and went back to sleep.

On February 9, Patrick Breen noted that "Milt at Murphys not able to get out of bed." Milt Elliott, the Reeds' teamster and friend, had moved back from the Donner camp and was staying with the Murphys. He had collapsed on the floor and could not get up. He was one of the most beloved members of the entire company and a young man that the Reeds considered part of their family. His health had gradually declined, but he refused to call attention to it, and no one had noticed. His only wish was not to die alone. He tried to move into the Breen cabin to be close to Margaret Reed and the children, but Breen was concerned about the man's condition and did not want his children to witness his death. Margaret, who Milt had always called "Ma," helped him make his way to the Murphy cabin, where he died. He was only 28.

Virginia later wrote about him. "When Milt Elliott died - our faithful friend, who seemed so like a brother - my mother and I dragged him out of the cabin and covered him with snow. Commencing at his feet, I patted the pure, white snow down softly until I reached his face. Poor Milt! It was hard to cover that face from sight forever, for with his death our best friend was gone."

But life, such as it was, went on at the lake camp.

Virginia Reed knew how close death was to all of them. "One night we had all gone to bed - I was with my mother and the little ones, all huddled together to keep from freezing - but I could not sleep. It was a fearful night and I felt that the hour was not far distant when we would all go to sleep - never to wake again in the world. All at once I found myself on my knees with my hands clasped, looking up through the darkness, making a vow that if God would send us relief and let me see my father again, I would be a Catholic."

Finally, God decided to answer one of the desperate prayers from the emigrants trapped in the snowy nightmare of the Sierra Nevadas.

14. "DO YOU COME FROM HEAVEN?"

James Reed, the subject of his daughter's fervent prayer, was still in California. He had been busy since early November when he and William McCutchen had tried to reach the trapped emigrants but had to turn back because of impassable snow. After that fiasco, Reed had kept fighting against the laws of nature and against the bothersome war in Alta California.

There was nothing more important to Reed than reaching his family and the rest of the Donner Party. At the same time, he was trying to carve a place for himself in California. As he tried to carry out a rescue mission, he was also paving the way for his family's new home in the West.

I can only believe that he had no idea of the dire situation that his family was facing in the Sierras. I'd like to think that if he had, he would've been a little less worried about becoming an important man in California. To believe otherwise is to believe James Reed was a monster.

Reed was painfully aware that he had made enemies among others in the Donner Party. He could have been the party's most effective leader, but what was perceived as his arrogance and his overbearing personality worked against him. So did his insistence that they take the Hastings cutoff, which arguably had directly caused the predicament the rest of the party was still in. Even though the emigrants who went along with Reed had done so of their own free will, that decision had not made him any friends - and neither had the death of teamster John Snyder.

Perhaps to make up for his failing along the trail, Reed looked for property in California while he also planned a rescue mission back to the Sierras.

On October 20, Reed, Edwin Bryant, and Reverend James Dunleavy, a Methodist minister, drafted a petition to seek land rights on an island in the Sacramento River. The men knew each other from the trail. Bryant, of course, was the leader of the pack mule train and Dunleavy had been asked to leave the Russell Party early on because his 140 head of cattle were slowing down the wagon train. The document was sent to Washington Bartlett, the chief magistrate in Yerba Buena, soon to be an important city called San Francisco. Bryant had discovered the island while exploring territory around Sutter's Fort. He recorded his favorable impressions of the river and the potential of the land, which could be used for grazing and farming.

Acting solely based on Bryant's word, Reed invested in land he had never seen. Reed did it again after returning from the first failed rescue mission. He desperately wanted to save his family, but since opportunities had arisen, he kept making deals and conducting business.

Again, because I believe that he didn't know the danger the stranded emigrants were in - although he probably should have - Reed was not dissuaded when John Sutter told him that any further rescue attempts would have to be postponed until after the winter storms had passed. There were few men in the area who were available for relief parties. Most of them had gone off to fight in the war.

But Reed didn't want to sit around waiting for winter to end. After discussing it with Sutter, he left the fort to seek help from Commander Joseph B. Hull, the senior military authority and highest-ranking naval officer at Yerba Buena. Reed rode south with a letter of introduction to Hull, as well as official papers allowing him "and three companions to pass to Pueblo de San Jose without molestation."

When he arrived, he discovered a problem - the Yerba Buena side of the bay was occupied by Mexicans.

Forced to wait in San Jose, Reed put his time to use looking for a new home for his family. Founded in 1777, El Pueblo de San Jose de Guadalupe was the oldest settlement in Alta California. The town, with irregular streets lined with adobe houses, was strange and exotic to Reed. Most appealing was the town's proximity to the sea, the many freshwater sources, and the open land for farming.

Reed made many friends and sought out people from Illinois or those he'd met on the western trail, using this network of contacts to look for opportunities. He also wisely used some of his secret stash of money to pave the way.

One of his most important new contacts was John Burton, a Massachusetts man who had left New England behind for San Jose in 1830. He married a Mexican woman, assumed the title of captain, and now made his living as a rancher and merchant. Among the Anglo residents, Burton was known as the "pioneer of pioneers," but the natives called him "Capitan Viejo," the Old Captain. In October 1846, he was appointed the first Anglo *alcalde*, or magistrate, of San Jose. Although he had little formal education, he was regarded for his honesty and had won the confidence of both the new settlers and the native population of the area.

Reed was soon a regular visitor at the Juzgado, the hall of justice that housed the courts, the jail, and Burton's office. This was where Burton listened to citizen's grievances, settled disputes, and carried out the duties of his position. One of those many duties was approving requests for purchasing property.

Reed had arrived at the perfect time. There were huge changes coming to the government, legal system, and daily life of the region. The war with Mexico, at least in Alta California, was coming to an end and Burton would not remain chief magistrate for much longer. He used his free time to grab as much land as he could by filing claims with the accommodating Captain Burton. It's doubtful if Burton even bothered to read the documents before he gave them his blessing. On a few occasions, Reed turned in petitions to purchase land in the names of family members and friends and forged their signatures on the paperwork. They were all approved.

In the middle of buying land, Reed also had to deal with an important obligation he'd committed himself to weeks before - his promise to serve in the military. When he had first arrived at Sutter's

Fort, he, Edwin Bryant, William Russell, George McKinstry, Lilburn Boggs, and several others had signed a document that committed them to helping the American forces in the war against Mexico. The only caveat was that he be given a chance to rescue the Donner Party emigrants. That mission had failed and now he had to accept his commission as a lieutenant in the army.

Reed was hesitant. He remained hopeful that he could get to Yerba Buena and find enough men for a rescue party, but Captain Joseph Maria Weber, a stern, German-born commander of U.S. volunteers at San Jose, would not allow it. "You must fight," he told Reed. "If you don't, it will be murder. You have been in the Black Hawk War, and you understand fighting. Besides, unless you help us, you'll never reach Yerba Buena alive. Every gringo's life is in danger."

Reed accepted that Weber was right. He could participate in the war and, in so doing, expedite the assembly of a rescue team. Helping other Americans would also be of benefit in the future. Reed took command of 33 mounted riflemen - later described as a "motley band of sailors, whalers, and landsmen" - and went to war. By most accounts, his short time as a lieutenant went well. He cut a fine figure leading his men on routine patrols through the countryside and the forests.

His one problem was with Jotham Curtis, the emigrant from Missouri that Reed and McCutchen had stumbled across during their failed rescue attempt. Reed said Curtis and his wife had "hailed us as angels" when they encountered their starving in the snow at the foot of Emigrant Gap. He and McCutchen had shared the couple's supper of roasted dog and later led them to safety at Sutter's Fort.

But en route to the fort, McCutchen and Curtis had argued about the couple's slow pace of travel. Curtis decided that he now had a grudge against Reed, too. He suffered the defiant Curtis's abusive tongue and, neither patient nor forgiving, Reed finally had enough. Curtis was discharged from further military service for insubordination and failure to follow orders.

That winter, Reed and his soldiers stayed on the move. While scouting, they lived off the land, making few friends among the natives, who were angry about the massive land grab by Anglo newcomers.

The Californios had never been happy about Mexican rule and had long contemplated a revolution. Still, they had little reason to be supportive of the American emigrants who wanted to take their land.

The Americans wanted to turn California into an independent territory, like Texas, then make it one of the largest states in the Union. The Mexican War divided the American people. Most supported the conflict - believing in Manifest Destiny - while some important political and public figures considered it a folly. Among the most vocal critics was James Reed's friend and former attorney, Abraham Lincoln. He considered the war immoral and a threat to America's values.

Reed managed to carry out his orders and keep up the morale of his men, even after the weather turned nasty. The long days and nights of riding with hardly any sleep took a toll on the men. Then, at last, Reed and his men were ordered into combat. It was not exactly a battle, but even a skirmish alleviated the boredom.

The incident was triggered by Reed's commanding officer, Captain Weber. Acting with no legal authority, he ordered his junior officers to confiscate as much livestock as they needed to feed the militia that had been recruited from the local American population. Instead of paying cash for the animals, the locals were given worthless scrip. And it didn't stop there. Fueled by aguardiente - a potent brandy made from grapes, apples, or pears - the men repeatedly raided the horse and cattle herds of every ranch between Yerba Buena and San Jose.

When a delegation representing the ranchers asked Naval Commander John B. Montgomery to remove Weber from his post, the request was denied. Montgomery said that Weber had not violated any rules or regulations and he berated the delegation for questioning the integrity of one of his officers.

Weber and his volunteers were also not the only ones who were stealing - or commandeering, if you like - horses and livestock. Lieutenant Washington Bartlett, the naval officer in charge at Yerba Buena, had also scoured local ranches for fresh provisions and stock. He didn't pay for anything either, so the "requestioning" was really nothing more than pillaging. The local ranch owners, including the highly respected Don Francisco Suarez, a former *alcalde* of Yerba Buena whose family had come to California in 1776, lost all patience.

When Lieutenant Bartlett and five armed sailors from the U.S. ship *Warren* came ashore to take more cattle and horses, they rode to Suarez's San Mateo ranch. A large force of men led by Sanchez captured the Americans and held them hostage. This was not an act of defiance against the United States but was in protest of the shenanigans being perpetrated by officers like Bartlett and especially Weber, who was considered to be "the principal culprit of the misdeeds."

On January 2, 1847, an expedition led in part by Weber stumbled over Sanchez and his sizable force of Californios, just west of the mission Santa Clara de Asis. Intending to rescue Bartlett and the sailors, the Americans, including Reed's company of volunteers, backed up by a detachment of U.S. Marines, engaged the Californios at what would be called "The Battle of Santa Clara," or perhaps more fitting, the "Battle of the Mustard Stalks." The site was covered by a large mustard field and the "battle" only lasted a few hours before a truce was called.

Four of the Californios were killed in the fighting while another four men were wounded. The Americans lost one horse and two men were wounded. A treaty was soon signed, and the prisoners were returned.

Reed wrote to John Sutter on January 12 and said, "I am heartily glad that I had such an opportunity to fight for my country... Every man in the fight acted well his part. The reason that there were so few killed was because we could not get close to them. Their horses were fine, while ours were broke down."

It was not, by any means, exactly a patriotic battle to remember.

The Mexican-American War in Alta California effectively ended after the skirmish at Santa Clara. Reed not only emerged unscathed, but his good luck continued. Although his short military hitch had slowed his efforts to assemble a rescue party, the war proved beneficial for him and his family. Soon after Reed returned to San Jose, Naval Lieutenant Robert F. Pinkney appointed him the officer in charge of the Mission San Jose. Years before, it had been one of the 21 missions established in Alta California by Catholic priests to convert and "civilize" the Native American population. However, when Mexico gained its independence from Spain, everything changed. The Mexican government, unable to support their upkeep, secularized the missions and eventually divided up their vast land holdings.

Pinkney had given Reed not only control of the mission buildings but also of the surrounding land, which included orchards and vineyards, some of which had been planted even before the mission was established in 1797. In December, Reed had already filed land claims near the mission for his family. He enlisted men to help plant crops, fulfilling the homestead provisions that stated he had to improve the land. Later, Reed would enter into an agreement that allowed him to lease all the orchards and vineyards, sharing in all the profits from them.

Now the only thing that was keeping Reed from going ahead with plans to rescue his family was his release from military service. On January 26, Captain Weber signed a discharge document and Reed immediately left for Yerba Buena.

In the city, he hoped to raise funds and enlist men for the rescue party. It was already February when he arrived. Reed was unaware that word was starting to spread about the missing Donner Party. On January 16, William Eddy had staggered to safety just ahead of the rest of the Forlorn Hope, but little was printed about the disaster at first. There was only a brief news item in the *California Star*, which had been in operation at the time for only one week. Under a small headline that read "Emigrants in the Mountains," the report did not name the company or any of the people involved, but did say that a party of about 60 had been prevented from crossing the mountains because of a heavy, early snowfall. It also mentioned that John Sutter had provided mules and provisions, but an early rescue attempt had failed. The story ended with a plea:

"We hope that our citizens will do something for the relief of those unfortunate people."

As he rode, carrying a letter signed by friends in San Jose asking the authorities in Yerba Buena to help the stranded emigrants, Reed didn't know that a rescue party had already been formed. He knew nothing of how dire the situation had become in the snowbound camps where people were dying. He didn't know that the Forlorn Hope had made it over the mountains or that they had survived by eating the flesh of their comrades who fell along the way.

Reed arrived in San Francisco on February 1, 1847, just two days after Yerba Buena's new name had become official. At the time, it was a village of no more than 500 people, not counting the Indians, even though they outnumbered every other racial group in California at the time.

The day felt like spring but there was winter weather still coming

San Francisco in the late 1840s

- especially in the makeshift emigrant camps in the Sierras.

Reed started by looking for funding for a snowshoe expedition to find the stranded emigrants. The letter that he carried was addressed to Commodore Robert F. Stockton, but he was away, so Reed called on Captain Joseph B. Hull instead. Reed later recalled, "I presented my petition to Hull, also making a statement of the condition of the people in the mountains as far as I knew; the number of them, and what would be needed in provisions to help get them out. He made an estimate of the expense that would attend the expedition and said that he would do anything within reason to further the object but was afraid that the department in Washington would not sustain him, if he made the general outfit. His sympathy was that of a man and a gentleman."

In other words, good luck, but the military wasn't paying for a rescue party.

Obviously, Reed wasn't giving up. He spent the rest of the day drumming up support. He sought out acquaintances from the California Trail as well as men who had served in the recent military actions. One of Reed's most enthusiastic supporters was Reverend Dunleavy, who he'd first met in the Russell wagon train. Dunleavy was a fellow Freemason, and he was willing to use his influence and oratorical skills to further Reed's cause.

An illustration of the City Hotel in San Francisco in the late 1840s.

Washington Bartlett was another staunch advocate. After briefly being held hostage by the Californios, Bartlett was still the magistrate of San Francisco. He conferred with Captain Hull and then called for a public meeting so that Reed could make an appeal to the people for manpower and financial aid. The gathering was arranged for the evening of February 3 at the City Hotel. News of the event spread quickly.

By the time it started, the popular hotel saloon was crowded with "nearly every male citizen" of the town in attendance, including Sam Brannan, the publisher of the city's first newspaper, the *California Star*.

While he was waiting to take the stage, Reed reunited with a trail comrade, Andrew Grayson, who had been in the Donner Party until wisely opting not to take the Hastings cutoff. Grayson pledged whatever help he could offer.

At 7:00 p.m., there was standing room only. Bartlett welcomed everyone and introduced Reed, who told the story of his family, the families of George and Jacob Donner, and the others they had traveled with on the trail to California. Reed became more emotional than he usually would have. His voice cracked and when he could no longer speak, he sank into his chair, sobbing and allowing tears to run down his face.

James Reed was anything but arrogant on that night.

When Reed faltered, Reverend Dunleavy picked up where the other man left off, spinning the rest of the tale from what he had learned from Reed. Dunleavy told them of the probable fate of the starving company. Unless relief arrived soon, he said, it would be too late.

Dunleavy had only just finished when the saloon erupted in cheers and huzzahs. A mass of men, many of them crying and clutching fistfuls of silver dollars, rushed the stage and handed the money over to a stunned James Reed. It took Lieutenant Bartlett and a few of his Marines to restore order. Committees were quickly appointed, including one to receive donations, and lines formed with donors. At least $800 was collected that night, along with offers of provisions, horses, and mules for a rescue party. In the following days, that amount rose to $1,500.

Just before the expedition was ready to depart, everything came to a temporary halt when a boat sent by John Sutter arrived in the harbor. It carried an urgent letter for Bartlett. It was dated January 19, 1847, and was written by John Sinclair, the magistrate of the Northern District. It told the story of how two men and five women from the snowshoe party had stayed alive by eating the flesh of those who died along the way. Sinclair's letter was based on a letter dictated by William Eddy, who was recovering in a nearby settlement.

Sinclair also reported that a party of able-bodied men was being raised to rescue the remaining members of the Donner Party, and he urged Bartlett to do the same.

The shocking news from Sinclair - and from William Eddy - caused serious concern to Reed and his rescue committee. The condition of the Donner Party was far worse than had been thought. Knowing that another relief party was also being formed, the group in San Francisco decided that more preparation was needed before they left. It seemed wise to recruit additional men and collect more food and supplies. In addition, the second party would establish a base camp along the way for replenishing supplies.

Everyone agreed this was a solid plan, even the anxious James Reed. A rescue would not be as easy as they initially thought - but there was still a chance to be successful. Reed and his friends frantically went back to work. They still needed to be ready to leave within days.

If only they had known the difference that only a few days could make to the struggling and starving survivors of the Donner Party.

While James Reed and his committees were still raising money and putting together food and supplies, a few of the men at Sutter's Fort and the surrounding settlements were preparing to go into the wintry wasteland of the Sierra Nevadas. They were going to try and reach the stranded party as quickly as possible and bring back anyone who was still alive.

Their plans had started almost as soon as the seven survivors of the Forlorn Hope had arrived in the valley. Talk spread among the men who had retrieved them that they needed to get into the mountains and find the rest of the group. There was a lot of talk but not much else at first. Because of a serious shortage of manpower among the scattering of emigrants wintering in the area, it took almost two weeks to find volunteers because so many of the able-bodied men had not yet returned from the war. Even when help was found, provisions were in short supply.

To try and rally men, it was decided that William Eddy should make an impassioned plea. Still weak but much improved after sleep and a few hearty meals, he dictated a letter to Magistrate John Sinclair from his bed. The letter was then given to a Miwok runner who crossed the flooded Bear River on a raft and reached Sinclair's ranch that night. Unfortunately, Sinclair was away for a few days so his wife, Mary, took delivery of the letter. She didn't let the Miwok messenger leave empty-handed. Mary gave him a bundle of undergarments for the women in the snowshoe party.

Mary Sinclair had no intention of delaying the rescue of the Donner Party because her husband was away from the ranch. She took Eddy's letter to Sutter's Fort the next morning and delivered it to Captain Edward M. Kern. He now had the task of enlisting volunteers for the rescue party. He called for a meeting at the fort's armory, but only a few men showed up - mostly emigrants still somewhat fresh from the trail and some sailors who had deserted their ships to work for John Sutter.

By all accounts, Kern was not the best recruiter. He was an epileptic that suffered from many health problems and was not a trained military officer, but an accomplished illustrator who came west

Illustrator, topographer, and military officer Edward M. Kern

to be outdoors and collect botanical specimens. He would have been better off talking about flora and fauna with Tamzene Donner than trying to convince strangers to risk their lives on a dangerous mission.

Kern did his best to describe the importance of the expedition, but he got little interest from those present until he announced that he would make sure the volunteers received $3 per day, which was a good sum at the time. However, when he was pressed for details about how they'd be paid, he admitted that he lacked the authority to pay them - he could only request it. That changed everything. Without a guarantee of payment, only three men stayed at the armory.

The oldest of the recruits was Aquilla Glover, a 40-year-old Kentuckian. He had left Missouri for California in the spring of 1846, with his wife and son, in a wagon train headed by Reverend James Dunleavy, the same man who was now helping James Reed in San Francisco.

Another volunteer was Riley Moutrey, another recent emigrant who had crossed paths with the Donner Party.

The third man to sign up was Joseph Sels, about whom little is known. He was remembered as being "good humored" and was thought to have been a runaway sailor. He signed the rescue party's roster under the name Joe Foster.

Recruitment efforts stalled out until Sinclair returned to the area. After reading Eddy's letter, he recorded the details of the Donner party's plight and sent them to Lieutenant Bartlett in San Francisco. Next, Sinclair and John Sutter jointly announced they would pay each member of the rescue party $3 per day if the U.S. government didn't come through with what Kern had offered. They also provided horses, pack mules, and supplies. When word spread, they wound up with four more volunteers.

One of them was Daniel Rhoads, a strapping young emigrant who'd spent five months on the California Trail with his wife, Amanda, in 1846. They had made the journey with 51 members of their family in a caravan led by his father, Thomas Rhoads, a Mormon elder. It was the largest single-family wagon train to ever make the trek to California.

Rhoads later wrote, "They gave the alarm that the people would all die without assistance. It was 2 weeks before any person would consent to go. Finally, we concluded we would go, or die trying for not to make any attempt to save them would be a disgrace to us and California as long as time lasted."

Daniel Rhoads, a member of the First Relief, photographed in the 1870s, a little less than 30 years after the rescue mission.

Sinclair, knowing his letter to San Francisco would bring more help, set out on foot to the winter settlements to help oversee the preparations for the rescue party. As soon as he arrived, he made sure that as many horses as possible were being rounded up for the expedition. Men, supplies, and mules were on the way.

On January 31, the rescue team from Sutter's Fort was ready. Seven mounted men, leading a line of pack mules left the fort, crossed the American River, and headed north. Aquilla Glover led the slow-moving train, which was forced to wade through heavy mud left by recent rains. It took them two days to reach the winter settlements but when they got there, not a moment was wasted. They immediately joined in with the others already hard at work butchering the half-dozen cattle that had been donated to the cause.

"We killed some beef cattle and dried the meat over fires. We pounded some wheat in Indian stone mortars and ground some in coffee mills," Daniel Rhoads recalled, "We cut the hides of the animals we killed into strips for future construction of snowshoes. Although we worked night and day without intermission, except for short intervals for sleep, these preparations occupied us three days."

One of the volunteers chosen to command the First Relief was Reason Tucker, shown here.

What came to be called the First Relief Party was finally ready to depart. It was a rough and tumble bunch, numbering 14 men. Some of them would be in support roles and not on the team that went all the way to the camps. None of the men were experienced with the mountains, but all of them were game and ready for the danger.

Captain Kern was originally planning to lead the party - which was a terrible idea - and had to be convinced to remain at the base camp to oversee the logistics and make sure that the supply line stayed open. The man must be admired for his bravery.

The two volunteers chosen to lead the First Relief were Aquilla Glover and Reason Tucker, level-headed men who had the respect of everyone in the party. One of Tucker's neighbors, John Rhoads, also joined the team. Daniel Rhoads was his brother, and he was not about to allow him to go without him. Tucker chose his own son, 15-year-old George, to go along and assigned him to guard a stockpile of provisions and spare horses at the base camp in the foothills. Another young man, William Coon, was chosen to help George. There are some accounts that say William was "feebleminded."

Glover and Tucker knew most of the men in the party, including Matthew Ritchie. He had been the one who had taken in the exhausted William Eddy when he came down from the mountains. His 19-year-old son, William, came along to haul supplies to the rescuers as they descended the Sierras.

Some of the members of the First Relief were not emigrants or settlers. Nel Coffeemeyer was a sailor who had deserted a whaling ship. A German named Adolph Brueheim also hired on, as did a French-Canadian named Joseph Verrot. He was an adventurer who had ridden with John C. Fremont to California in 1844. A skilled woodsman, he had helped bring in six of the survivors of the Forlorn Hope.

Oddly, Jotham Curtis also signed up with the party. He had been rescued from the snow by James Reed and William McCutchen but had caused so many problems for Reed during his recent military service that he'd been drummed out.

The last man to join the party was none other than William Eddy, who was still emaciated and feverish from his ordeal. Although Sinclair and others tried to discourage him from going, he was determined to return to the camp where he'd last seen his wife and children. He said that he was going along even if they had to tie him to his saddle, so Glover and Tucker finally relented.

The First Relief was ready to leave on February 4, but while the horses were being saddled, some of them broke away. By the time they were rounded up, a storm moved in and it began to rain. Since most of the day had already been wasted, they decided to wait until the next morning to move out. They were glad they waited - one of the men later described the storm as "torrents accompanied by one of the heaviest hurricanes ever experienced on the Sacramento."

It was still raining on February 5, but they could wait no longer. The string of pack animals was made ready and the volunteers ate a hot breakfast and mounted up. William Eddy was still so weak that he had to be helped into the saddle. He was still hopeful about the rescue, of course not knowing that just the night before, his daughter, Margaret, had died in the camp at Truckee Lake. His wife, Eleanor, died two days later.

The long procession moved out but were still in sight of the settlements when the travel became challenging. The path was a marshy swamp, thanks to the rain. More than once, the pack animals - with heavy loads of food and supplies - bogged down in the mud to their bellies. This required removing all their goods so they could be hauled out by a team of other mules. By the end of the first day, they had only traveled 10 miles but over the next two days, they only traveled 15 more combined.

When the skies finally cleared, the party spent an entire day in the sun, drying out their soaked clothing and provisions. They made scaffolds from tree branches and hung their stores of meat, blankets, and clothes on rope lines to dry. In the morning, they set out again, now only stopping for the horses and mules to eat when they found good grass.

George Tucker later wrote, "The next day, we got to Steep Hollow Creek, one of the branches of the Bear River. The stream was not more than 100 feet wide, but it was about 20 feet deep, and the current was very swift. We felled a large pine tree across it, but the current swayed down so that water ran over it about a foot deep. We tied ropes together and stretched them all across to make a kind of hand railing and succeeded in carrying over all our things."

It did not go well when they tried to get the animals to swim across the stream. The first two horses had to be forced into the water and they were swept away by the current and almost drowned. They managed to get all of them across using the ropes, with men on each side of the river, pulling and guiding them along the way. It took them half the day to get past the river.

"That night we climbed a high mountain and came to snow," Tucker wrote. "Camped that night without any feed for our horses."

The next day, the First Relief made it to Mule Springs, located on a high ridge above the Bear River. In some spots, the snow was four feet deep, making it impossible to go any farther on horseback. They decided to continue on foot and use Mule Springs as the base camp. Some of the men unloaded the pack animals while others cut poles and cedar boughs to build a shelter for the men staying behind and for the provisions.

In the morning, Verrot and William Eddy took the pack animals back down the mountain to the winter settlements. Eddy, desperate to reach his family, objected at first, but then had to admit that he was still too weak to make the journey on foot. The youngest boys, George Tucker and William Coon, made themselves comfortable at the camp. They had to guard the supplies and tend to the extra horses until other people returned.

On February 11, the 10 remaining members of the First Relief left Mule Springs. Each man carried with him a hatchet, a tin cup, and a blanket. Each man also hauled between 50 and 75 pounds of meat and flour - except for Curtis, who said he could carry only half that load. They hiked in single file in the hard-crusted snow, each man walking in the footprints of the man in front of him. When the leader who broke the trail wore down, he took the spot at the back of the line and the next man took his place.

There was no guide to lead them - only the dead reckoning skills of Glover and Tucker. When they had left Fort Sutter, they'd be told that others would be following them so as a way to mark the trail, they set fire to

A temporary camp was set up for the storage of supplies and provisions at Mule Springs, just above the Bear River.

every dead pine tree that they encountered. At the end of every three days - making 15 or 20 miles - they tied a small bundle of meat and hung it up in a tree. This lightened their load and also ensured that they would have food for the return trip.

As the party climbed higher, the snow became deeper. Frustration grew with every step. Eventually, they stopped to craft some snowshoes from pine boughs and rawhide strips. They were clumsy, at best. When the snow became soft and wet from the sun, it stuck so badly to the shoes in heavy clumps that they were useless.

But the First Relief marched on.

On February 13, they reached Bear Valley. The snow was at least 10 feet deep, but the crust was hard, so they didn't sink into it. Curtis led them to the far end of the valley where the remains of his wagon still rested. Back in November, Reed and McCutchen had stashed some food there. Some of the men dug through the snow, but found that the hidden provisions had been ripped apart, probably by bears or wolves.

It was raining when they made camp that night, but the rain turned to snow in the darkness. The sun came out the next morning, but morale was low. Once again, the men stayed in camp to dry their soaked clothing and blankets.

Another day closer to the Donner Party was lost.

Bear Valley, the snowy stretch of wilderness that the First Relief had to cross before they could ascend to the summit and get to Truckee Lake.

Worse, three members of the party announced they'd had enough. Matt Ritchie, Adolf Brueheim, and, of course, Jotham Curtis said they wouldn't go any further. Ritchie, one of the older men in the party, admitted that he didn't think the trek would be so demanding. Brueheim pointed out that he had signed on to go only as far as Bear Valley. And Curtis, after finding nothing he could salvage from his wagon and old camp, said he had no interest in continuing a mission of mercy for people he didn't know.

This sudden change of heart from the three men rattled the other members of the party. They were discouraged, fearing that others might decide to quit, and the mission would end in failure.

That was when Reason Tucker spoke up - he'd guarantee $5 per man, payable on the day of their return, to every man who completed the rescue. The offer, although a generous one, was not enough to change the minds of the three men who were already going to quit, but all the other members of the party assured Tucker they would stay.

Aware that food was waiting for them back at the Mule Springs base camp, the men who were leaving cached most of their provisions for when the party returned with survivors. The three men, free of their heavy packs, left the next morning and the seven remaining members of the First Relief pressed on into the snow.

Storms continued to dump fresh flakes on the trail, but the team kept moving. They burned dead pine trees as markers, left more caches of food for themselves or others to use, and gradually ascended the western slope of the Sierras. When Aquilla Glover and Daniel Rhoads became ill from altitude sickness, others carried their packs.

Just as the party thought the worst was behind them, they were hit by another major snowstorm. But they kept going, climbing another 15 miles closer to the summit. They camped above the Yuba River bottoms and after a good night's sleep, had to face more snow. After a few miles, conditions became so poor that they had to stop and fashion more snowshoes. They climbed higher and Glover and the younger Rhoads brother became sicker. Progress slowed, then stopped. The next day, though, brought clear skies and they kept going.

The First Relief made it almost to the summit on February 17. They had traveled eight miles since their last camp, wading through snow that was nearly 30 feet deep.

The next morning, the seven men looked out from the summit toward the east. They saw no signs of life - only an ice-covered lake and miles and miles of unending snow. They began to descend just after noon and walked the entire afternoon. By the time they reached Truckee Lake, the sun was starting to go down.

They decided to save time by crossing the frozen lake, walking toward the trees where William Eddy had assured them they would find cabins and - hopefully - people who were still alive. They saw nothing, though. No trace of cabins or shelters, just piles and piles of snow.

Daniel Rhoads recalled, "We looked all around but no living thing but ourselves was in sight and we thought all must have perished."

The men began shouting so that anyone alive in the camp would be able to hear them. As they did so, they suddenly saw a movement in a snowbank. A woman emerged from a hole in the snow and as they approached, more people began to appear. They looked like wraiths, skeletal figures that Rhoads and the others would never forget.

The first woman that appeared choked out the words that greeted the rescue party. "Are you men from California?" she cried, "Or do you come from Heaven?"

15. THE SECOND RELIEF

While the members of the First Relief were discovering the starved specters at Truckee Lake, James Reed was anxiously trying to leave Northern California. By this time, his family and the rest of the Donner Party had been trapped in the mountains for four months.

Reed was just finishing his recruitment of volunteers and his gathering of horses and supplies from the Sonoma and Napa Valleys. He wasn't riding alone. After the public meeting in San Francisco, the old trail guide Caleb Greenwood - the man who tried to talk Reed out of the Hastings cutoff - had arrived to help Reed raise volunteers.

Greenwood, 83-years-old, had learned of the Donner Party's predicament from William McCutchen, who was in Sonoma with his own recruitment effort. McCutchen was just about to leave for Sutter's Fort and he sent a letter to Reed with the old guide urging him to hurry to the winter settlements. "There is no time to delay," he wrote.

Reed was well aware of the need to hurry. He also knew that Greenwood's many years of wilderness experience would be invaluable to the effort - and so did Mariano Vallejo, the influential California political and military leader. He had donated horses and mules from his ranch and sent hundreds of dollars for the rescue effort, including a sizable sum to be given to Greenwood for his help.

Reed and Greenwood spent almost two weeks enlisting personnel and gathering horses. At Fort Sonoma, they acquired 10 army horses and five men. Reed bought more horses at the ranch of George Yount and rounded up five more volunteers. He caught up with McCutchen at Yount's ranch. McCutchen was healthy again and ready to leave for the Sierras.

On February 13, Reed and his rescue party started for Sutter's Fort, unaware that a story that criticized the Donner Party had appeared that day in the *California Star* newspaper. It appeared under the headline "Distressing News" and it was written by George McKinstry, one of the bachelor emigrants who had left the wagon train to make better time. He had arrived at Sutter's Fort in October. When poor health prevented him from serving in the military, he accepted an appointment as sheriff of the Sacramento District.

In the article, McKinstry related what he knew based on his own experiences and what he later learned from Reed when he made it to Sutter's Fort. According to McKinstry, the fate of the party was all James Reeds' fault. He said that the decision to carve out a new trail in Utah to avoid the narrow Weber Canyon was the worst error in judgment the party had made.

McKinstry wrote, "Mr. Reed and others who left the company, and came in for assistance, informed me that they were 16 days in making the road, as the men would not work a quarter of the time. They were then some 4 or 5 days travel behind the first wagons, which were traveling slow, on account of being obliged to make an entire route for several hundred miles through heavy sage and mountains, and delayed 4 days by the guides out hunting passes in the mountains; and these wagons arrived at the settlement about the first of October. Had they gone around the old road, the north end of the great Salt Lake, they would have been in the first of September."

McKinstry also described the snowshoe party's "horrid journey over the mountains" and how some of them had "made meat of the dead bodies of their companions" to stay alive.

The editor had used a blunt note to introduce McKinstry's story, summing up the attitude he had toward the Donner Party and their situation. He wrote: "The writer who is well qualified to judge, is of the opinion that the whole party might have reached California before the first snow fall, if the men had exerted themselves as they should have done. Nothing but a contrary and contentious disposition on the part of some of the men belonging to the party prevented them from getting in as soon as any of the first companies."

The newspaper stories spread scores of rumors about the Donner Party, and with each telling, the story changed. Whether Reed ever read what McKinstry wrote about him is unknown. If he did, he never mentioned it, but if he had, I would imagine he would not have taken it lightly.

But on the day the story appeared, Reed was busy with the new rescue party. He was pleased with the men they'd gathered. Greenwood had recruited several mountain savvy men who were younger and heartier versions of himself. The rest of them seemed quick and capable and they rode hard through the hills to the Sacramento Valley. They seldom stopped for water or to camp. Reed made one quick stop to buy more horses at William Gordon's ranch on Cache Creek and then they moved on.

Reed had all the men and horses that he needed, but instead of going straight at the Sierras, the rescue team was on its way to the winter settlements, the designated rendezvous site for the team. The boat from San Francisco was going to meet them there with supplies and provisions.

When they arrived, though, no one was there. Reed sent a man to follow the river and look for the boat and he found it - at Sutter's Fort. It was supposedly taking refuge there from strong winds.

The overdue ship was under the command of Passed Midshipman Selim Woodworth, a young emigrant who had once left a note in a deserted cabin along the trail for family friend George McKinstry, who was then still part of the Russell Party. In early February, Commander Hull had put the junior officer in charge of relief operations. This was at the same time that Reed was putting together the rescue party known as the Second Relief.

On the morning of February 18 - when the First Relief was starting the final leg of its journey to the lake camp - Reed was checking the supplies and provisions on Woodworth's boat. The amount of donations and purchased goods was overwhelming. There were barrels of flour and pork, 400 pounds of sugar, tins of ground coffee, 100 pounds of cocoa, and a cash gift from Commander Hull. The funds collected paid for frying pans, hatchets and axes, blankets, woolen stockings, adult and children's shoes, bolts of calico and flannel, deer skins, comforters, and 17 pounds of tobacco.

It was wonderful - but it was a disaster. There was no other boat to take the men across the river and to get the supplies to the winter settlements.

But, thanks to Greenwood and the other mountain men, Reed came up with a daring new plan. They would not wait for Woodworth and the stalled boat. Instead, elk hides would be used to fashion bullboats by making bowl-shaped frames with bent willow branches and covering them in animal skins with the fur side out. Often used by Indians and trappers, the tub-like crafts were slow and difficult to steer but since it would take a good deal of time to swim the horses across the river, there would be time to transport men and supplies in the small boats.

This wouldn't solve all their problems, but it was a start.

But then, just as Greenwood and the other men were starting to construct the small boats, a schooner sailed upriver in their direction. It was the *Indian Queen*, commanded by Perry McCoon, and sent by John Sutter to help with the efforts. They'd use it to get the men and the horses across. Then, Woodworth would bring the relief boat with all the provisions to the settlements.

As soon as the boat was tied up, a ramp was put into place for loading the horses and mules. Reed didn't want to waste any more time. He and McCutchen coaxed their horses aboard before the rest of the party and the schooner started for the opposite bank with Reed shouting orders back to the men. He urged them to follow and ride as fast as possible to the winter settlements. By the time that McCoon had turned the boat to bring the rest of the party across the river, the wind had picked up and he was forced to wait before returning to the other side. By then, Reed and McCutchen were gone.

When they reached the settlements, they went right to work. A herd of cattle was there waiting, and rancher William Johnson urged them to take whatever they needed for meat. They shot five of them and stayed up all night to get them butchered and hung over fires to dry. Johnson and several others spent the night grinding 200 pounds of flour and packing it into bags.

In the morning, the rest of the party arrived at the settlements. They helped to bag the dried beef and pack up supplies. Unlike the brave but inexperienced men of the First Relief, Reed's company was mostly made up of veteran frontiersmen, all of them with honed survival skills. Greenwood had recruited his teenage son, Britton, for

Johnson's Ranch at the winter settlements, where Reed and the other rescue parties prepared to go into the mountains in search of Donner Party survivors.

the expedition. He was the youngest man but had spent his entire life in the wilderness with his father.

Another addition to the relief party was John Turner, a big and burly man who had recently left serving with John C. Fremont. He was considered one of the best trappers west of the Rocky Mountains and was notorious for his large vocabulary of profanities.

Little was known about most of the other men in the party, which consisted of two French-Canadians - Matthew Dofar and Joseph Gendreau - and three young men - Charles Cady, Nicholas Clark, and Charles Stone - who had little wilderness experience, but were hardworking and eager. Reed liked them and referred to them as "the boys."

Reed's longtime friend, Hiram Miller, the blacksmith who left Springfield to work as a teamster for the Donners, had also joined the group. He had left the caravan on July 2 to join the other single men in the mule train, but when he heard about the predicament of the Donner Party, he wanted to help. He had many friends trapped in the mountains, along with Margaret Reed and the children, who he considered family.

Several more men were added, mainly to tend the horses and shuttle supplies to Mule Springs. Most of them would remain at the base camp. Reed had complete faith in the 10 core members of the party, but had lost all confidence in Selim Woodworth and his relief boat.

There was still no sign of him and the supplies. Reed would not wait any longer. The meat and flour that he and the other men had prepared during the night would have to be enough for now.

Just after sunrise on February 22, the men were ready to ride. Reed left instructions that when Woodworth finally arrived at the settlements, the provisions that he brought with him should then be transported into the mountains to Mule Springs.

And with that, the Second Relief rode off along the Bear River. They started for the mountains, following the same path taken by the men of the First Relief, who had left frozen Truckee Lake that same morning with 23 members of the Donner Party who were considered strong enough to travel.

Most of them were children.

And not all of them would survive.

16. THE HUNGER

When the seven men of the First Relief arrived at the lake camp on the evening of February 19, some of the emigrants, delirious and overcome by starvation, truly did mistake the men for angels. It had been so long since they had seen a face from outside the community that they could only imagine they came from heaven. They didn't recognize the seven men who appeared out of the gloom and those who didn't think they were angels were convinced it was all a dream.

But most of the emigrants would not have recognized themselves if they had looked in a mirror at this point. The men from the rescue party were shocked by what they found. The emigrants had been turned into creatures that seemed human but had been stripped of their humanity. Withered figures of the walking dead, shrouded with torn and ragged clothing, crawled and stumbled out of the cabins. Many of them could barely walk and some of those who managed, soon collapsed into the snow.

Others stood silent and staring with blank eyes, their chapped lips quivering as they whispered to the rescuers. The cabins, infested with lice and vermin, reeked of wood smoke, soiled bedding, human waste, body odor, and rotting rawhide roofs, mixed with the stench of boiled hides and bones that were crusted into the cooking pots. Those who didn't have the strength to come outside huddled under stiff blankets, oblivious to the smell around them.

It didn't take long for many of the emigrants to realize that the men who had appeared had come to save them. They flocked to them, hugging them, thanking them, shouting praises to God, and weeping with joy. Reason Tucker later wrote, "The sight of us appeared to put life into their emaciated frames." He would recall that his men were so moved by the emigrants' reactions that they "cried to see them cry and rejoiced to see them rejoice."

Among the most vocal were the Reeds, especially after they learned that James was alive. Virginia remembered the vow she had made to God one dark night, that if he would send relief to the camp and let her see her father again, she would become a Catholic.

Finally, one of the prayers sent up from the camps had been answered.

Years later, Virginia wrote about the night the

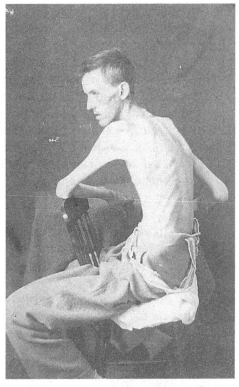

This man is not a member of the Donner Party but rather a survivor of a Civil War prison camp, who lived under the same kind of starvation conditions of those trapped in the Sierra Nevadas that winter. This photograph is used to offer the reader some idea of the physical conditions of those the First Relief found at Truckee Lake.

First Relief arrived at the camp. "All were starving. They shouted to attract attention. Mr. Breen clambered up the icy steps from our cabin and soon we heard the blessed words, 'Relief, thank God, relief!' There was joy at Donner Lake that night, for we did not know the fate of the Forlorn Hope and we were told that relief parties would come and go until all were across the mountains. But the joy and sorrow were strangely blended. There were tears in other eyes than those of

261 | T h e   F o r l o r n   H o p e

children; strong men sat down and wept. For the dead lying about on the snow, some even unburied, since the living had not the strength to bury their dead.

Trying to avoid making a terrible situation worse, the men from the First Relief had to lie to the emigrants. When they asked the men about the welfare of family and friends from the snowshoe party, they were assured that everyone was safe. It was better to lie. Soon enough, these tragic survivors would learn the fate of those who were not so lucky - the fallen who had died and been eaten by the others.

The relief party made the rounds of the camp, visiting all the cabins and shelters and handing out small amounts of dried beef and biscuits. They knew the dangers of giving a starving person too much food.

Dan Rhoads later wrote, "They had been without food, except for a few work oxen since the first fall of snow. We gave them food very sparingly and retired for the night having someone on guard until morning to keep close watch on our provision to prevent the starving emigrants from eating them which they would have done until they died of repletion."

By the time the First Relief had arrived, nine members of the company had died at the lake camp. When the first deaths occurred, survivors had buried them deep in the snowdrifts, but later, after they became weaker, they only managed to drag them outside and cover them in a quilt.

Dan Rhoads wrote, "So far, the survivors had not been compelled to partake of human flesh." As he checked the corpses that were scattered about the camp, he made another interesting note - most of the dead were adult males. "I remember seeing but 3 living men. Lewis Keseberg was lying on his back, unable to rise. Patrick Breen and one other were the only ones left. Very few women or children had died up to that time."

But on the morning of February 20, there was another death in camp - little Catherine Pike, who was less than a year old. The tiny, malnourished child died in the arms of her grandmother, Levinah Murphy. She had become the sole caretaker of Catherine and her three-year-old sister, Naomi, when their mother had left with the snowshoe party. When Harriet had left the lake camp with her sister - at Levinah's insistence - she had been so starved that she was no longer able to produce milk to feed her nursing baby. Levinah did her best to care for the baby, feeding her a thin gruel of flour and water, but it wasn't enough. It was a miracle that she had survived for as long as she had.

Her death was barely noticed by the ravenous survivors. They were only concerned for their families or themselves - which may have been the reason that no one sent the relief party to the camp at Alder Creek right away.

Finally, after some breakfast on the second day, Reason Tucker, John Rhoads, and Sept Moutrey packed up some provisions and went to check on the Donners and those in the other camp. Tucker later wrote, "We found them in a starving condition. Most of the men had died and one of them leaving a wife and 8 children. The two families had but one beef head amongst them... There were two cows buried in the snow, but it was doubtful if they would be able to find them."

Fortunately, there had been no deaths since Jacob Donner and the three other men had died in late December. But when the rescuers found George Donner, it was apparent that death would be coming for him soon. His wounded hand was rotted with infection and when the men knelt by his side, they could smell his sickly-sweet breath. Despite Tamzene's valiant efforts, the infection had spread and now his arm was so gangrenous that he was unable to move.

John Rhoads never forgot the moments when he tried to boost George Donner's spirits. Many years later, when he was dying himself, he confessed that his conscience had always bothered him because he had told Donner that he would come back and get him, all the time knowing he could not keep that promise.

Tamzene was the only one who seemed to be in decent health, especially when compared to the other adults. The relief team decided that she was strong enough to make the return trip, but she flatly refused. She told them that her stepchildren were strong, and they should go with them. She would not leave her husband and three daughters behind. They tried to convince her, but it was no use, so Elitha and Leanna were bundled up for the trail and went back with the men to the lake camp.

Betsy, Jacob's widow, also chose to remain with her youngest children. Solomon Hook, Betsy's oldest son and Jacob's stepson, also stayed behind. Eliza later explained that Solomon had become "snow blind and demented, and at times restless and difficult to control." Solomon's younger brother, William, and stepbrother, George, Jr. joined their cousins when they left with the rescue party.

Besides the four young people, two others were taken from the Alder Creek camp - Dorthea Wolfinger, the young widow, and teamster Noah James. Jean-Baptiste stayed behind to cut firewood and look after the women and children.

Before they departed, the rescue party cut a large stack of firewood and gave each person in camp a cup of flour, two biscuits, and some sliced jerked beef. That was all they could spare until the next relief party arrived.

Tucker told Tamzene and Betsy to stay strong - more help was on the way. Tamzene told him that she prayed this was true for once the little food they had left was gone, there would only be one way to keep the families alive.

Tucker knew what she meant - and knew she was serious.

Elitha Donner, shown later in life, after the events of that terrible winter.

Just before the party left for the lake camp, Tamzene took Leanna and Elitha aside and told them never to speak about what they had seen and experienced in the Sierras.

After many tearful goodbyes, the rescuers and their six charges left. Even after they were out of sight, those left in camp watched the empty trail and cried.

Eliza Donner wrote, "Mother stood on the snow where she could see all go forth. They moved in single file - the leaders on snowshoes, the weak stepping in their tracks made by the strong. Leanna, the last in line, was scarcely able to keep up. It was not until mother came back with Frances and Georgia that I was made to understand that this was the long-hoped-for relief party... Oh, it was painfully quiet some days in those great mountains, and lonesome upon the snow. The pines had a whispering homesick murmur, and we children had lost all inclination to play."

Back at the lake camp, the other four members of the First Relief spent the day trying to decide which emigrants to take back with them. Priority was given to families with no food, single adults, older boys, and small children who could be carried. Parents would remain to care for the younger children, as would anyone who was physically impaired or seriously ill. In the end, 17 of the 34 emigrants at the lake were chosen to return with the rescue party.

Those chosen were Margaret Reed, her four children, and Eliza Williams; Edward and Simon Breen, two sons from the family who still had the most hides left to eat; William, Eleanor, and Lovina Graves; William Murphy and his sister, Mary; Philippine Keseberg and her daughter, Ada; John Denton, a Donner driver; and little Naomi Pike, who would be wrapped in a blanket and carried by John Rhoads. With the addition of the six from the Alder Creek camp, the rescuers were prepared to bring 23 survivors out of the mountains. Knowing that there were several food caches along the trail, the rescuers passed out most of the remaining food in their packs to the emigrants who were staying behind.

On the morning of February 22, Patrick Breen started the day by burying the body of tiny Caroline Pike in the snow. After that, he turned his attentions to prayer. He prayed for the men of the First Relief and the survivors who they were leading west toward the summit.

Once again, though, God chose not to listen to the prayers of Patrick Breen.

The return trip of the First Relief was soon underway. They were backtracking on the same trail from a few days earlier but had not gone far when they were faced with their first problem. Following in the footsteps of the adults, through heavy snow, was so difficult for the younger children that they were falling behind. All the children but two - Naomi Pike and Ada Keseberg - were too big to carry so they had no choice but to walk. John Rhoads already had Naomi slung over his shoulder in a blanket and Philippine was carrying her daughter as best she could while struggling through the snow.

After spending so much time confined to their cabins in camp, even some of the older children and adults found that the hike was more challenging than they'd thought it would be. They were stiff and out of shape, plus they were weak from starvation and hypothermia. Those with family and friends fared better than those who were alone, like John Denton. The sickly but determined young man relied on sheer will power to keep him on his feet. On the other hand, Leanna Donner, who had a tough time getting from Alder Creek to the lake camp, faltered often but managed to trudge along with help from her sister.

Leanna later remembered, "I was one of the weakest in the party, and not one in the train thought I would get to the top of the first hill. We marched along in single file, the leader wearing snowshoes, and the others following after, all stepping in the leader's tracks. I think my sister and myself were about the rear of the train, as the strongest were put in the front."

There were others in worse shape than Leanna, however. Tommy Reed, just three-years-old, and his sister, Patty, who was almost nine, were exhausted after traveling only two miles. As their sister Virginia put it, "they just gave out." This brought the entire group to a stop. Neither Margaret nor the other children were strong enough to carry Tommy and Patty. Aquilla Glover and Reason Tucker quickly conferred, and it was decided that the children would have to go back to the lake camp.

Virginia wrote, "They were not able to stand the fatigue and it was not thought safe to allow them to proceed, so Mr. Glover informed mama that they would have to be sent back to the cabins to await the expedition. What language can express our feelings? My mother said she would go back with her children - that we would all go back together."

But Glover refused to let Margaret return to camp. He knew how difficult this was for her, but in the best interest of herself and her family, she needed to remain with James and Virginia in the rescue party and stay the course.

Virginia added, "Mr. Glover promised mama that as soon as they reached Bear Valley, he himself would return for her children. Finally, my mother, turning to Mr. Glover, said, 'Are you a Mason?' He replied that he was. 'Will you promise me on the word of a Mason that if we do not meet their father you will return and save my children?' He pledged that he would. My father was a member of the Mystic Tie and mama had great faith in the word of a Mason."

Glover looked directly into Margaret's eyes and said, "I thus do promise."

He chose Sept Moutrey to help him take Tommy and Patty back to the lake camp. Once they were safe, the men would catch up to the First Relief.

Virginia recalled that it was "a sad parting - a fearful struggle." But Patty and Tommy took it in stride. All the Reed children were close but as the youngest, the two had a special bond. Before leaving, Patty turned to Margaret and told her, "I want to see papa, but I will take good care of Tommy."

After hugs from the rest of the family, Glover and Moutrey knelt down so that the two youngest Reeds could climb onto their backs for the hike back to the lake.

Patty hesitated for a moment - she had something else to say. "Well, mother, if you never see me again, do the best you can," she said in her sweet voice.

It was enough to put tears in the eyes of Glover and Moutrey, two of the toughest men the children would ever know.

When Glover and Moutrey arrived back at camp with Tommy and Patty, the reception they received from Patrick and Peggy Breen was as cold as the weather outside. The Breens, happy to have five fewer hungry mouths to feed in their crowded cabin, had celebrated the Reeds' departure.

Now, two of them had come back.

At first, Patrick Breen - good Christian that he was - refused to allow the two children back into the cabin. Glover stayed calm, even though he wanted to knock a few of the man's teeth out. Instead, he played on the Breens' sympathy, reminding them that other relief parties would soon arrive. The children had nowhere else to go. But Breen didn't budge. Finally, out of desperation, Glover said he would leave extra food behind to support Tommy and Patty. Asking for help hadn't worked with Breen, as usual, but the extra

The always pious Patrick Breen believed in charity - as long as it benefited only his family - and was the first to utter a self-serving prayer.

food did. Breen reluctantly let the children back into the cabin.

The First Relief had advanced another mile down the trail by the time Glover and Moutrey caught up with them. They made camp at the head of the lake. The men cut down pines and built platforms for the fires. There wasn't going to be much food until they made it to the first of the caches, but they did what they could, dividing what they had into an ounce of smoked beef and a spoonful of flour twice a day for everyone.

The next morning, the group awoke to find their clothing and even their shoelaces were frozen stiff. Ned Coffeemeyer, the former sailor and relief party member, discovered that during the night, the rawhide strings of his snowshoes had been stolen, presumably by one of the hungry emigrants.

Virginia Reed wrote about the second day, "At break of day we were again on the road, owing to the fact that we could make better time over the frozen snows. The sunshine, which it would seem would have been welcome, only added to our misery. The dazzling reflection of the snow was very trying in the eyes, while its heat melted our frozen clothing, making them cling to our bodies."

Ascending to the pass took up most of the day for the bedraggled party. Travel was excruciatingly slow. The rescuers did all they could to support the emigrants, to boost their morale, and most importantly, to keep them moving. This required making sure they stayed on their feet, which was easier said than done, especially with a large group of children trudging through deep snow.

The exception among them was James Reed, Jr. The five-year-old acted like a little mountain goat. During the climb up the steep slope, he scrambled over icy rocks and followed in the tracks of the men who led the way. His mother and sister worried and called out to him to be careful, but he never slowed down. He made his way over the mountain through snow that was as high as his waist and Virginia later recalled that he told her, "Every step he took was a getting nigher to Pa and something to eat."

Just before leaving camp that morning, the emigrants had been told that there was a cache of food just over the mountain pass. After a few days of meager rations, this was an incentive to raise their spirits - and to keep them putting one cold foot in front of another. That afternoon, although worn down by the hike, their strides were quicker as they approached the place where the food had been hidden.

When the log platform that had been built for fires came into view, everyone picked up the pace. They knew what was waiting for them - a tall pine tree with tied bags and bundles of meat and other provisions safely cached high up in its branches.

But when they reached the pine, all they found was the tree. There were no bundles of food. What was left of the cache was scattered on the ground. Although it had been tied up high in the tree, suspended with rawhide, animals had climbed the tree and chewed through the ties. The bags had fallen to the ground and the food had been devoured.

At first, the party just stood there, staring in silent disbelief. A few of them began to weep. Others got angry and walked away. The rescue party took stock of the situation. Other than what little could be salvaged from the ground, combined with the little they had in their packs, the closest food was 20 miles away, cached in the next site. But what if it was gone, too? That was a four-day hike with no food, and they didn't know if anything would be waiting for them when they got there.

Before the sun rose on February 24, Moutrey, Coffeemeyer, Glover, and Dan Rhoads - all chosen by Tucker - slipped out of camp and got a head start on the rest of the party. They headed west toward Bear Valley, hoping that animals had not gotten to the next cache of food. If they found it intact, they would bring back as much food as they could carry. In the meantime, Tucker, Sels, and John Rhoads would keep the emigrants moving - and try to keep them alive.

The party had only traveled about two miles that morning when Tucker realized that John Denton was falling behind. It was not the first time the young man had been unable to keep up. He had been one of the slowest since the start of the trek. Until then, though, he had held his own, refusing to let his physical ailments hold up the group. John Denton had many friends in the Donner Party and was well-liked by everyone. Although most of the emigrants had become callous about the well-being of others in the group, several of them were genuinely concerned about Denton.

When the young man finally caught up, he literally collapsed into Tucker's arms. He was exhausted and snow blind and simply could not go any farther. He had become a burden to the party, he said, and

- true to his nature - wanted to be left behind. The only favor that he asked was that if they met another party on the trail, to send them his way.

Dan Rhoads later wrote, "He tried to keep a hopeful and cheerful appearance, but we knew he could not live much longer. We made a platform of saplings, built a fire on it, cut some boughs for him to sit on and left him."

Tucker left behind a ration of food for him, then fetched a spare blanket and wrapped it around Denton to shield him from the cold. He also left some wood within reach so that he could keep the fire burning as long as possible. Tucker admired him for his sacrifice.

Tearful goodbyes were said, and the emigrants took their places in line. Virginia Reed wrote that Denton, wrapped in a quilt and smoking his pipe beside the fire, looked so comfortable that little James Reed wanted to stay with him for a while. Virginia couldn't bear to explain to the boy why he couldn't.

Tucker shook Denton's hand one last time and joined the others. "I very unwillingly left him, telling him he should soon have assistance, but I am afraid that he would not live to see it."

And the First Relief rescue party marched on.

As they hiked, Tucker kept an eye out for the blackened pines they had burned on their way up the mountains. The hike continued to be slow. Even though they were on the other side of the pass and gradually descending, it was still difficult to make any distance. Because of the afternoon sun, some of the men found themselves buried in the snow when they broke through the melting crust. They were exhausted, scared, and had a constant, gnawing hunger. Frostbite affected many of them. They were in pain; their clothing was torn and barely suitable for the freezing temperatures, and they were blinded by the glare on the snowpack.

And they had just left one of their own behind to die.

As they continued to walk, the most pathetic of the party was undoubtedly Philippine Keseberg, stumbling through the snow with her daughter. Devastated by the loss of her baby son in January and the earlier death of Ada's twin sister, Philippine was determined to keep Ada alive at all costs.

At first, she had managed to carry the little girl and keep up with the rest of the party. But by the second day, she was gasping for air and making frequent stops to rest and reposition Ada in her arms. At one point, she became so tired that she put the girl down and begged her to walk. Ada tried, but soon gave out and had to be carried again. At one point, in sheer desperation, she called out to the others that she would give them $25 and a gold watch if they would carry Ada, even for a little while. But none of them could. They all had their own children to watch, were breaking the trail, or, in the case of John Rhoads was already carrying Naomi Pike.

The relief party traveled seven miles after leaving John Denton. Somehow, Philippine made it into camp with her daughter. Fires were built on platforms, snow was melting for drinking water, and the last bits of dried meat were handed out for supper.

At some point during the night, nestled in the warmth of the campfire and her mother's arms, little Ada Keseberg died.

Philippine was inconsolable when she awoke to find that her daughter was dead. She clutched the child to her as she cried and screamed, rocking back and forth, and refusing to let her go. Tucker waited as long as he could but, at last, he gently told her that they had to leave. But Philippine told him that she would not go without her daughter.

Tucker convinced her to leave with the others by reminding her that she was a young woman with her whole life ahead of her. She had to go on - for herself and for her husband. Numb with shock, she stumbled on. Some of the women comforted her as best they could.

Tucker sadly recounted, "I told her to give me the child and her to go on. After she was out of sight, Rhoads and myself buried the child in the snow the best we could. Her spirit went to heaven, her body to the wolves."

The party continued for five miles before stopping to make camp as darkness was approaching. There was nothing to eat but roasted rawhide cut from snowshoes. That became their only source of food for the next three days.

On February 26, they stopped at noon to rest and eat more rawhide strings and some pieces of rawhide that they managed to tear off Tucker's tattered pants.

They resumed the trek but had only gone a half mile before they saw two men walking toward them - Sept Moutrey and Ned Coffeemeyer. They were carrying dried beef from the cache in Bear

Valley - it had not been touched. A fire was built right on the trail and the band of survivors hunkered down in the snow and ate all they could. By the time they had finished, the afternoon sun had softened the snow, making hiking difficult, and they made it only one more mile before making camp for the night.

The next morning brought an even better surprise. The party's other two scouts - Aquilla Glover and Daniel Rhoads - had an encounter of their own. Instead of all four of the rescuers returning to the First Relief, Glover and Rhoads set out for the base camp at Mule Springs. Their plan was to get more provisions and then return to help get the party to safety. They were on the Bear River Trail when they saw movement in the distance. As they got closer, Glover and Rhoads saw 10 men, all wearing snowshoes and toting heavy packs. They called out a greeting and when they all met, the leader of the party shook their hands and made introductions.

It was James Reed and the nine other members of the Second Relief.

The shouts and cheers of the dozen men echoed through the valley. After handshakes and back slaps, questions began to be asked and answered. Reed asked about his family and was relieved to hear that not only were they all alive, but his wife and two of his children were behind them on the trail, coming in his direction.

Reed knew he would see them soon, but travel had also been slowed for the Second Relief. As the first rescue party had learned, it was impossible to get horses and mules loaded with provisions through the deep snow. Earlier that morning, they had removed the packs and the animals were taken to the camp at Mule Springs. Caleb Greenwood, unable to make it into the mountains on foot, returned with them. The remaining men had loaded the supplies on their backs, tied on snowshoes, and started walking.

Of all the men of the Second Relief, only Bill McCutchen received bad news from the Donner Party camps. Although McCutchen had been able to reunite with his wife, Amanda, a survivor of the Forlorn Hope, he learned from the First Relief that his daughter, Harriet, had died three weeks earlier while in the care of Elizabeth Graves at the lake camp. He was shaken by the loss but remained committed to the rescue mission.

That night, after everyone else was sleeping, Reed baked bread and sweet cakes over the fire. He had done the same thing the night before. Reed was bringing dried meat and supplies to the starving emigrants, but he also wanted them to have fresh bread. Baking each night gave him something to think about instead of worrying about his family.

But on this night, when he was finished, he was unable to sleep. He could only think about how close he was to Margaret and two of his children. He woke the men earlier than usual in the morning and got them on the trail. He wanted to gain ground before the sun melted the snow crust, he told them, but none of them were fooled. They were happy to leave a little early so that Reed could see his family sooner.

They left early on the morning of February 27 and had only gone about four miles before they came upon, what Reed called, "poor unfortunate starved people" on the trail. He knew right away it was the rescuers and the rescued of the First Relief.

As the Second Relief marched closer, one of the men at the front of the line called out to the first party. "Is Mrs. Reed with you? If she is, tell her Mr. Reed is here!"

When she heard this news, Margaret collapsed with relief and tumbled into the snow.

Virginia Reed, though, didn't hesitate. She pushed past the leaders of the relief party and stomped through the snow toward new arrivals. When she saw her father, she stumbled and started to fall but Reed leapt forward and caught her, sweeping the girl up into his arms. Together, they hurried toward Margaret, lifted her up, and embraced her, too. Little James pushed his way into the cluster of family and soon they were all laughing, crying, and talking at once.

James Reed controlled his emotions this time, not like when he broke down during his speech in San Francisco. His restraint was even evident in his journal entry for that day. "Here I met my wife, Mrs. Reed, and two of my little children. Two still in the mountains. I cannot describe the death-like look they all had. Bread, bread, bread was the begging of every child and grown person. I gave to all what I dared and left for the scene of desolation."

The reunion was a short one. Margaret and the children needed to get out of the mountains and to safety. Reed was anxious to get to the stranded emigrants that had been left behind. He and his party continued east and the other Reeds, along with the First Relief, went west.

The First Relief group camped that night at the head of Bear Valley, where William Thompson, one of the men Reed had recruited in Sonoma, was posted to hand out food from the large supply of provisions there.

During the night, twelve-year-old William Hook, one of Jacob Donner's stepsons, was tormented by hunger. He had eaten his nightly rations but was still hungry. All he could think about was the stockpile of food that had been raised off the ground and into a nearby tree so that it would be protected from animals.

But it wasn't protected from this animal.

William climbed the tree and tore into the cache of food. He ate until he was stuffed, but then ate some more. The emigrants had all been warned about how dangerous it was for a starving person to overeat, but William was just too frenzied to stop.

When he was found in the morning, everything possible was done to try and help him. He was given a cup of tobacco juice to drink to induce vomiting, but it failed to work. He was left behind with John Gordon, who Reed had put in charge of the post, and two other emigrants. They had also overeaten, although not as much as William had. They recovered quickly. William Murphy stayed behind in camp because his feet were so badly frostbitten that his shoes had to be cut off.

Many years later, he recalled the horrible predicament of William Hook, describing how the boy was out in the snow on his knees and elbows. "The camp-keeper called to him to come in. He then told me to make him come to camp. I went out and put my hand on him, speaking his name, and he fell over, being already dead. He did not die in great agony, as is usually alleged. No groan, or signs of dying, were manifested to us. The camp-keeper and myself took the biscuits and jerked beef from his pockets, and buried him just barely under the ground, near a tree which had been fired, and from around which the snow had been melted."

He was placed in that shallow grave on March 1, dead from a cardiac arrest.

The First Relief, meanwhile, were in camp about 10 miles to the west. They stopped for the day when Margaret Reed became sick, probably from one of her intense migraines. Most of the party continued on the next day, allowing the Reeds and a few others to follow the trail at their own pace.

They all met up again at Mule Springs, where the emigrants were stunned to find Selim Woodworth waiting with about 400 pounds of supplies. These were the provisions intended for James Reed and the Second Relief to take to the mountain camps, but Woodworth had failed to make it to the rendezvous point in time because of bad weather. It had taken him four days to get from near Sutter's Point to the winter settlements. When he arrived, he reportedly declared, "I shall not return until all are safely in camp." But soon after leaving the settlements, Woodworth began to have serious concerns that led to a change in plans. By the time he reached Mule Springs, he decided that it would be more prudent for him and his men to remain there and disperse provisions to the various rescue parties.

An illustration created later in life depicting Selim Woodworth, who was supposed to be leading a supply party to help the relief groups in the mountains. Woodworth made it no farther than Mule Springs, where the useless, bombastic officer reclined in camp, complaining about the cold. He turned out to be quite lucky that James Reed was an honorable man.

Tucker, Glover, and others who knew the importance of the supplies to the emigrants and rescuers didn't think much of Woodworth, his courage, or his leadership skills. Woodworth did nothing to change their opinion of him. None of the arrivals in camp would ever forget the image of the effete naval officer lying on a blanket while two of his men rubbed his feet with ice to prevent frostbite while he sipped brandy.

The First Relief skipped the strong drink but, according to Tucker, they settled in at the camp "where we were met with nourishing tea and sugar which revived us a good deal."

The next day, everyone was surprised to see a barefooted Billy Murphy limping into camp with camp-keeper John Gordon and the other emigrant who had eaten too much but had survived. William told his sister, Mary, and the others who greeted him that he had been inspired to walk despite pain after seeing William Hook die in front of him.

Fortunately for Billy and all the others, they would be able to ride for the rest of their journey. There were horses in camp and the trail before them was green, fresh, and free of snow. Virginia Reed wrote, "How beautiful it looked. We stayed a day or so, getting the horses and mules ready to ride. No more dragging over the snow, when we were tired, so very tired, but green grass, horses to ride, and plenty to eat."

The closer the 18 survivors got to the winter settlements, the more hopeful and optimistic they became. They were going to live after all, they slowly realized, not starve to death in a frozen, snow-covered landscape. They finally had something to smile about again.

And Virginia's smile could apparently light up a room. The 13-year-old may have been very thin -- and likely needed a bath and a few more meals - but the pretty girl caught the eye of some of the younger men who had been charged with escorting the emigrants out of the foothills and into the valley. One of them, Edward Pyle, 22, had been hired along with his father to haul supplies to Mule Creek Camp. After a day or so, he worked up the nerve to speak to Virginia - and he asked her to marry him. It was a bold move considering the two of them had never spoken before. Virginia turned down the proposal with a smile and a laugh to gently send him away without damaging his ego. The two of them became good friends instead of husband and wife.

The relief party stopped at the winter settlements for a short rest and a hot meal. They also talked with some of the survivors of the Forlorn Hope, who were still there, and brought them news from the camps. There was little talk about what the snowshoe party had gone through on their journey.

And there was no mention of what was undoubtedly on

An illustration of the John and Mary Sinclair's Ranch Del Paso

everyone's mind - cannibalism.

On March 4, the First Relief arrived at Sutter's Fort - more than five months later than the Donner Party had planned. Many of the survivors burst into tears when the fort came into view. Sutter greeted them all warmly and provided them with all the comforts they had been dreaming about during the horrific months trapped in the mountain camps - hot baths, fresh clothing, food, and drink. A questionable physician that Sutter kept around to tend to his constantly sick Indian workforce tended to the emigrants with physical complaints, like William Murphy's painful feet.

They were all provided with quarters at the fort or were invited to stay with families living in the area. It was the Reeds' good luck to be taken in by John Sinclair and his wife, Mary, at their Rancho Del Paso on the other side of the American River. Virginia loved the kind couple. She wrote, "I really thought I had stepped over into paradise. Mrs. Sinclair was the dearest of women. Never can I forget their kindness." Mary was only a few years older than Virginia and the two of them became close friends.

James, Jr. now on a regimen of milk, eggs, and calves' liver, had made a full recovery. The rambunctious boy was as energetic as ever.

And even Margaret was starting to heal - physically anyway. She was having difficulty sleeping and felt uneasy at night, worrying still about her husband and her children left in camp. She couldn't help but feel that something was wrong.

Later in that first week of March, the temperature dropped again and a cold, hard rain started to fall across the area. The chill that accompanied the rain seeped into Margaret's bones and sent a cold finger of fear into her heart.

If it was raining in the valley, she knew, then it was snowing in the mountains.

17. HORROR IN THE MOUNTAINS

James Reed and the Second Relief were pushing into the mountains by the time his wife and two children were arriving at the winter settlements in the valley. He knew that far too many members of the Donner Party had already died, but it was not too late for the others - the ones that he was desperate to save.

The men of the Second Relief had become more than just comrades during their expedition. Reed had great respect for all of them, especially the hardened trappers among them who had braved many mountain winters. And the others respected Reed, too. Those who knew about Reed's killing of the teamster believed Reed's version of events about what happened. All of them understood the need to make quick decisions and plenty of these men had also taken lives. They also admired Reed's willingness to shorten the reunion with his family and continue with the rescue mission. They were all driven by the urgency to reach the mountain camps and save as many people as possible.

Once the Second Relief was back on the trail to the summit and the camps beyond it, they slowed down as little as possible, only to stopping to eat and to leave caches of food for the return trip. When the hardpack snow became soft under the afternoon sun, John Turner, the most experienced mountaineer in the group, suggested that the men sleep in the daylight hours and travel at night, when the crust was frozen, and it was easier to pick our landmarks in the moonlight. The idea worked and the party picked up speed.

The next night, three of the men - Charles Cady, Nicholas Clark, and Charles Stone - wanted to keep moving rather than set up camp. Reed gave his approval of their plan. After Turner schooled them about the route and the landmarks to watch for ahead, the young men left as an advance party.

And then took a wrong turn and got lost.

After wandering around for a little while, looking for the trail, they came upon a clearing and made a macabre discovery - the frozen corpse of John Denton, still sitting up but with his head bent forward and his chin on his chest. The once stalwart young man had now become a landmark for the rescuers. They knew they were back on the trail.

They hurried on, crossed the summit, and were nearing the camp when they spotted a party of Indians. They had no firearms and feared the Indians might have raided the cabins and killed the survivors. The three men took cover behind a snowbank for the rest of the night, huddling close together because they didn't dare build a fire that might be spotted.

While Cady, Clark, and Stone were hiding out ahead of them, the rest of the Second Relief made good time. With Tucker and young Brit Greenwood serving as guides, there was no chance of getting lost. These men also came upon the body of John Denton. Reed later wrote, rather poetically, "I found him dead. Covered him with a counterpane, and buried him in the snow, in the wildest portions of the earth."

Early on March 1, with barely enough light to see, Clark, Cady, and Stone moved down the trail to the emigrant camp by the lake. They dreaded what they might find there. They watched the trees for Indians and the snowbanks for signs of blood, but there had been no massacre. They now quickly approached the camp.

The snow had started to melt, and they could see the top of a cabin. They called out and some of the emigrants began to emerge, looking like dirty, starving scarecrows. The young men went from shelter to shelter, letting people know that another relief party would be arriving very soon. They handed out small amounts of dried meat and did their best to comfort those who seemed to be in the worst

Most of the surviving emigrants were found along the shore of Truckee Lake in the same snow-covered cabins where they had started the winter - although conditions there had become much, much worse.

condition.

At the Breen cabin, the stench from inside made them gag, but they found all five of the Breen children and Patty and Tommy Reed alive.

Once they had checked on everyone at the lake camp, Stone stayed behind while Cady and Clark hiked to the Alder Creek camp to see how the Donners and the others there had fared.

They would be horrified by what they found.

Around noon that day, Reed and the remainder of the rescue party arrived at the lake camp. They went directly to the Breen cabin. As Reed walked up, he saw Patty sitting on the corner of the cabin's roof. The rest of the structure was still buried in snow. When she saw her father, she let out a shriek of joy and ran to greet him. Reed, just as joyful, scooped her up into his arms and swung her around. She hardly weighed anything. She had always been a small child, but now she was skin and bones.

Inside the cabin, Reed found his son, Tommy. At first, the little boy didn't recognize him, but after hearing Reed's voice, he finally realized that it really was his father with a beard and a face tanned by the sun and wind. Reed made a large pot of soup and filled Patty's apron with biscuits. She proudly handed them out to everyone in the cabin.

While they ate, Reed talked with Patrick Breen, who told him that no further deaths had occurred at the lake camp since the First Relief had left with the first group of survivors.

But then he lowered his voice and told Reed that he feared that cannibalism had been taking place at the Alder Creek camp. He assured him, though, that it had not happened at the lake and neither of his children had tasted human flesh.

More information would eventually be revealed, but Breen told Reed that the mood had changed in camp after the First Relief departed. A feeling of doom settled over those left behind. Stuck caring for the two Reed children, Breen got it into his head that the rations left for them, along with his supply of oxen hides, would not last so he killed the last dog left in camp. It was dressed, cooked, eaten but not shared outside the cabin. A short time later, he turned away Elizabeth Graves when she came begging for dog meat or hides.

On February 26, Breen had written "hungry times in camp" in his journal. He also noted that Levinah Murphy had visited the Breen cabin and told him that she could hear wolves howling every night. She predicted that the wolves would soon dig up the dead bodies that had been buried near her shelter - and indicated that they should dig up the bodies before the wolves did. Breen wrote, "Mrs. Murphy said her yesterday that she thought she would commence on Milt. I don't think she has done it yet, it is distressing. The Donners told the California folks that they would commence to eat dead people 4 days ago, if they did not succeed that day or next in finding their cattle under ten or twelve feet of snow and did not know the spot or bear it, I suppose they have done ere this time."

Reed and McCutchen - after hearing this disturbing bit of news - went to the Murphy cabin and found it in much worse condition than the Breens' place. Reed later wrote, "The Murphy cabin conditions

Deep snow photographed in the Donner area in 1866, two decades after the Donner Party's ordeal. This is an indication of how the cabins looked when the Second Relief arrived in early March 1847.

passed the limits of description and almost of imagination."

Just outside the cabin, Charles Stone - who had stayed behind when Cady and Clark went to Alder Creek - started a fire and began washing a pile of lice-infested clothing and bedding in a large pot. After they went inside the cabin, Reed and McCutchen stripped off their own clothing to also be washed.

In the cabin, they found that Levinah Murphy's physical and mental condition had deteriorated so badly that she was unfit to remain with the children. She was in the grips of dementia, alternating back and forth between crying and laughing. Her son, Simon, was eight-years-old and had been taking care of himself, but George Foster, Jr. was only a year old and James Eddy was three. They were hungry, dirty, and barely alive. Stone had given them some food, but Reed took a chance and fed them a little more and then he and McCutchen gently bathed the little boys and wrapped them in fresh flannel blankets.

The two men then entered the shelter of Lewis Keseberg, who was still disabled from his foot injury, was in terrible pain, and lying in his own excrement. When Reed began washing him, Keseberg was humiliated and angry. He and Reed had constantly been at odds while on the trail, but Reed tried to convince him that none of that mattered now. When he left the Murphy and Keseberg shelters, he asked Charles Stone to keep an eye on them and to make sure they didn't try and eat too much all at once.

Later, in an interview, Keseberg recalled, "When Reed's relief party left the cabins, Mr. Reed left me half a teacupful of flour and about a half pound of jerked beef. It was all he could give. Mrs. Murphy, who was left with me, because she was too weak and emaciated to walk, had no larger portion. Reed had no animosity toward me. He found me too weak to move. He washed me, combed my hair, and treated me kindly. When he left me, he promised to return in two weeks and carry me over the mountains."

Not far from the Murphy cabin, Reed and McCutchen found the mutilated body of Milt Elliott, Reed's old friend and teamster, who had taken such good care of the Reed family for as long as he could. His face and head had not been touched but his body had been dismembered. Most of the flesh had been cut from his torso and limbs. They found bones and small pieces of flesh scattered about, offering proof that someone in the camp had eaten the dead.

They assumed it was Mrs. Murphy - who allegedly announced her plans to Breen - but they had no way of knowing for sure.

The last cabin the two men visited belonged to the Graves clan. Like the others in camp, Elizabeth Graves and her surviving children had lost so much weight they were almost unrecognizable. The emaciated, hollow-eyed family devoured the small rations of food that were given to them and then they simply turned away and crawled under the blankets. They offered no words of gratitude - or words of any other kind. They had become almost animal-like.

Before Reed and McCutchen joined the others in the rescue party, who had set up camp outside to avoid the dank, vermin-infested cabins, they took the time to find the body of McCutchen's baby daughter, Harriet, in the snow. They dug a shallow grave for her in a small piece of land where the snow had melted and laid her to rest.

At his cabin, Patrick Breen wrote the last entry in the journal that he had started in November: "Mond. March the 1 So fine and pleasant froze hard last night there has 10 men arrived this morning from Bear Valley with provisions there is amongst them some old they say the snow will be here until June."

On the morning of March 2, Reed and three of the other men headed for the tents at Alder Creek. They left four of the rescuers behind to prepare the emigrants for the trip west.

When they arrived at the Donner camp, Cady and Clark were waiting for them. The faces of the two men were pale and their entire beings had been shaken. They had spent the last two days in a state of horror.

They grimly recounted to Reed that when they arrived, they found Jean-Baptiste Trudeau leaving the camp of Jacob Donner's widow with the leg and thigh of Jacob Donner. It had been sent for by his brother, George, and it was the last flesh they had left. Jacob's widow, Betsy, was helpless by this time. There was no food left and she stated that she would rather die that eat her husband's body.

The camp had already consumed four bodies and when they arrived, Cady and Clark found the children, sitting on a log, with their faces stained with blood, devouring Jacob's heart and liver. Around the fire were hair, bones, skulls, and pieces of half-eaten limbs. It was a scene of horror like nothing the two men had ever seen before.

The scene was largely unchanged when Reed and the others arrive, although Jean-Baptiste had returned Jacob's leg and thigh to his grave after Cady and Clark arrived. Most of the rest of Jacob was gone. His head had even been cut off and was found lying face upwards in the snow a few feet from his mutilated corpse. There were other graves, too, but nothing remained in them but a few scattered pieces of flesh and bone.

Reed and the rescuers inspected the camp. At George Donner's tent, they found him on the brink of death. He had become so weak that he could no longer lift his head or his arms. Tamzene - unlike her husband or her sister-in-law, Betsy - was still strong enough to travel. Reed noted that Tamzene's daughters - Frances, Georgia, and Eliza - all seemed fit and hearty. It was apparent to him that the girls' appearance was the result of survival cannibalism. They had stayed alive by eating the bodies of the dead teamsters and their uncle, Jacob.

But Reed discreetly chose to omit all references to cannibalism in his relief report. However, at least one widely published newspaper article in 1847 - written by J.H. Merryman from notes written by Reed

- did contain vivid accounts of the cannibalism at both of the Donner Party camps.

In describing what he called the "deplorable condition of the camps," Merryman wrote of Reed and the rescuers finding "the fleshless bones and half eaten bodies of the victims of famine." He also wrote about the human flesh and organs that the starving emigrants consumed as an "unholy feast" and described how some of those stranded in the mountains were so desperately starving that they didn't bother cooking the flesh but consumed them raw. Merriman wrote, "To Mr. Reed this was a horrid sight. Among the bones and skulls that filled the camp kettles, he saw the remains of many an old and well-tried friend."

For the rest of their lives, some of the survivors - including some of the Donner family - not only refused to discuss cannibalism, but claimed that it had never occurred in the camps. Other survivors, though, did not become angry or defensive when the subject came up. Many of them freely admitted that they had eaten human flesh to stay alive - they simply had no choice.

It came down to eating what was there or dying.

Georgia Donner, one of the three daughters of George and Tamzene, was never ashamed of the fact that as a five-year-old girl, she had survived because of the human flesh she was given to eat. Many years later, she shared some of her vivid memories with historian C.F. McGlashan: "My

Georgia Donner was only five-years-old when her family became trapped at Alder Creek. She was never ashamed of the fact that she consumed human flesh - she did what she had to in order to survive that winter.

uncle was the only one they could find for some time. His wife expressed her wish to unbury the body, so that the limbs might be used. And from these, food was prepared for the little ones in both camps.

While eating I chanced to look up. My mother had turned away and my father was crying. Samuel Shoemaker was the only one I knew of being found afterward."

In a letter she wrote, Georgia added a curious note about Shoemaker: "Jacob Donner's wife came down the steps one day saying to mother 'What do you think I cooked this morning?' Then answered her own question herself, 'Shoemaker's arm.'"

Jean-Baptiste Trudeau was also identified as one of the cannibals in camp, based on the eyewitness accounts of the rescuers who had seen him carrying Jacob Donner's leg. Trudeau was later interviewed by Henry Wise, a career naval officer and writer. Parts of that interview were also included in a book called *Los Gringos*, which also contains a lot of sensationalistic and untrue accounts of the Donner Party - so fact must be separated from fiction with his stories.

Many of the accounts in the book used a source that was only identified as "an officer of the navy in charge of the expedition," which turned out to be the unreliable Selim Woodworth, who never got any closer to the camps than Bear Valley. One of the statements credited to this "officer of the navy" claimed, "Mothers possessing portions of their dead companions, refused to divide it with their own children, while alive, and when the children died, actually devoured the bodies of their own offspring!"

We know this is a blatant lie, considering the many examples of mothers among the party like Margaret Reed, Peggy Breen, and others, who did everything possible to keep their children alive.

And there was no better example of a caring mother than Tamzene Donner - as Reed and his men were reminded once again. No matter how hard they tried, they were unable to persuade her to leave her children in camp and go with the rescuers. Just as she had told the First Relief, Tamzene said she would never abandon her husband and leave him to die alone. Instead, she and the three girls would wait for the next relief party, which was supposed to be led by Selim Woodworth. If George was still alive when they came, then she would remain and allow the girls to leave. Reed agreed, believing that Woodworth was only a few days behind them.

But, of course, he wasn't. He was still sitting at the relief camp that had been established in Bear Valley - and he wasn't moving.

Reed ended up taking three emigrants from Alder Creek - Mary

Donner, two weeks away from her eighth birthday; her brother, Isaac, who was five; and Solomon Hook, the 15-year-old stepson of Jacob Donner. Jean-Baptiste, irritated that he had not been chosen again, stayed behind in Betsy Donner's tent, as did her son, Lewis, who was three-years-old. Reed left behind rescuer Nicholas Clark to care for Betsy and to help the others until the next relief party arrived.

Reed asked Charles Cady to stay behind with Tamzene and her daughters to help care for George. They also moved Samuel, Betsy's four-year-old son, into their tent to give his mother some relief.

Cady and Clark were left with nine pounds of jerked beef and 11 pounds of flour to carefully ration out between the nine remaining emigrants. They figured this would be enough food for a week - more than enough time for Woodworth's relief party to make it to the camps.

Before they returned to the lake camp, Reed and Hiram Miller oversaw a sale of items from Jacob Donner's estate. This seems like an odd time to do such a thing, especially since the only buyers were the men from the rescue party, but I suppose it had to be done at some point. They bought shawls, silk handkerchiefs, vests, shoes, and boots. Nicholas Clark bought a knife for $1. Joseph Verrot bought books and a comb. Reed gave $4 for a pair of boots that he gave to the shoeless Lewis Keseberg that day when the party returned to the lake camp.

When they arrived, they found the rescuers and 14 emigrants who had been deemed strong enough to make the long hike out of the mountains. Those chosen were seven members of the Breen family, five members of the Graves family, and Patty and Tommy Reed. Only three of them were adults - Patrick and Margaret Breen and a confused Elizabeth Graves, who fretted about the safety of a stash of gold and silver coins she was taking with her. They had been secreted in the family wagon, but it had been burned months before when they had all become snowbound. The coins had been removed and hidden somewhere else and now she insisted on bringing them down the mountain with her.

Five emigrants were left behind at Truckee Lake - Lewis Keseberg, Levinah Murphy, her son, Simon, and the young Foster and Eddy boys. Charles Stone from the rescue party was placed in charge of the camp to keep some semblance of order and to check on Keseberg and Mrs. Murphy.

On March 3, the Second Relief left the lake camp with 17 more emigrants. Most of them were younger than 10 and some had to be carried by the rescuers. Any adult who was not carrying a child had to tote blankets or supplies. A few still held on to personal belongings. Besides the dried beef and biscuits the relief party had handed out, the Breens also had a bundle with some strips of beef, coffee, tea, and sugar in it that they had managed to save. They would, of course, not be willing to share those supplies with others.

Elizabeth Graves had entrusted her bag of coins to one of the rescuers to carry. Unaware that her son-in-law, Jay Fosdick, had died - and had been eaten - with the snowshoe party, she carried his violin with her. He had left it behind at the lake camp.

With all these encumbrances, the party moved slowly, and they did not get far on the first day. They camped on bare ground on the north side of the lake. That night, as they huddled around a fire, laughter was heard among them for the first time in quite a long while. Patrick Breen borrowed Fosdick's fiddle and played every Irish jig and ballad he knew for two hours.

In the morning, just before they left camp, Elizabeth Graves overheard some of the relief party, including the man she'd entrusted with her coins, make a joke about stealing them. Already concerned about the money, Elizabeth took the coins from the man and told Reed that she had a few chores to handle and would catch up with the group. As soon as the party moved off, Elizabeth and her older children moved the bag of coins to a spot that she marked behind a large rock. She quickly dug a hole and buried the bag. When they made it to safety, Elizabeth would return for her buried treasure.

After memorizing the location, Elizbeth, holding her baby daughter, hurried to rejoin the party. It was not long before the end of the Second Relief came into view.

The party marched on but made little progress again that day. Despite prodding from Reed and McCutchen, the emigrants tired quickly.

Camp was set up in the late afternoon and Breen put the violin to use for a second night. Spirits were high, but the food supply was nearly gone. There was still no sign of Woodworth and the next relief group.

They managed a small breakfast the next day and moved on, cold, hungry, and tired. It was imperative that they get over the summit

Even with help from James Reed and the Second Relief, the weak and hungry emigrants faced brutal conditions to make it out of the Sierra Nevadas.

and make better time. They finally made it over the summit by afternoon and reached a campsite that had been used by the First Relief. It was in a long meadow in Summit Valley on the west slope of the mountains and near the head of the Yuba River. The men rebuilt the log platform for a fire, cut pine boughs to sleep on, and gathered firewood. There was very little food and even the stronger rescuers were tired and worn down.

As the emigrants and rescuers sat by the fire that night, there was no fiddle playing and no laughter. They were hungry and exhausted. They simply sat and stared at the fire.

And then the storm came.

The temperature dropped and the moan of the wind became a howl. Far away at the Sinclair Ranch, Margaret Reed had watched it rain and knew that it would be snowing in the mountains - she was right. The storm became a sort-of grand finale for the winter of 1846-47.

Reed would call it a "perfect hurricane." He wrote, "The men up nearly all night making fires, some of the men began to pray. Several became snow blind. I could not see even the light of the fire when it was blazing before me."

As had happened to other parties, the fire blazing on the platform melted the snow beneath it, creating a deep pit. It had already snowed more than a foot when 14-year-old John Breen suddenly collapsed, or, as he put it, "fainted or became stupid from weakness." He had started to slide into the fire pit when one of the others grabbed him and dragged him back to safety. His mother managed to pry open her son's clenched jaws and pushed some sugar into his mouth, which quickly revived him.

The storm was still going strong the next morning. Reed handed out the last of the food - a spoonful of flour for each person. The wind and driving snow pelted the rescuers as they chopped wood and kept the fire going.

None of the other adults offered any help at all. Patrick Breen, of course, appeared to be in constant prayer.

The rescuers did their best to shield the children, who wailed constantly from under their blankets and cried themselves to sleep. Peggy Breen and Elizabeth Graves clutched their infant daughters to their chests and checked constantly to make sure they were still breathing. When the children slept, the camp was silent, aside from whimpering that was drowned out by the wind.

Reed, although exhausted, took the first fire watch so that the others could get some sleep. He didn't last long. He lost consciousness and when he did, the flames died down. At the same time, the logs that formed the foundation of the platform slipped, dumping much of the fire into the pit of melted snow. It only took a few minutes before icy air overwhelmed the camp. The cold awakened the emigrants and chaos erupted. The children screamed, their mothers cried, and the rescuers rushed to try and do anything they could - except for Brit Greenwood. Although he'd been raised in the woods, he fell to his knees and joined Patrick Breen in his pointless prayers.

Several - perhaps all - would have died if not for the quick-thinking of William McCutchen and Hiram Miller. Without hesitation, they sprang into action. As McCutchen recalled in 1871, "The rest of the men were disheartened, and would not use any exertion, in fact they gave up all hope and in despair, some of them commenced praying. I damned them, telling them it was not time to pray but to get up, stir themselves and get wood, for it was a matter of life and death to us in minutes. The fire was nearly out; the snow falling off the trees had nearly extinguished it before discovered; it was only rekindled by the exertion of Mr. Miller and myself."

Once the fire was going again, McCutchen and Miller went to Reed's aid. He had not fallen asleep - he'd actually fainted. They pulled him close to the fire and rubbed his feet and hands until he slowly began to regain his senses. When he could sit up and sip some water, his two friends finally looked after themselves. Miller attended to the splayed skin of his frozen hands and fingers and, like McCutchen, got as close as he could to the fire. McCutchen was so cold that he accidentally burned the back of his shirt as he hovered near the heat.

Reed recovered but not all the emigrants survived the night. Isaac Donner had quietly died in the excitement. He was lying on some pine boughs between his sister, Mary, and Patty Reed but slipped away so silently that neither of the sleeping girls awoke.

Mary was shocked and troubled by her five-year-old brother's death. During the night, as she tossed and turned in her sleep, one of her feet slipped into the fire. The foot was so numbed by frostbite, though, that she didn't wake up until it was badly burned. It was an injury that would prevent her from walking. She remained huddled at the fire while McCutchen and Miller placed Isaac's body in the snow.

The storm raged for two terrible nights and then finally began to slack off on the third day. The wind began to die and by noon, the snow stopped falling. Reed was finally feeling better and after talking with McCutchen, announced that the party would take advantage of the lull in the storm and keep moving toward Sutter's Fort.

No one was excited by this news. They had been without food for two days. Elizabeth Graves and her children were so exhausted that they were barely able to move. Margaret Breen was likely the strongest member of her family and might have been able to walk, carrying her youngest child, but she didn't want to leave her husband and other children behind.

Patrick Breen refused to leave the camp. He said that he would rather die there than out on the trail. Reed argued with him, trying to make him see that his family would die if they stayed there, but Breen waved him away angrily. Frustrated and not wanting to be responsible for the family's deaths, Reed summoned the other rescuers to listen to the conversation.

McCutchen later wrote, "Then Mr. Reed called myself and others to witness, that if any of Mr. Breen's family died, their death be upon him and not upon us. Before leaving, we did everything in our power for those who had to remain, cutting and leaving wood enough to last for several days."

Mary Donner was anxious to leave with Reed and the others. She promised that she could keep up, even with her painful feet. But she only took a few steps before falling down in the snow. She wept softly as a place was made for her with the Breen and Graves families. They were sitting around the edge of what had become a very deep fire pit with only a small stash of the Breens' seeds and some sugar.

A relief party would eventually reach them but not before the place was forever dubbed "Starved Camp."

What was left of the Second Relief - Reed, Miller, McCutchen, and Brit Greenwood, who had eventually regained his courage - took three young survivors with them and continued the journey. It was not the rescue effort that Reed had envisioned but at least he had his two lost children with him. Tommy was being carried by the always resilient Hiram Miller, but Patty wouldn't let her weary father carry her. She insisted on walking. The other survivor, Solomon Hook, was distraught over the death of his stepbrother, Isaac, and was concerned about leaving his stepsister, Mary, at the camp, but he was strong enough to make his way without help.

Patty Reed soon found that walking in the deep, soft snow into a biting wind had not become any easier than her first attempt to make it out of the mountains. After a few miles, everyone but Miller was suffering from frostbite. By then, Patty, who had been valiantly following in her father's footsteps, was slowing down, and becoming wobbly. She started muttering to herself and then suddenly cried out about how she was surrounded by an incredible vision - a band of angels dancing among beautiful stars. Reed was alarmed. Patty was hallucinating, a sure sign that a person was freezing to death.

He picked her up and wrapped her in his arms, hoping to restore some of her warmth. The others wrapped a blanket around them both and McCutchen and Miller vigorously rubbed her hands and feet.

Virginia Reed later wrote about the incident: "Patty thought she could walk, but gradually everything faded from her sight, and she seemed to be dying. All other sufferings were now forgotten, and everything was done to revive the child. My father found some crumbs in the thumb of his woolen mitten; warming and moistening them between his own lips, he gave them to her and thus saved her life."

The idea that a few bits of a biscuit saved Patty's life became a bit of Reed family folklore - but it was really the massaging of her hands and feet and the blanket that raised her body temperature and restored her senses. When she felt better, the party moved on. Patty was now being carried, cocooned in a blanket that hung like a sack across her father's back. She was kept warm by the heat from Reed's exertions as he cut a trail through the snow.

They made 10 miles that day and late in the afternoon, they made camp next to the Yuba River. The hours of traversing the loose snow had left them drained. They built a fire and melted snow for water but there was nothing to eat. The party was now on its fourth day with no food.

There was still no sign of Woodworth's relief party.

They would have been able to find them easily if the party had been looking, though. The Second Relief's feet were so frostbitten that, as Reed later wrote, they "could have tracked the whole distance by blood." The group was in so much pain that it made them forget about how hungry they were, at least for a little while.

They crowded around the fire and rubbed their cracked feet and toes with handfuls of icy snow, unknowingly making the situation worse. Brit Greenwood's feet were so bad that they would end up permanently damaged. A few of the others eventually lost toes.

That same night, as they huddled near the fire, two figures walked into camp from the darkness - Charles Cady and Charles Stone, members of the Second Relief who had been left behind at the mountain camps. They had decided to leave after determining that their comrade Nicholas Clark and Jean-Baptiste Trudeau could oversee the two camps on their own. Curiously, the two men had no one with them. Instead of carrying a child, they both had heavy packs. They had no food, only seriously frostbitten feet.

There is no record of the conversation that occurred that night around the fire, but I cannot imagine it was a pleasant one. It turned out that what Cady and Stone had done was nothing short of criminal and some might say, it was downright evil.

The crimes of Cady and Stone were, luckily for them, not pieced together until much later, when everything was finally revealed. Legally, there was nothing that Reed could have done to them if he had known what had transpired that night, but I imagine that he and the other rescuers would have been quite angry - even angrier than they probably were.

Soon after the Second Relief had departed, Stone left the lake camp and hiked to Alder Creek, where Reed had left Cady and Clark to care for the Donners. Clark was out hunting, hoping to supplement their supplies with fresh game. He had spotted some bear tracks and found a black bear and her cub. Clark got off a shot and wounded the mother. Both bears ran off, but Clark was following the trail of blood they'd left behind.

While Clark was gone, Cady and Stone began talking and bemoaning the predicament they faced. With little food and signs that another winter storm was coming, they concluded that they'd be better off if they left and got back to the valley on their own. With an agreement reached, they made plans to leave right away.

When a horrified Tamzene Donner heard that Cady was going to abandon her and the rest of the Donner family, she struck a desperate deal with the two of them - for a good sum of gold, and possibly as much as $500, they agreed to take her three daughters - Frances, Georgia, and Eliza -- over the mountains. They also agreed to carry the girls' keepsakes and belongings, including some silver spoons and a bundle of silk that Tamzene wanted her daughters to use to cover their expenses when they reached the settlements. She combed their hair, dressed them warmly, and then took them to see their father so they could kiss him goodbye.

Eliza later recalled, "The men helped us up the steps and stood us up on the snow. She came, put on our cloaks and hoods, saying, as if talking to herself, 'I may never see you again, but God will take care of you.'"

Soon after leaving the lake camp, leaving a weeping Tamzene behind, Cady and Stone discovered that six-year-old Frances was able to walk on her own but the other two girls would have to be carried.

That wasn't going to work for these two.

When they reached the lake camp, they deposited all three girls in the dank and squalid cabin of Levinah Murphy, who was so physically and mentally broken that she could barely take care of herself, her son, and grandson, let alone three little girls. The only other occupant of the cabin was the bearded, wild-eyed Lewis Keseberg. He scowled at the three Donner girls as they cowered in the corner.

Cady and Stone only stayed for a few minutes, leaving before dark to camp in the Breen cabin for the night. That night, the same furious storm arrived that trapped the Second Relief at the Starved Camp.

Fearing they would be trapped if they stayed at the lake camp, Cady and Stone decided to venture out into the storm the next morning and head for the summit. It is unknown whether they planned to take the Donner girls with them if the storm had not struck or if abandoning them was the plan all along. Regardless, they left them at the Murphy cabin and shuffled off to the west. Instead of carrying the children, they carried away the silver spoons, fancy silks, and gold coins that Tamzene Donner had given them to save her children.

For the Donner girls, it must have been a terrifying realization when they realized they had been abandoned in a fetid cabin with four people who were more dead than alive.

Although cold and hungry, the two men made good time. After crossing the pass, they came to a campsite with a deep, wide hole in the snow with a blue curl of smoke rising out of it. On the edge of the hole were two corpses - a woman and a child - and they looked below to see a ragged woman, a few children, and an emaciated man lying on his back. He stared up at them with hollow eyes.

Instead of trying to help the Breens and the Graves, who had been left behind at Starved Camp, Cady and Stone backed away from the pit and quickly resumed their westward trek. Later that night, they caught up with Reed and the Second Relief.

No mention was made of the Donner girls, the gold and valuables, or those left at Starved Camp. Reed likely asked why they had left the mountain camps and the two men undoubtedly came up with a story that would appease Reed and the others.

The Second Relief - two men larger with the addition of Cady and Stone -- was up and moving again the next morning. It was their fifth day without food. Frostbite made every step painful, although spirits were lifted when they came upon a parcel of provisions dangling from a tree. It had been left there by Matthew Dofar, one of the three mountaineers that Reed had sent ahead several days before to look for food.

The first parcel that Dofar, traveling with John Turner and Joseph Gendreau, had found had been eaten by animals but they had pressed on. They were soon buried under the snowstorm that swept through the Sierras and had to dig in. They had no food, but they had a fire and managed to survive. Once they were on the move again, they found the next food cache. Animals had been into it, but most of the provisions had been spared. It was enough to give the three men some energy to keep going. By then, John Turner was so badly frostbitten that he had to be helped along the trail.

Dofar, the strongest of the three men, backtracked a short distance and left the cache for Reed and his party to find. He returned to Gendreau and Turner on his bleeding feet and they continued on the trail. Soon, they were carrying Turner by his shoulders. They hadn't gone far before they encountered some members of Selim Woodworth's elusive supply party finally coming up the trail from Bear Valley.

Reed and the Second Relief - crippled by the cold but strengthened by the food left in the cache - weren't far behind the other three men. When they made camp that night along the Yuba, he sent Cady and Greenwood ahead of them. The sounds of voices were heard in the distance and Reed knew that another camp must be nearby. He was right. They were some of Woodworth's party and they brought food to the Second Relief that evening.

The next morning, Reed was finally reunited with Woodworth, the naval officer that he and the others no longer trusted - and for good reason.

While Reed and the Second Relief were suffering on the mountain trail - and those left in Starved Camp were dying from hunger - Woodworth, with an abundance of food and supplies was idling in camp at Bear Valley.

If Reed had not been so exhausted, he would have been enraged. He confronted Woodworth and demanded that he dispatch men and supplies immediately to the emigrants at Starved Camp and to those still trapped in the two camps on the other side of the mountains. Woodworth was aghast at the suggestion. He had absolutely no interest in going further east once he saw the physical state of Gendreau, Dofar, and especially Turner. He would not proceed, he told Reed, without a guide.

Reed found Woodworth's behavior to be a serious dereliction of duty. Those of the Donner Party who didn't care for James Reed often accused him of arrogance, but they could never say he was a coward. The same could not be said of Woodworth, who seemed to be both arrogant and afraid. As Reed later noted, if Woodworth had not been so concerned about his own welfare, he would not have been so dangerous to others. "Much suffering would have been prevented," he wrote, "but he relied upon his own judgment, and that judgment belonged to a man young in years and of little experience."

Woodworth seemed to have forgotten his vow at the winter settlements - "I shall not return until all the people are in camp" - but others who took part in the rescues did not forget. Still, Woodworth was given the benefit of the doubt and was largely portrayed in a positive light by the newspapers of the day. History, though, would not be as kind about his complacency and about his unwillingness to leave his base camp. Bernard DeVoto later wrote, "Woodworth was not coming; he never came. He was taking his comfort in camp and nourishing what, compared with the courage of the others, can only be called ignominious cowardice. So, the return of the Second Relief, which should have been the most successful, constitutes the final catastrophe of the Donner Party."

But if Woodworth failed to grasp the seriousness of the situation left behind in the mountains, James Reed certainly understood it. He knew that rescuers needed to get into the Sierras as soon as possible, but he also knew the Second Relief had a responsibility to get the survivors off the western slope and back to the settlements. Woodworth was not up to the task but, fortunately, there were other men in the base camp who were.

To Reed's surprise, two of those men turned out to be old comrades from the trail, William Eddy and William Foster. As two members of the Donner Party who still had sons trapped in the mountains, they had a compelling need to take on the rescue mission.

Eddy and Foster were the only two men who had survived the Forlorn Hope. They had both eaten the dead to stay alive and they'd also had their differences. Just weeks before, when trying to escape the snowy mountains, the two men were ready to kill one another. Eddy angrily disagreed with Foster's intention to kill and eat the two Miwoks,

Luis and Salvador, who were guiding the snowshoe party. Despite his protests, Eddy was unable to stop Foster from killing them a short time later and the two stayed away from each other for the rest of the journey. But after their rescue - and the recovery of Foster's senses - the animosity between them vanished and they formed a solid bond over the mutual goal of saving their sons.

Eddy had been a member of the Second Relief when it left the winter settlements for the mountain camps, but quickly found that he had not recovered well enough to make the trip. He got as far as Mule Springs and had to return. After more rest and better food, he was ready to try and again and rode out with Foster. They used horses for as long as they could and then hiked through the snow to find Woodworth. They tried everything they could think of to get Woodworth to cross the summit, including shaming him, but it was no use. He did agree to move forward on the trail - likely just to placate them - but not very far.

It was later said that Woodworth had ordered the company to halt and make camp after he grew tired from carrying his own blanket.

With the arrival of Reed and the Second Relief, Eddy and Foster were inspired to travel into the Sierras with a third company that would hopefully bring back their sons.

But the two men would find tragedy waiting for them in the mountains.

18. STARVED CAMP AND THE THIRD RELIEF

Eddy and Foster, the leaders of the Third Relief, were so anxious to get on the trail that when they called for volunteers to join a new rescue party, but no man stepped forward, they decided to go alone. Reed stopped them. He had just returned from the same trail and knew how bad it was. It was too dangerous for only two men to brave the elements and try and get the sick and starving emigrants back over the mountains. Reed convinced them to wait. Come back to the Bear Valley base camp, he insisted, and regroup.

They still had trouble recruiting men when they made it back to the base camp. Finally, Selim Woodworth stepped in - or rather, the government's deep pockets did. He offered to pay anyone who accompanied Eddy and Foster $3 per day for their trouble and then offered an additional $50 fee to any man who would bring out a child that was not his own. Eddy separately agreed to pay Hiram Miller, who had just come down with the Second Relief, to return with them. Foster paid the same amount to another man, William Thompson.

Three other men agreed to go on the terms offered by Woodworth. One was a volunteer from San Francisco, Howard Oakley. Another was Charles Stone, who might have been feeling guilty about leaving the Donner girls behind or might have simply wanted the extra money he could earn - or could steal, if there was more booty hidden in the mountains. The third man was a former traveling companion of the Graves family, a tall, bear-like man named John Schull Stark.

While the seven men of the Third Relief prepared for their expedition, Reed readied his own party for the final part of their journey. Hiram Miller said a warm goodbye to little Tommy Reed, his traveling companion in the mountains and placed him in the care of another rescuer. Patty Reed climbed onto her father's back with the little doll that she had been carrying with her since the plains. Now that she finally felt safe, she took the doll from its hiding place and she clutched it in her hand. She kept the tiny figure close as they traveled first to the base camp at Mule Springs and then on to the winter settlements, Sutter's Fort, and across the American River to the Sinclair ranch. Waiting there were Margaret, Virginia, and James, Jr.

Virginia later wrote, "At last my father arrived at Mr. Sinclair's with the little ones, and our family was again united. The day's happiness repaid us for much we had suffered; and it was spring in California."

After embracing, Margaret and Virginia pulled the filthy rags off Tommy and Patty, scrubbed them clean, and dressed them in fresh clothing. The entire family sat down for the first good meal that a few of them had enjoyed for a long time.

As Patty ate, she continued to clutch her little doll in her hand. Margaret finally realized that her daughter had saved it - along with a lock of hair from Sarah Keyes' head - and she was so moved by this that she cried.

As for James Reed, he was filled with both gratitude and hope. All six of his family members were safe and alive. They had not come through their ordeal without scars, but they were alive. Their lives in a new place could finally begin and the long, hellish nightmare of the Reed family was finally over.

The same could not be said for others in the Donner Party.

In the frigid and foreboding Sierra Nevada Mountains, the struggle continued for the emigrants and their rescuers. The Third Relief discovered the dangers ahead of them almost as soon as they left Bear Valley, even though the weather was clear, and they made good time on the crusty snow. Each man carried a 50-pound pack of provisions taken from Woodworth's stockpile of supplies.

A reminder of the dangers ahead of them was found in the frozen body of John Denton. Stone led them to the place, taking a slight detour. Denton's body was still sitting there, although it was now showing signs that passing animals had stopped to gnaw at it. The rescuers took the time to search Denton and found a small diary, a pencil, and some sheets of paper in his pockets. On one sheet was a poem that Denton had written, but whether it was done while traveling or as he was dying is unknown. The first part of it read:

O! after many roving years,
How sweet it is to come
Back to the dwelling place of youth,
Our first and dearest home;
To turn away our wearied eyes
From proud ambition's towers,
And wander in the summer fields,
The scenes of boyhood's hours.

The men packed up Denton's few belongings, including the paper and poem, and quickly moved on. Eddy and Foster knew that more death awaited them on the trail the next day when they reached Starved Camp. They expected to find that most of the emigrants left there were dead.

Instead, when they arrived, they found 11 survivors sitting around a fire at the bottom of the deep pit.

For nearly a week after Reed and the rest of the Second Relief had left the camp, those they had left behind struggled to survive in the pit their fire had melted into the snow. The hole had grown deeper and wider until it was nearly 15 feet in diameter and an astonishing 24 feet deep, reaching now all the way to bare earth.

The rescuers learned that Elizabeth Graves had died the first night after Reed and his party had left - and with her had died the location of her sack of buried gold coins.

As the days dragged on, Patrick Breen simply gave up living. He lay listless on the muddy ground, staring at the sky above and likely wondering why his hollow prayers were never answered. But Peggy Breen struggled to care for the nine children trapped with them - her own five, Mary Donner, and the orphaned Graves children. Soon after Reed and McCutchen left, five-year-old Franklin Graves joined his mother in death. The Breens dragged the boy's body up out of the pit and laid it in the snow next to his mother's and Isaac Donner's bodies.

For the first few days, Peggy brewed small amounts of tea from her diminishing supply of tea leaves and gave it to the children to keep them warm and offer a little nourishment. She also gave them little bits of the sugar and handed out the seeds that she brought along. Every few hours, day and night, Peggy or her oldest son, John, crawled up one of the trees that had fallen into the pit and wandered through the forest in search of firewood. Whenever they left the pit, they scanned the trail for any sign of rescue but there was nothing to be seen. When the relief parties failed to arrive, Patrick Breen sank deeper into despair.

An image of Mary Donner created long after the events of this book.

During the day, the weather was fair and relatively warm. Some of them crawled up to the edge of the pit and stood in the sun, trying to store up warmth for the night ahead. After the sun went down, things were brutal. With no cloud cover, the warmth of the day quickly vanished. As they lay in the pit, staring at the vast array of stars above, they shivered and ached with the pain of the cold. When morning came, they found their blankets and clothing were crusted over with frost.

A week passed and the seeds and the tea began to run out. Finally, there was nothing left to alleviate the hunger pains of the children in the pit. Emaciated and with no body fat to insulate them, the children hovered just at the edge of freezing to death.

Finally, Mary Donner, a little girl with frostbite and burns from where she fell into the fire, couldn't stand the hunger any longer.

She suggested that they eat the dead.

On March 12, William Eddy, William Foster, and the Third Relief trudged up the length of the Summit Valley on snowshoes. Ahead of them, they saw a large, dark void in the snow from which smoke was curling toward the sky.

As they got close to Starved Camp, they saw the bloody bones of what appeared to be a woman strewn about in the snow. Elizabeth Graves' body had been stripped of most of its flesh. Her heart and liver had been cut out of her chest and abdomen and her breasts had been removed. There were other bones nearby, too. They appeared to be those of children.

Nancy Graves was only eight-years-old when she was forced to consume her mother's flesh while starving in the mountains. She was haunted by this for the rest of her life.

Down in the pit, they saw the circle of survivors, pale and skeletal, around a fire. They had survived on bits of meat that had been roasted over the fire.

One of the children, eight-year-old Nancy Graves, did not yet know that the flesh she had been eating was her mother's. It was a revelation that when it came was so devastating that it would lead to bouts of sudden weeping during the rest of her childhood and a sense of guilt from which she would never recover.

The men of the Third Relief were stunned by what they found at Starved Camp and were uncertain what to do next. It seemed unlikely that any of those in pit - aside from Peggy Breen and her son, John - could get out of the mountains without help, and Peggy refused to go without her husband and children.

Eddy and Foster wanted to push ahead immediately to look for their sons but knew they had a responsibility to the stranded and starving emigrants. Charles Stone and Harold Oakley saw a possibility of making extra money and could do so without ever crossing the summit - they would carry two children down from the mountain. Stone picked up Elizabeth Graves, who was weak and close to death, and Oakley gathered up Mary Donner with her badly burned feet. They volunteered to go back down the trail with them. This was a good plan and yet it left some of the Graves children and all the Breens behind to wait for yet another relief party, or for those going on to the lake camp to return.

The men stood in the snow and discussed it for a bit before finally calling for a vote. All except for John Stark were for leaving the Breens again. When his name was called, Stark stepped forward and firmly stated, "No, gentlemen, I will not abandon these people. I am here on a mission of mercy, and I will not do half the work. You can all go if you want to, but I shall stay by these people while they and I live."

Early the next morning, the party divided. Before dawn, Eddy, Foster, Miller, and Thompson continued traveling up the mountains toward the camps. Stone and Oakley picked up the two girls and John Stark took charge of the rest, placing Jonathan Graves on his wide back with his blankets and other gear. He led the rest of them down the length of Summit Valley, traveling westward. As the smaller children grew tired from stomping through the snow, they took turns riding on the back of the gentle giant with Jonathan.

Stark made sure that every emigrant from Starved Camp made it out of the mountains alive - a feat that, while largely unheralded, should be remembered as one of the greatest moments in the history of the West.

Years later, James Breen recalled being a little boy at Starved Camp. He vividly recalled a time when his mother thought he had stopped breathing and Peggy was shocked when Patrick told her to "let him die, he will be better off than any of us." An even greater memory, though, was the arrival of the Third Relief and the heroic John Stark.

James wrote, "To his great bodily strength, and unexcelled courage, myself and others owe their lives. There was probably no other man in California at that time who had the intelligence, determination, and what was absolutely necessary in that emergency, the immense physical powers of John Stark. On his broad shoulders, he carried the provisions, most of the blankets, and most of the time the weaker

Left -- An image of James Breen as an adult. On the right - Isabella Breen was only an infant when her mother carried her out of the mountains and away from Starvation Camp.

children. In regard to this, he would laughingly say that he could carry them all if there was room on his back, because they were so light from starvation."

When the survivors faltered, Stark would carry two of the children ahead on the trail, leave them, and return for two more. While Stark shuttled the children, Patrick Breen limped along, and Peggy carried baby Isabella. When they finally made it to Mule Springs, they were able to use horses to navigate the muddy trail to the winter settlements.

Stark got every member of the Breen family and two of the Graves children to the safety of the settlements, but Charles Stone couldn't do the same with little Elizabeth Graves. He made it all the way to Sutter's Fort with her, but she died on April 1. She lived just long enough for him to collect his $50 bonus.

There was grave concern at the fort for the health of the emigrants. James Breen looked like a skeleton and his frostbite and burns were so worrying that there was talk of amputating one of his legs. He fully recovered, however, and went on to become a prominent attorney and judge who died in 1899.

During his lifetime, James was quick to defend the decision made by the Second Relief to leave the Breens behind at Starved Camp. "No one can attach blame to those who voted to leave part of the emigrants. It was a desperate case. Their idea was to save as many as possible, and they honestly believed that by attempting to save all, all would be lost."

This was a belief shared by Eddy, Foster, Miller, and Thompson of the Third Relief when they continued on to Truckee Lake. They planned to save as many people as possible, but they could only take those who had a chance of surviving the return trip.

They both hoped their boys would be among those who were strong enough to travel. Neither of them had seen their sons since December 16. They were left to pray they were still alive.

The four men of the Third Relief arrived at the lake camp before noon on March 13. Eddy and Foster began calling out, rushing ahead of the others, and racing toward the Murphy cabin, from which smoke ribboned into the sky. They rushed inside and found a group of spectral figures in the darkness, crouched in corners and lying on beds of pine boughs. In the dim light, they could make out the three youngest Donner girls, Simon Murphy, and a feral-looking Lewis Keseberg.

Foster recognized his mother-in-law, Levinah Murphy. She was huddled in the shadows, gaunt, wild-eyed, and disheveled. Foster called out to her and, nearly blind, she turned in his direction just as Foster and Eddy asked for the whereabouts of their sons.

"Dead." Levinah muttered, stunning both men.

Apparently, three-year-old James Eddy and two-year-old George Foster had died only days before - and then both of their bodies had been eaten.

As the two fathers struggled to regain their composure, Levinah offered more unnerving news. Ironically, she had been one of the first emigrants to engage in cannibalism, but now, she pointed an accusatory finger at Keseberg, who was cowering in a corner. She claimed that Keseberg had grown so impatient for little George to die on his own that he took the boy to his bed - allegedly to keep him warm - but had strangled him in the night. Keseberg denied the charge, stating that the boy had died from natural causes.

He did, however, freely admit to butchering and eating the two little boys but emphatically insisted that he did not murder them.

Eddy and Foster were outraged. Eddy threatened to kill Keseberg then and there, but the man was so emaciated and frail that he resolved to wait until they got to California to do it. Later, Eddy attempted to make good on his threat in San Francisco but was talked out of it by James Reed.

In 1879, Georgia Donner delved into her memories of that horrible season and the death of George Foster. She remembered Keseberg taking the child into bed with him, but had no memory of anything out of the ordinary happening that night. She was only five-years-old at the time, but recalled the boy being dead the next morning. She wrote, "Mrs. Murphy took it, sat down near the bed where my sister and myself were lying, laid the little one on her lap, and made remarks to other persons, accusing Keseberg of killing it. After a while, he came in, took it from her, and hung it up in sight, inside the cabin, on the wall."

Eleanor Eddy

When William Eddy returned to the camp at Truckee Lake, he learned that his wife, Eleanor, son, and daughter had all died and been cannibalized while he was leading the Forlorn Hope.

In a separate letter, Georgia provided further details about the gruesome scene: "The dead child that Keseberg hung on the wall was not eaten by him alone. A part was given to my sisters and myself, and Simon Murphy, whom I remember kindly cut a piece, laid it on the coals, cooked, and ate it."

Even though William Eddy suspected that Keseberg had killed his son, too, he made another horrible discovery that day at the lake camp. Eddy learned that, like his son, his wife and daughter had also been cannibalized.

But William Eddy, even with his entire family gone, willed himself to continue with the mission.

He and Foster were in no mood to linger in the presence of

Keseberg and walked outside to try and figure out what to do next. They needed to decide who among the emigrants still had a chance to make it out of the mountains alive.

Levinah Murphy was only 37-years-old but now looked at least twice that age. Her death was quickly approaching, and she would not be taken away by the Third Relief.

And neither would Lewis Keseberg. He had been disliked since the overland journey and now with a cloud of suspicion hanging over him, Foster and Eddy had no intention of risking their lives to save his.

This left the Donner sisters and Levinah's son, Simon, who would turn nine the next day. It was decided that with help from the rescuers, all four of them were strong enough to make the trip. All that remained was for them to find out how the emigrants at the Alder Creek camp had fared.

As they were talking, Simon Murphy saw a haggard woman wander out of the woods as if in a daze. It was Tamzene Donner, coming to search for her daughters. When she was brought into the cabin, her girls threw themselves into her arms and kissed her.

Tamzene had hiked over from the Alder Creek camp after learning of the treachery of Cady and Stone from Nicholas Clark. He had recently visited the lake camp and discovered that the sisters had been left there by the other men. As if the news that her daughters had not made it to safety wasn't upsetting enough, she also learned that Keseberg was talking about killing the girls for food.

Once the Third Relief rescuers had calmed the girls, Tamzene related to them what had occurred since Reed had departed with the earlier relief party.

Just as the big storm that hit the Sierras was lifting, her nephew, Lewis Donner, Jacob and Betsy's three-year-old son, had died. Betsy, stricken with grief, had made her way to the other tent and laid the dead child in Tamzene's lap. With Clark's help, she had buried the little boy in the snow. Soon after, Betsy, physically and emotionally drained, had quietly died, too.

Clark was finally successful with his bear hunt. He had shot and killed the cub he'd been chasing when he trapped it in a cave. The fresh meat lasted a bit longer than the rations left by the Second Relief, but soon, it was also gone. At that point, the survivors returned to eating the dead, carving up the corpses and Betsy and the others left in the snow.

Then, one day before, Tamzene had learned that her daughters had been left behind at the lake camp and decided to go and look for them. She left Clark and Jean-Baptiste to look after young Samuel Donner and her husband.

When she finished telling her story, Tamzene asked Eddy to go back with her to Alder Creek. Perhaps they could take Samuel with them when they left or do something about George's gangrenous arm.

Foster, Eddy, and the others went

Georgia and Eliza Donner, with their guardian Mrs. Brunner in the middle. This photograph was taken in 1847, not long after the two girls were rescued from the mountains by Eddy's and Foster's relief party.

outside to discuss how to proceed. They were worried that another storm was approaching. If it arrived, they would be cut off in the camps. It was time to leave - now. When they reentered the cabin, they said that everyone who was able to travel had to leave now.

Tamzene and her daughters were going to be torn apart again.

Hiram Miller picked up Eliza, Eddy picked up Georgia, and Thompson picked up Frances. Foster hoisted Simon Murphy onto his back. Levinah Murphy, unable to watch her youngest son be taken away, rolled over on her bed to face the wall. The men took the children outside into the snow and hurriedly bundled them into warm clothes.

Tamzene was frantic. Eddy urged her to come with them. She begged them to give her time to return to Alder Creek to see if her husband was still alive, but the men couldn't take the chance of getting stuck if they remained in camp another night.

Tamzene still continued to argue, to beg, and to plead. What about Clark and Trudeau? They were healthy and could still be rescued. She asked them to wait just a little while so she could return to camp and fetch Samuel to go with them. Mostly, she just pleaded for her daughters to be saved and offered Eddy all the money she had left to make sure the girls were rescued.

Eddy told her to keep the money. He would "save her children or die in the effort." Clark and Trudeau could make it out of the mountains on their own, he said, it was too late to save the others. The rescue party had no extra provisions and could not risk being stranded by a storm.

Once again, Eddy asked her to come with them but, for the third time, Tamzene refused to leave. She could not abandon her husband. While George drew breath, she would stay by his side.

She once again told her daughters goodbye. This time, she was very aware that it was unlikely she would ever see them again. As the men carried the girls away with them, Tamzene cried out, "Oh, save, save my children!"

The men trudged off through the woods and onto the ice of Truckee Lake.

Eliza Donner later wrote of that final day at the lake. "Now, she was about to confide us to the care of a party whose leader swore either to save us or die with us on the trail. We listened to the sound of her voice, felt her goodbye kisses, and watched her hasten away to father, over the snow through the pines, and out of sight, and we knew we must not follow."

When Tamzene turned and walked away, she did not look back. At Alder Creek, Nicholas Clark and Jean-Baptiste Trudeau had already departed on their own journey out of the mountains, leaving only four living members of the Donner Party behind - George and Tamzene Donner, Levinah Murphy, and Lewis Keseberg.

The Third Relief carried on with the march, pausing on a mountainside overlooking the lake for a small meal of bread and water. Eliza Donner later wrote, "When we reached the head of the lake, we overtook Nicholas Clark and Jean-Baptiste, who had deserted my father in his tent and were hurrying toward the settlement."

When the two men appeared unexpectedly on the trail, Eddy and the others couldn't help but notice that Clark was carrying a heavy sack that turned out to contain more of the Donners family's belongings, including a pair of Jacob's guns. Clark claimed that Tamzene had given them to him for safekeeping, which seemed hard to believe since the two men had slipped away from the Alder Creek camp before Tamzene had returned.

Worse still, Clark had chosen to carry away a heavy sack of loot instead of little Samuel Donner. When questioned, Clark said that Samuel had died before they left Alder Creek. Only later did Eddy find out that Samuel had not died that day but on March 20, a full week later. Clark and Trudeau were treated with suspicion but, were allowed to travel with them down to the winter settlements.

Compared with the other return trips, things went relatively smoothly for the Third Relief. The weather had greatly improved and they made good time. A few days along, one of the rescuers found a bundle alongside the trail. It was some of the stolen Donner belongings that Cady and Stone had made off with but had been forced to leave behind when Cady's feet swelled from frostbite. William Thompson turned out to be handy with a needle and thread. He pulled the fine silk dresses from the pack and turned them into cloaks for the three girls, which they wore proudly for the rest of the journey.

The Third Relief caught up with some of the emigrants that Stark was still bringing out of the Starved Camp. Soon, they were below the snow line at Mule Springs, where they rested for a few days and then rode horses to the winter settlements. Local women were waiting for them there and took away the girls' silk robes and dressed them in calico, much to the displeasure of the Donner sisters.

The next stop for the girls was the Sinclair ranch, where Margaret Reed cared for them and then took them to Sutter's Fort, where they were reunited with their half-sisters, Elitha and Leanna.

The mission of the Third Relief was complete. Soon, though, plans began to be made to return to the Sierras and rescue anyone who was still alive. Some of the men from the three rescue parties were game to go back and in late March, another party set out. Again, the weather turned bad and an onslaught of storms stopped them before they could even leave Bear Valley.

After this attempt failed to come together, there were some who began to question whether they should even muster another team. It seemed unlikely that anyone was still alive, and even if they were, Lewis Keseberg hardly seemed worth saving and Tamzene Donner had refused to be rescued on three separate occasions.

But the final horrific chapter of the Donner party saga was yet to be written.

19. MAN EATER

There is a Native American legend that tells the story of a malevolent creature called a "Wendigo." This creature can appear as a monster with some of the characteristics of a human, or as a spirit that possesses a person to make them into something monstrous with a taste for human flesh. It seems that the Wendigo is most prevalent in the winter, during times of cold, isolation, and starvation.

And it's not just a supernatural creature. The Wendigo is a monster of our own making.

According to the Ojibwa tribe, the Wendigo "was a large creature, as tall as a tree, with a lipless mouth and jagged teeth. Its breath was a strange hiss, its footprints full of blood, and it ate any man, woman or child who ventured into its territory. And those were the lucky ones. Sometimes, the Wendigo chose to possess a person instead, and then the luckless individual became a Wendigo himself, hunting down those he had once loved and feasting upon their flesh."

But it wasn't a random selection. The Wendigo was apparently made, not born. It was created whenever a man resorted to cannibalism to stay alive. This occurred when Native Americans - or white settlers - found themselves stranded in the bitter snows and ice of the mountainous regions. Trapped, the survivors were compelled to cannibalize the dead in order to live. Other versions of the legend say that humans who displayed extreme greed, gluttony, and excess, might also be possessed by a Wendigo, thus the myth served as a method of encouraging cooperation and moderation.

As noted by the Ojibwa, the Wendigo became a monstrous creature, cursed to wander the land, always seeking to fulfill its incredible appetite for human flesh. If there is nothing left for it to eat, it starves to death.

But it's not just a legend. Being forced into cannibalism was highly traumatic and completely against all rules of society. When people were in such dire straits that they had to eat the dead, most survivors ended up with trauma-related anxiety, or PTSD, which can be disabling. Others, more resilient by nature, survived without long-term emotional consequence.

And then there were those who were driven to insanity.

There is a disease called Kuru, which is caused by eating other people's brains and nervous tissue. The infectious agent is a type of mutant protein that spreads and multiplies. It can be deadly - a person's brain develops lesions and atrophy, and they lose motor skills cognitive abilities and eventually die. A person with an advanced case of Kuru would be unable to tell right from wrong, progressing to the point that they would be considered insane in a court of law.

But there are other kinds of insanity connected to cannibalism, too. They are the reason that the legend of the Wendigo was created. In these cases, persons driven mad by hunger turn on other people for food. In times past, such cases developed in the winter, usually in people who were isolated by heavy snow for long periods. They may have started with cannibalism for survival, but then acquired a taste for human flesh.

In 1661, a report written by Jesuit priests discussed men who were driven mad by hunger and the consequences that resulted. The report told of men "who had met their death the previous winter in a very strange manner. Those poor men were seized with an ailment unknown to us, but not very unusual among the people we were seeking. They are afflicted with neither lunacy, hypochondria, nor frenzy; but have a combination of all these species of disease, which affects their imaginations and causes them a more than canine hunger. This makes them so ravenous for human flesh that they pounce upon women, children, and even upon men, like veritable werewolves, and devour them voraciously, without being able to appease or glut their appetite - ever seeking fresh prey, and the more greedily the more they eat. This ailment attacked our deputies; and, as death is the sole remedy among those simple people for checking such acts of murder, they were slain in order to stay the course of their madness."

What should be done about a man that develops a voracious taste for human flesh - and will murder, if necessary, so that he can satisfy it?

That's a question that many were asking in April of 1847 when the so-called Fourth Relief was sent into the Sierra Nevada Mountains.

By April 1847, the weather had cleared, and winter had finally turned to spring. What was dubbed the Fourth Relief was organized in late March, not as a rescue party but as a salvage party that would recover belongings and anything of value that had been left at the Truckee Lake and Alder Creek camps.

Magistrate John Sinclair drew up an agreement that stipulated that anything recovered would be divided among survivors, heirs, and the salvage crew. Half of what was recovered would go to the estates of the Donner brothers and the other half to the salvage party for their services. The two Donner families were believed to have been carrying a large amount of gold and silver with them, as well as silks, linens, jewelry, books, and other valuable goods that were precious commodities in California.

If they found any survivors? That was a bonus.

William Fallon, a mountain man of "prodigious size," was the leader of the expedition. He and two others - Joseph Sels and John Rhoads - were in charge and were to operate under the conditions set by John Sinclair. Since Elizabeth and Jacob Donner were both known to be dead, the men would receive half of whatever they found. If George and Tamzene Donner were found alive, the party was to negotiate with them the terms on which they and their property would be recovered from the mountains. It they were dead, then their goods would be shared with the Donners' orphaned children.

Along as the rest of the party was Reason Tucker - for both financial and humanitarian reasons - and William Foster, who presumably wanted to salvage what he could of his own possessions before someone else did.

On April 10, just three days before the mission departed, the *California Star* newspaper printed a controversial article about the Donner Party, the condition at the camps, and the inept behavior of the emigrants who'd been stranded. The story was filled with outrageous lies and factual errors but peppered with just enough of the truth to create a perception of the Donner Party that still exists today. They were portrayed as failures who were unworthy of America's divine right to expand across the continent.

That article set the stage for how future generations would view the Donner Party, but a barrage of stories that followed earned the wagon train its infamous place in macabre American history. The stories were gruesome, sensational, morbid, and, unfortunately, mostly true.

The Fourth Relief left the winter settlements on April 13 and arrived at the lake camp four days later. There were no signs of life, but there was plenty of death. Scattered about were dismembered corpses, limbs stripped of flesh, and several skulls that had been split open.

Reason Tucker, who had already seen bodies lying in the snow during his previous visit, was nevertheless shocked by how horrifying the cabins had become since he had last been there. He later wrote, "Death and destruction. Horrible sight. Human bones. Women's skulls sawed to get the brains. Better dwell in the midst of alarm than to remain in this horrible place."

Eleanor Eddy's and Levinah Murphy's partially butchered bodies could be identified, but the other remains they found were unknown.

There was nothing they could do for the dead and since there was no living person in the camp, they spent the next two hours rummaging through the cabins, enduring the smell of death, and searching for valuables. They found little that was worth packing out over the mountains, so they set off for the Alder Creek camp.

Along the way, they found fresh tracks from a lone person who had recently traveled the same trail, apparently moving away from Alder Creek. But when they got to the camp, they again found no one alive. However, they did find that trunks had been broken open and belongings had been scattered out in all directions. There were tools, personal items, bolts of calico, shoes, schoolbooks, and broken furniture. It appeared that someone had been looking for something, but there was no way of knowing if they had found it.

But the men did find another ghastly scene. In a kettle outside of a tent, they found chunks of human flesh that had been cut up into serving sizes. They assumed the meat came from George Donner, whose body was nearby, wrapped in a sheet, most likely by Tamzene.

But she hadn't butchered him. George's head had been severed and his skull split open. His brains had been removed.

The men searched but there was no sign of Tamzene.

Fallon and the other men ransacked both Donner tents looked for the stash of gold and silver they were rumored to have. Failing to find it, they began packing up the most valuable of the other goods and made camp for the night. They continued gathering things the next day, taking anything of value - but still no gold or silver coins were found.

Frustrated but still determined, some of the men remained at Alder Creek to dig through the snow and Foster, Rhoads, and Sels went back to Truckee Lake. They had decided to try to follow the mysterious tracks in the snow they had come across the day before.

When they arrived at the lake cabins, they were stunned to find Lewis Keseberg, alive, at the old Breen cabin. He was shivering and looked dazed, wrapped in a blanket on the floor and surrounded by human bones. Next to him was a pan of water and what appeared to be a fresh human liver and lungs.

The rescuers moved closer to Keseberg and began asking questions. How had he managed to survive? Keseberg freely admitted that he had done so by eating the flesh of the dead. Then they demanded to know what had happened to Tamzene Donner. She had been in good health when the last relief party left her a month before. Keseberg looked up at their angry faces and his expression told them what they already suspected - Tamzene was dead.

And, in fact, part of her was in the cooking pot that was sitting in front of them, even though some of the supplies left from the last rescue remained untouched. There were also the carcasses of cattle that had been lost in the winter storms that were now thawing in the melting snow. They were intact because, as Keseberg later explained to his men, the oxen meat was "too dry eating."

They asked him where the Donners' money was and Keseberg swore that he knew nothing about any money. But when they searched his belongings, they found silks, jewelry, two of George Donner's pistols, and $225 in gold coins. They demanded to know the true story of what happened in the camp after the last rescue team had departed.

Did Lewis Keseberg deserve the reputation he received as the "Killer Cannibal" of the Donner Party? According to what the men of the Third and Fourth Relief parties found - and thanks to Keseberg's own statements - he certainly did!

Keseberg told them but he had already lied to the men once. Was what he told them now the truth? As far as they could tell, Keseberg had violated a taboo even greater than cannibalism for survival - he had murdered a woman so that he could consume her body.

Keseberg had never been well-liked among others in the wagon train. He was cruel to his family - ignoring his daughter and abusing his wife - and usually didn't treat other members of the party much better. After the incident with James Reed and the teamster, which ended in the other man's death, Keseberg had vocally called for Reed's execution. There was also the incident with Hardcoop, when Keseberg ejected him from his wagon. The old man's legs gave out and he vanished, dying somewhere along the trail.

Keseberg was described as an eccentric, antisocial man who mostly kept to himself. He was once described as "predisposed to derangement of mind," and this was before he was trapped in the mountains without food.

But, as we know, Keseberg was not the only member of the Donner Party who engaged in cannibalism. Roughly half of them, including most of the Forlorn Hope, ate the dead that winter. All of them were haunted by their actions for the rest of their lives.

But Lewis Keseberg seems to be a different story. He didn't deny eating Tamzene and, according to the Donner sisters, he ate others before the Third Relief party arrived. But he refused to admit that he had killed Tamzene. He said that he waited to butcher her only after she died of natural causes - but then again, he'd said the same thing about little George Foster, who had mysteriously died after a night when Keseberg had taken him into his bed.

Levinah Murphy had also died of natural causes, he said, a few days after the Third Relief left camp. Keseberg had remained in the cabin, living off her flesh, and listening to the wolves scratching at the door of his shelter each night.

Then, on March 29, George Donner had died and Tamzene had become mad with grief. She ran all the way to the lake from Alder Creek to see if anyone there was still alive. Along the way, she fell into the water and her clothing froze. Shivering, weak, and unable to stop crying, she managed to make it to the cabins, where she found Keseberg. Tamzene was sick, he claimed, burning with fever and he wrapped her in a blanket and put her to bed.

Tamzene raved. She told Keseberg that she had to see her children in California, and she was willing to cross the mountains on foot, at that very moment, if necessary. He told her to sleep and, in the morning, when he went to check on her, he found that she was dead.

It was only then, he said, that he'd eaten her remains.

But they didn't buy his story. They accused him of killing Tamzene and stealing the Donners' money and valuables. He denied this, but they continued to pressure him to admit his guilt. When Fallon, a very intimidating figure, grew tired of the denials, he threatened to hang Keseberg unless he could explain how he had gotten the money.

Finally, he admitted that he had taken the valuables from the Donner's camp - but only upon request of Tamzene herself. As he told it, Tamzene knew she was dying when she went to bed on that last night and asked Keseberg to gather up the money that she'd left at Alder Creek and give it to her children at Sutter's Fort.

Suspicious, disgusted, and frustrated, the men left Keseberg alone and went back to Alder Creek, where the others had remained to pack up the Donners' goods. The next day, they returned to the lake camp, still convinced that Keseberg had murdered Tamzene for food and concealed the rest of her money.

This time, they were rougher with him. Fallon formed a noose and looped it around Keseberg's neck and shoved him to the floor. Then he began to tighten it. Keseberg gasped and choked and finally cried out that he would show them where the money was as long as they didn't kill him. Fallon loosened the rope and Keseberg led Tucker and Rhoads off into the snow towards Alder Creek. They returned with $273 that Keseberg had buried near the tents.

Keseberg - liar and cannibal - was begrudgingly taken out of the mountains by the Fourth Relief. They wanted to leave him, but then decided it would be better to have the law decide his fate.

They left the camp bearing packs that weighed at least 100 pounds each. Keseberg - able to walk with only a little pain - was with them, wearing the boots that had been given to him by James Reed.

During a rest stop along the Yuba River, Keseberg noticed a piece of calico cloth sticking up out of the snow. Curious, he pulled on it and discovered the blue-faced body of his own daughter, Ada, who had starved to death on the return trip with a rescue party.

Until just that moment, Keseberg believed that his wife and daughter had survived.

On April 29, 1847, a little more than a year after the original Donner-Reed party had left Springfield, Illinois, the last surviving member - Lewis Keseberg - arrived at Sutter's Fort.

But Keseberg's story wasn't quite over. After his return to civilization, news of the "Donner Party Tragedy" spread across the nation. Keseberg, thanks to members of the Fourth Relief, was portrayed as a monster who ate humans not just for survival, but for pleasure.

I'm not convinced they were completely wrong.

Journalists dubbed him a "human cannibal" and a ghoulish thief and began reporting the murder of Tamzene Donner, even though it was never verified as fact.

But the additions to the horrific legends of Lewis Keseberg came from an unlikely source - Keseberg himself. It was said that after settling in California, he would frequent local saloons and talk about being a cannibal to anyone who would listen. He claimed that human flesh was more delicious than beef and described Tamzene Donner's liver as the sweetest bite he had ever tasted. Even so, some claim that even if Keseberg said these things, they don't necessarily prove his guilt. Post-traumatic stress disorder is known to provoke psychotic symptoms, like hallucinations or delusions, but I've never seen anything

PHŒNIX BREWERY
—AND—
DISTILLERY.
L. KEESBERG,........Proprietor.
SE. Cor. M and Twenty-eighth Streets,
SACRAMENTO.

L. Keseberg

Keseberg's only successful business was the Phoenix Brewery in Sacramento, which he ran for nearly eight years. It was destroyed by a flood in 1861. Keseberg was either the unluckiest man alive, or, as some might say, his failures were divine retribution.

that shows this was the case with Keseberg.

Whatever the reason for his grisly stories, they got him into legal trouble. Keseberg was ultimately accused of murdering six of his fellow party members but was acquitted on all counts due to lack of evidence. He later returned to court, but this time, he sued the members of the relief party who found him at Truckee Lake, claiming they had fueled the terrible rumors about him. The jury ruled in his favor - but awarded him only $1 in compensation and forced him to cover the court costs.

The jury didn't believe him either - they just couldn't prove what he'd done wrong.

John Sutter eventually gave Keseberg a job, putting him in charge of one of Sutter's schooners that traveled regularly between Sutter's Fort, Hock Farm, and Monterey. But that didn't end the stories and rumors. Keseberg's reputation followed him wherever he lived or worked. In 1851, he was the proprietor of the Lady Adams Hotel, but the business suffered from its owner's reputation. No one wanted to stay in the place owned by the Donner Party cannibal. The hotel was burned to the ground. The cause of the fire was undetermined.

Keseberg spent the next eight years operating the Phoenix Brewery located at the corner of 28th and M Street in Sacramento, until an 1861 flood destroyed the brewery.

Life never got easier for Keseberg, but he was allowed to tell his story again when C.F. McGlashan wrote his book on the history of the Donner Party. He reached out to the surviving members of the company to interview them, including Keseberg, who was then 65-years-old. He now had the platform to tell his version of the events of that winter and address the rumors that had followed him for years. He changed his story, although still admitted that he had cannibalized other members of the group. He told McGlashan, "The flesh of starved beings contains little nutriment. It is like feeding straw to horses. I cannot describe the unutterable repugnance with which I tasted the first mouthful of flesh. There is an instinct in our nature that revolts at the thought of touching, much less eating, a corpse. It makes my blood curdle to think of it!"

Keseberg's greatest chance for redemption came when McGlashan arranged for him to meet Eliza Donner Houghton, the now adult, married daughter of the woman he'd long been accused of killing. Eliza had been a young girl when Keseberg knew her and when he saw the grown woman standing in front of him, he collapsed to his knees. He didn't deny eating Tamzene's body but swore again that he hadn't murdered her. Hearing the sincerity in the voice of this man that she barely remembered from childhood, Eliza decided to take him at his word.

Keseberg's wife, Philippine died in 1877 and he lived out the rest of his life poor and struggling to care for the couple's two children - both born after the Donner Party events - who both had intellectual disabilities. He died in 1895, nearly a half century after the winter that had defined him in the public eye. He took his last breath in a hospital for the poor, penniless and only remembered as the last cannibal at Truckee Lake and the survivor that the newspapers referred to as the "man eater."

law for a time but was never successful. During the Civil War, he proposed leading an army of southerners west to seize the Arizona Territory for the Confederacy. After the war, he went to South America and published *The Emigrant's Guide to Brazil.* He died in Brazil in 1870 while trying to establish a colony for Confederate veterans.

Most of the survivors of the Donner Party were absorbed into the growing population of California. Some of the survivors lived as unhappy recluses, while some like William and Mary Graves, Virginia Reed, and Eliza Donner published accounts describing their ordeal.

The Reed family in San Jose in the 1850s

The various families of the Donner Party almost never saw each other after they were rescued and it's easy to understand why. They had endured a horrific experience and during the ordeal had engaged in what is still considered as one of the greatest human atrocities -- cannibalism.

James Reed settled his family in San Jose, made a fortune in real estate and in gold after the discovery of the precious metal in John Sutter's creek in 1849, and became one of the leading citizens of the new state. Several of the streets in San Jose were named for members of the Reed family. James never spoke in public about the killing of John Snyder.

His wife, Margaret, lived a peaceful life, no longer bothered by the migraines that had plagued her for so long.

When eight-year-old Patty Reed had arrived in California, she still had the bundle of special things with her that she had hidden in her dress, like the little wooden doll and the lock of her grandmother's hair. That doll later ended up in a display in a museum at Sutter's Fort.

In 1847, Patty wrote a cousin that lived back in Illinois. In the letter, she said, "Oh Mary, I have not wrote you half of the trouble we had, but I have wrote you enough to let you know now that you don't know what trouble is." She then added, "Thank God we have all got through... the only family that did not eat human flesh."

More than 20 years after the tragedy, that letter was reprinted in a newspaper. "We shall never forget the manuscript of that letter," the editor recalled. "It was blotted all over with the tears which the poor girl shed while describing the sufferings of her famished parents, the death, and the flesh of the dead bodies furnishing food for the starving children! Horrible, horrible!"

Patty Reed was 93 when she died in 1931.

Virginia Reed died 10 years earlier at the age of 87. She wrote her own account of the trail and that winter in the mountains and never forgot what she went through. Until the day she died, Virginia always made sure that she had cookies or candy with her at all times. Long before, when she'd been rescued from the mountains, she vowed that she would never again be caught without food - and she never was.

The Breens were the only other family in the company, besides the Reeds, who all managed to survive that winter in the mountains. They did so mostly by refusing to share their supplies with anyone else.

Patrick Breen, the man whose prayers God never seemed to hear, settled his family in San Juan Baptista and he became a prominent rancher. Of the six infants in the Donner party, Isabella Breen was the only one to survive to adulthood. She was also the last survivor of the entire Donner party, passing away in Hollister, California, in 1935.

William Eddy, leader of the Forlorn Hope, remarried and started a new family in Petaluma, California. He did try and make good on his promise to kill Lewis Keseberg - the man who had cannibalized his family - but James Reed talked him out of it.

Because many of the survivors were women and children who were orphaned, the young women were forced to marry to survive.

At 13-years-old, Mary Murphy became an orphan after the death of her parents. Just three months after her rescue - and with no other options - she married a man who turned out to be abusive. In a letter, she wrote, "I hope I shall not live long for I am tired of this troublesome world and I want to go to my mother."

But Mary survived that marriage and found a better man, Charles Covillard, a miner who founded the town of Marysville, California, which he named for his beloved wife.

Mary Graves, a 20-year-old survivor of Forlorn Hope, married again after her rescue. The next year, her husband, Edward Pyle was murdered. "I wish I could cry but I cannot," Mary wrote. "If I could forget the tragedy, perhaps I would know how to cry again."

Mary's sister, Sarah Fosdick, also remarried and she tried her best to support and care for their younger siblings, who had lost the rest of the family in the mountains. The more fortunate were adopted, while some had to survive without any home or family of their own.

The Donner children were left as orphans. Some of the younger Donner children were adopted by various families, while the older girls, some as young as 14, married young Californians. The oldest of the Donner survivors, Elitha, died in 1923 at the age of

Eliza Donner Houghton and her family. Her husband, Sherman, later became mayor of San Jose.

90. She had spent the last 50 years on a ranch near Sacramento. She never talked about what happened at her family's camp, but every year, when a local school offered a mandatory unit on the Donner Party, she would sit in the classroom, listening silently from the back row.

After the publication of C.F. McGlashan's book about the Donner Party was published in 1879, the husband of one of the Donner sisters claimed that the book's description of cannibalism was untrue and filed an injunction against it. But a judge allowed the publication to proceed, citing numerous pieces of evidence that proved it had actually occurred.

In 1911, Eliza Donner published her own book about the Donner Party. Eliza had been one of the last survivors to be rescued from the lake camp and she and the two sisters who were with her mostly raised each other in the San Francisco area until 1861, when Eliza married Sherman Houghton, the widower of another Donner Party survivor.

Houghton became the mayor of San Jose and Eliza wrote her book, stating, "Who better than survivors knew the heart-rending circumstances of life and death in those mountain camps?"

Who better indeed?

As time marched on, the cabins, shelters, and corpses left at Alder Creek and Truckee Lake vanished with time.

In June 1847, General Stephen Kearney visited the site of the Truckee Lake camp and buried the remains of all the emigrants whose bodies had been left to the elements. His men dug a grave for them at the site where the Murphy, Pike, Foster, and Eddy families first took shelter after the caravan became stranded.

The chilling reminders of the Donner Party encouraged new emigrants to hurry along the California Trail for years to come, avoiding the shortcuts that promised more than they could possibly deliver.

Eventually, the railroads put an end to the Oregon and California Trails and time - that great enemy of the westward emigrants - wiped away the physical remnants of the Donner Party's suffering, but it would not erase the memories.

Truckee Lake - which would be renamed Donner Lake - was frequently visited over the years. The tracks of the Union Pacific Railroad ran along a nearby ridge and the Lincoln Highway, the first automobile route across America, followed along the north shore of the lake and then climbed to the summit, which became known as Donner Pass. This is still Route 40 today.

On the east end of the lake is Donner Memorial State Park, which offers campsites, hiking trails, picnic areas, and beaches. Of course,

The Lincoln Highway - the first automobile route across America - traveled through Donner Pass and along a ridge above Donner Lake.

these are all things that none of the trapped emigrants of that terrible winter could have imagined.

In 1901, work began on a monument to the ill-fated wagon train near the site of the cabins that had given them shelter. It was erected in honor of all the pioneers who made the difficult trek across the plains and mountains in the 1840s, but there was no doubt that the Donner Party was central to the idea.

On June 6, 1918, the monument was dedicated. Atop a 22-foot-high pedestal - the same height as the depth of the snow that winter - stood a bronze depiction of a pioneer family. The monument had been partially funded by selling more than 5,000 glass vials that contained splinters from the ruins of the cabins. The rest of the money was provided by the Native Sons of the Golden West

The ceremony was attended by hundreds, including the governors of California and Nevada, dignitaries, area residents, and visitors from across the country. A band played music, the politicians made speeches, and the onlookers erupted into thunderous applause when two young girls dressed in white pulled the drape off the giant bronze statue.

But there were three in attendance who were not as excited as the crowd around them. They were the guests of honor and were given a place to stand at the foot of the monument so they could witness the honors bestowed on the emigrants who had once survived and died

Left - The Emigrants Memorial in Donner State Park was dedicated in 1918.

Left to right: Governor Emmet D. Boyle of Nevada, Patty Reed Lewis; Eliza Donner Houghton; Frances E. Donner Wilder; and Governor William D. Stephens of California.

there.

The guests of honor were three old ladies, wearing their Sunday finest - Patty Reed and sisters Eliza Donner Houghton and Francis Donner Wilder. They represented the last eight surviving witnesses to what had taken place at Donner Lake.

More than 70 years before, they had been little girls who were fighting to stay alive. Now they had returned to the place where they had been frozen and famished to witness another moment in history. Much had changed and, yet, much had stayed the same. The rocks, the lodgepole pines, and the white firs remained, watching over the place where the camp had been. The meadow still stretched out toward the lake and the flat place where the shelters had been was now hiding the buttons, spoons, coins, and bones that remained under the earth.

The women didn't cry. They had used up all their tears long ago. The children became women who married and became mothers and grandmothers.

The people they once knew were now ghosts.

Only 46 of the emigrants who made camp east of the pass on the night of October 31, 1846 survived that terrible winter.

Is it any wonder that so many consider it haunted?

The Summit from Donner Lake, Calif.

For decades, Truckee Lake was considered a cursed and shunned place. The stories of the doomed emigrants were widely told and those who passed by the place on their own journey west hurried past rather quickly, avoiding any urge to linger there.

As the years passed, stories grew. Early legends of the lake claimed that the restless ghosts of the doomed expedition still wailed and cried in the night, reliving their fear and starvation over and over again. Tales were told by travelers who weren't aware of the dark history linked to the ruined cabins along the lakeshore. Many of them stayed the night before they crossed the pass and experienced the phantoms of those who died - or were murdered --- years before. Those same accounts tell of mournful wails and ghostly figures who wandered about in panic and confusion.

There were many who told tales of the spirit of Levinah Murphy, who slowly went mad, trapped in the cabin with children she could no longer care for as the winter days stretched on with no end in sight. They often said she lingered near the site of the family's cabin - now marked by a large rock that had been part of the chimney - and asked travelers for help. When they approached her, the emaciated woman in rags simply vanished.

She was an unnerving figure, but not the one that so many

The pass that the Donner Party tried so desperately to cross is now known as Donner Pass and it looms above the area that is now been given the name of the tragic party of emigrants.

travelers feared. It is strange that a woman who was so widely loved and respected in life went on to become so frightening in death - but that's exactly what happened to Tamzene Donner.

For decades, stories told of a woman's wailing voice that echoed in the night around the ruins of the old cabins. Many passing emigrants saw the woman, staring at them as they went by. The story never changed, whether the travelers were in wagons, on horseback, or traveling by automobile. She was frequently there, looking for something - or someone - with her dark, hollow eyes.

This restless spirit, it was said, was Tamzene Donner, still trapped at the place where she met her end. It was said that the mystery surrounding her death may have kept her spirit at this spot.

According to Lewis Keseberg, after George Donner died, Tamzene lost her mind to grief and ran wildly through the woods, searching for someone - anyone - who was left alive. But she fell into a stream and her clothing froze. Shivering and weak, she stumbled to a cabin from which a ribbon of smoke curled from the chimney.

Keseberg claimed that Tamzene was burning with fever when she burst through his door and that he did all he could to save her. Keseberg, lost in his own madness, later admitted to cannibalizing Tamzene but always swore that he hadn't killed her - but few believed the "human cannibal." He was charged with her murder, but a jury found there was not enough evidence for them to convict him.

What really happened will never be known.

And for that reason, it's said, her spirit remains. She is trapped here by the lies that accompanied her death.

As years passed, the stories of Tamzene Donner lived on, so to speak. Visitors to the state park reported a wild-eyed woman in a pale dress who was there one moment and then gone the next. They heard a woman weeping and crying in the darkness. Often, they experienced an inexplicable cold chill around the site of the cabin where Tamzene took her last breath.

The site of the Murphy Cabin, where several of the emigrants died, is preserved by this marker, fixed to the stone that served as a fireplace hearth. The names of the Donner Party are inscribed on the marker.

Tourists taking snapshots in the area returned home to find the unsmiling face of a woman in old-fashioned clothing in their family photos.

Another tourist with a video camera was filming during a family picnic and when he watched the video later, he heard the far-off sound of a woman crying in pain. Was it the voice of Tamzene Donner still crying from the other side?

Many years ago, while living in Utah, I took a trip to Donner Lake to see where the wagon train had come to an end. Growing up in Central Illinois, I was familiar with the places where the Donners and Reeds had lived near Springfield. Their first night's camp was now the lawn of the State Capitol building. I currently live close enough to the square in Jacksonville where the Donner's camped that I see it every day.

But seeing the place where the journey came to an end was different. And it's not just the lake. Even the old highway - not Interstate 80, but the old Lincoln Highway route - that travels through the pass has a feeling of history about it. I'd been interested in the story of the emigrants who got lost and perished in the wild for many years. The promise of ghostly activity at the site where their journey concluded made the trip even more interesting. But, as it turned out, my night at the lake camp was without incident - and perhaps that was for the best.

I would be hard-pressed to think of a group of people - or the spirit of a woman like Tamzene Donner - who more deserved to rest in peace. The horrible days they endured at the lake, and along the trail to the Sacramento Valley, were terrible enough that they should not be subjected to an endless purgatory here on earth.

I would hate to think that the spirits of heroic figures like William Eddy, Charles Stanton, and Tamzene Donner are still lost out there, somewhere in the wilderness, forced to repeat their most hellish days over and over again.

Perhaps some ghost stories -- and the ghosts who create them -- just deserve to fade away.

BIBLIOGRAPHY

Brown, Daniel James - *The Indifferent Stars Above*, Harper, New York, NY, 2009

Brown, Dee - *The American West*, Simon and Schuster, New York, NY, 1994

Bryant, Edwin - *What I Saw in California*, G. Appleton, New York, NY, 1848

Burton, Gabrielle - *Searching for Tamsen Donner*, University of Nebraska Press, Lincoln, NE, 2009

Butko, Brian - *Greetings from the Lincoln Highway*, Stackpole, Mechanicsburg, PA, 2005

Campbell, Bruce Alexander - *The Sangamon Saga*, Phillips Brothers, Springfield, IL, 1976

Carlton, Genevieve - *Here's What Happened to the Surviving Members of the Donner Party*

Cleland, Robert Glass - *This Reckless Breed of Men*, University of Mexico Press, Albuquerque, NM, 1976

Constable, George - Editor, *The Pioneers*, Time-Life Books, Alexandria, VA, 1974

Croy, Homer - *Wheels West*, Hastings House, New York, NY, 1955

Debczak, Michelle - *How Lewis Keseberg was Branded the Killer Cannibal of the Donner Party*

DeVoto, Bernard - *The Year of Decision, 1846*, Little Brown, New York, NY, 1942

Dirck, Brian R. - Lincoln *the Lawyer*, University of Illinois Press, Champaign, IL, 2008

Dungan, Myles - *How the Irish Won the West*, Skyhorse Publishing, New York, NY, 2011

Fanselow, Julie - *The Traveler's Guide to the Oregon Trail*, Falcon Press, Helena, MT, 1992

Faragher, John - *Sugar Creek: Life on the Illinois Prairie*, Yale University Press, New Haven, CT, 1988

Feldman, George Franklin - *Cannibalism, Headhunting, and Human Sacrifice in North America*, Alan C. Hood and Co., Chambersburg, PA, 2008

Franzwa, Gregory M. - *The Oregon Trail Revisited*, Patrice Press, Tucson, AZ, 1972

Fremont, John Charles - *Memoirs of My Life*, Belford, Clarke & Co. Chicago, IL, 1886

Hall, Carroll D. - *Donner Miscellany*, Book Club of San Francisco, San Francisco, CA, 1947

Hardesty, Donald L. - *The Archaeology of the Donner Party*,

University of Nevada Press, Las Vegas, NV, 1997

Hastings, Lansford - *The Emigrant's Guide to Oregon and California*, George Conclin, Cincinnati, OH, 1845

Heilbach, Rose - *What Really Happened to the Donner Party?*

Holmes, Kenneth, Editor - *Covered Wagon Women Volume 1 1840-1849*, University of Nebraska Press, Lincoln, NE, 1995

Houghton, Eliza Donner - *The Expedition of the Donner Party and Its Tragic Fate*, A.C. McClung, Chicago, IL, 1911

Hurtado, Albert L. - *John Sutter*, University of Oklahoma Press, Norman, OK, 2006

Johnson, Kristin - "Donner Party Cannibalism," *Wild West*, 2013
--------------------- - *"Unfortunate Emigrants"*, Utah State University Press, Logan, UT, 1996

Kaufman, Richard F. - *Saving the Donner Party and Forlorn Hope*, Archway, Bloomington, IN, 2014

King, Joseph A. - *A Winter of Entrapment*, P.D. Meany, Toronto, 1992

Korns, Roderic K. - *West from Fort Bridger*, Utah State Historical Society, Salt Lake City, UT, 1951

Limburg, Peter R. - *Deceived*, IPS Books, Pacifica, CA, 1998

Luchetti, Cathy - *Men of the West*, W.W. Norton, New York, NY, 2004

Mayo, Matthew - Haunted Old West, Globe Pequot, Guilford, Connecticut, 2012

McGlashan, C.F. - *A History of the Donner Party*, Crowley and McGlashan, Truckee, CA, 1879

McLaughlin, Mark - *The Donner Party*, Mic Mac Publishing, Carnelian Bay, CA, 2007

Morgan, Robert - *Lions of the West*, Algonquin Books, Chapel Hill, NC, 2011

Mullen, Frank, Jr. - *The Donner Party Chronicles*, Nevada Humanities Committee, Reno, NV, 1997

Murphy, Virginia Reed - *Across the Plains in the Donner Party*, Outbooks, Golden, CO, 1980

Older, Cora Miranda Baggerly - *Love Stories of Old California*, Books for Libraries Press, Freeport, NY, 1940

Parkman, Francis - *The Oregon Trail*, Doubleday, Garden City, NY, 1946

Rarick, Ethan - *Desperate Passage*, Oxford University Press, New York, NY, 2008

Steele, Volney - Bleed, Blister, and Purge, Mountain Press, Missoula, MT, 2005

Stewart, George R. - The California Trail, University of Nebraska Press, Lincoln, NE, 1962
----------------------- *Ordeal by Hunger*, Houghton Mifflin, New York, NY, 1936

Tannahill, Reay - *Flesh and Blood*, Stein and Day, New York, NY, 1975

Taylor, Troy and Rene Kruse - *A Pale Horse Was Death*, Whitechapel Press, Decatur, IL, 2012

Teggart, Frederick J. Editor - Diary of Patrick Breen, Vistabooks, Dillon, CO, 1991

Thornton, J. Quinn - *The California Tragedy*, Biobooks, Oakland, CA, 1945

Tinkham, George Henry - *California Men and Events*, Record Publishing, Stockton, CA, 1915

Unruh, Johnd D., Jr. - *The Plains Across*, University of Illinois Press, Chicago, IL, 1979

VanDevelder, Pail - *Savages and Scoundrels*, Yale University Press, New Haven, CT, 2009

Wallis, Michael - *The Best Land Under Heaven*, W.W. Norton, New York, NY, 2017

SPECIAL THANKS TO

April Slaughter: Cover Design and Artwork
Lois Taylor: Editing and Proofreading
Lisa Taylor Horton and Lux
Orrin Taylor
Rene Kruse
Rachael Horath
Elyse and Thomas Reihner
Bethany Horath
John Winterbauer
Kaylan Schardan
Maggie Walsh
Cody Beck
Becky Ray
Tom and Michelle Bonadurer
Lydia Roades
Susan Kelly and Amy Bouyear
Cheryl Stamp and Sheryel Williams-Staab
And the entire crew of American Hauntings

ABOUT THE AUTHOR

Troy Taylor is the author of books on ghosts, hauntings, true crime, the unexplained, and the supernatural in America. He is also the founder of American Hauntings Ink, which offers books, ghost tours, events, and weekend excursions. He was born and raised in the Midwest and currently divides his time between Illinois and the far-flung reaches of America.

CPSIA information can be obtained
at www.ICGtesting.com
Printed in the USA
JSHW012124050623
42767JS00001B/12